The

Loss

of a

Pet

Third Edition

"Old Drum Memorial." The bronze plaque beneath the statue contains the entire text of a speech by the late Senator Vest of Missouri. In the 1870 trial of a man from Warrensburg, who had wantonly shot a neighbor's dog, Vest asked $200 in damages. After this brief but effective speech, the jury deliberated only two minutes and awarded the plaintiff $500.   *Photo by W. Sife. Courtesy of City of Warrensburg, MO*

The Loss of a Pet

Third Edition

Wallace Sife, Ph.D.

Howell
Book House™

Howell Book House
Published by Wiley Publishing, Inc., Hoboken, New Jersey

For general information on our other products and services or to obtain technical support please contact our Customer Care Department within the U.S. at (800) 762-2974, outside the U.S. at (317) 572-3993 or fax (317) 572-4002.

Wiley also publishes its books in a variety of electronic formats. Some content that appears in print may not be available in electronic books. For more information about Wiley products, please visit our web site at www.wiley.com.

Library of Congress Cataloging-in-Publication Data:
Sife, Wallace.
     The loss of a pet/Wallace Sife.—3rd ed.
          p.cm.
     Includes index.
     ISBN-13: 978-0-7645-7930-1(pbk.)
     ISBN-10: 0-7645-7930-4
     1. Pet owners—Psychology. 2. Pets—death—Psychological aspects. 3. Bereavement—Psychological aspects. I. Title.
     SF411.47.S54   2006
     155.9'37—dc22
                                                                                      2005012603

Printed in the United States of America

10   9   8   7   6   5   4   3   2

Third Edition

Book design by Scott Meola
Cover design by Monica Benalcazar
Book production by Wiley Publishing, Inc. Composition Services

To peace and permanence, in the loving memory of my pal,
Dachshund Edel Meister, MS, CD (1979–1987),
and all his soul mates who were beloved,
and the good people who mourn our common loss.

And . . .
Now, at the writing of this Third Edition
I wish to also dedicate this to the
Association for Pet Loss and Bereavement
and the special people who had originally come
to this organization for help
—and later stayed to become a vital part of its unique cadre
of caring, counseling friends.

TRIBUTE TO THE DOG

*T*he following speech was made by the late Senator Vest of Missouri in the trial of a man at Warrensburg, who had wantonly shot a dog belonging to a neighbor. Mr. Vest represented the plaintiff, who demanded $200 in damages. As a result of this speech, the jury, after two minutes of deliberation, awarded the plaintiff $500.

"Gentlemen of the jury: The best friend a man has in this world may turn against him and become his enemy. His son or daughter that he has reared with loving care may prove ungrateful. Those who are nearest and dearest to us, those whom we trust with our happiness and our good name, may become traitors to their faith. The money that a man has, he may lose. It flies away from him, perhaps when he needs it the most. A man's reputation may be sacrificed in a moment of ill considered action. The people who are prone to fall on their knees to do us honor when success is with us may be the first to throw the stone of malice when failure settles its cloud upon our heads. The one absolutely unselfish friend that a man can have in this selfish world, the one that never deserts him and the one that never proves ungrateful or treacherous is his dog.

"Gentlemen of the jury, a man's dog stands by him in prosperity and in poverty, in health and in sickness. He will sleep on the cold ground, where the wintry winds blow and the snow drives fiercely, if only he may be near his master's side. He will kiss the hand that has no food to offer, he will lick the wounds and sores that come in encounters with the roughness of the world. He guards the sleep of his pauper master as if he were a prince. When all other friends desert he remains. When riches take wings and reputation falls to pieces, he is as constant in his love as the sun in its journey through the heavens. If fortune drives the master forth an outcast in the world, friendless and homeless, the faithful dog asks no higher privilege than that of accompanying him to guard against danger, to fight against his enemies, and when the last scene of all comes, and death takes the master in its

embrace and his body is laid away in the cold ground, no matter
if all other friends pursue their way, there by his grave side will
the noble dog be found, his head between his paws, his eyes sad
but open in alert watchfulness, faithful and true even to death!"

Courtesy of The Daily Star-Journal Warrensburg, MO
Inscribed on the Old Drum Memorial Warrensburg, MO 1870

CONTENTS

FOREWORD

The first time I met Dr. Sife, it was to discuss his professional interest in pet loss counseling. He recognized the power of pet-person relationships and felt society had paid far too little attention to the pain that people experience when these relationships end. He wanted to join the small group of mental health professionals caring for the bereaved companions of pets who had died.

The next time I met Dr. Sife, he had become one of the bereaved. The sudden death of his dog, Edel Meister, prompted him to join the Animal Medical Center's Pet Loss Support Group, the first ongoing service of its kind.

In the midst of his sorrow, Dr. Sife found the strength to offer consolation to others who came to the group. Whether their losses were recent or many months old, he drew on his own experience to help others understand what they were feeling. He began to talk about writing a book that would be therapeutic and healing for others. *The Loss of a Pet* is that book.

Written from the perspective of a fellow mourner, while drawing on his training and experience as a psychologist, *The Loss of a Pet* supports the right of those people whose companion animals have died to feel whatever is natural for them. Sadly, many who are grieving have their pain increased by the awkwardness or apathy of friends and family. Dr. Sife describes how to protect oneself from additional hurt, while remaining open to any attempts, no matter how halting, to comfort.

People who have lost pets, and those around them, wonder why attachment and grief are so strong. Both groups question at what point these feelings become extreme, potentially harmful. Wallace Sife explains how companion animals offer a rich but safe kind of interaction. At the same time he offers a few examples from his professional practice.

Dr. Sife does more than describe feelings of grief and explain their origin; he suggests concrete steps to deal with the confusing and unpleasant sensations that go hand-in-hand with these feelings. Chapter 5 is a good example. First he ties anger, a normal stage of bereavement, to frustration at lack of control. He then outlines a technique for handling anger without hurting oneself or others. He suggests writing down all the reasons to be angry, then he recommends discussing these with trusted friends, practicing the perspective of each person involved.

The Loss of a Pet is a personal book that reflects Wallace Sife's unique views on pet loss. His passionate commitment to personal growth and happiness underscores his call to accept reality and let go of the past. Professional readers will find he has added a different dimension to old concepts. His caring for the relief of suffering shines through the entire work. In *The Loss of a Pet* he has taken his own advice, to create a living memorial to a very special dog.

Susan Phillips Cohen, MSW, DSW, ACSW
Director of Counseling
Animal Medical Center
New York City

INTRODUCTION

Grief must have a purpose and direction;
otherwise, it is unproductive and destructive.

*I*f you are the special kind of person who grieves deeply for the loss of a pet, this book is written for you. Or, if you have a beloved pet now, these pages can help enhance your overall awareness and joy in its companionship. Unfortunately, all living things die, and although you can never be really prepared for that, what is offered here can help you draw upon your love to minimize your grief and pain, when death eventually does happen. For all pet lovers, bereavement is actually an important part of our celebration of the joyous life and very special love we had together.

What is presented in these pages will help you realize that you are not alone. So many others have suffered the same anguish. What we have learned about this tragic experience can help you cope with it. This book reflects what I have learned from the collective experience and wisdom of many thousands of bereaving pet owners. It also incorporates the most efficient therapies dealing with their unique bereavement and grief. It will explain this exceptionally painful and mystifying impact on your life, and show how you can manage it. The shock of loss and bereavement is one of the most profound emotional traumas we can experience, and it should be nothing to be embarrassed by. The imposed stigma of shame and sense of isolation is something that you will now be able to better understand and productively deal with.

Since so little has been known about pet bereavement up until recently, it is natural to wonder whether such powerful reactions for a pet are normal. It is important to know that the exceptional feelings and irrational periods we go through at this time are common symptoms that we all experience. Unfortunately, because of this lack of information, many rational people question their own sanity at such nerve-wracking moments. Intellectually, we might understand the death of a beloved pet, but it is so hard to accept, emotionally. This is always so heartbreaking and out of proportion, when still in the grips of such deep privation and bereavement. What you will learn about yourself and your grief will convince you that you are not in any way losing your mind. The loss of a pet is a unique emotional trauma, and the pain and confusion you are experiencing will be demystified. This knowledge will help you deal with your grief and distress.

Nobody lives forever. And who would really want to? We can understand that when it applies to ourselves, and it would make a lot of sense if we were to apply this wisdom to the death of our beloved companion animals, as well. It can help you come to better terms with your bereavement. There is no way to exist in this world of change without accepting loss.

I am always asked how long the terrible pain will go on. But there is no easy answer. There are too many different personal factors involved in determining this. Some of these will be examined in later chapters of this book. However, it is good to know that we can help the healing process when we change or modify some daily routines that formerly involved the deceased pet. Also, too many constant physical reminders and associations left about the house become very upsetting. It would be useful to remove or reduce their numbers, for the time being at least. In addition, if we allow ourselves to speak about our loss and grieve freely, the mourning period will be shorter and more constructive. We let some of the pain out this way, which makes room for healing.

In clinical studies it has been found that some people never truly complete their mourning process. Therefore, they suffer more than they should, and bear their grief needlessly for many years—even for the rest of their lives. The heartbreak we endure can be so tragic that at first we feel we need to suffer, without end. It is absolutely essential to give ourselves permission to heal. Otherwise, we are "spinning our wheels" and will stay mired in our misery.

Human beings are creatures of habit and structure. We find security in routines and established orders. Our individual bondings form powerful subconscious templates for our behaviors. Living with a beloved pet for an extended part of our lives produces new patterns that become permanent. All of us lovingly adapt our lifestyles around this cherished adopted family member. We become completely conditioned to the routines. This habituated way of life with a dear pet and friend is taken for granted, and we go on as if it will never end. But it does end, and suddenly our beloved one is gone! Regardless of the pet's age or health, we can never be really prepared for this. The resultant shock is an unavoidable psychological reaction, and cannot be easily dismissed or glossed over. Our whole life goes through a violent emotional upheaval. It is as if a great jagged hole had been ripped out of one's life. We need time and patience with ourselves, and this book will help you achieve that.

You probably also have experienced situations in which you were forced to feel defensive and secretive about your bereavement. We cannot avoid all contact with others who say that we should not suffer real bereavement for a pet—which is only an animal and can easily be replaced. Such ignorant responses reflect their personal problems and should not become ours, especially at this very painful and vulnerable time of loss. These cynical critics have never known the unique love of a pet, proving themselves unqualified to judge us in this grief. They are not pet-oriented people, and they lack the wisdom of experience. But be grateful for any sincere attempts by others, however awkward, to ease your pain. You must learn to make this important distinction. Well-intentioned people will try to get us to act cheery. They get upset, seeing us cry and they just don't realize that we must go through a deeply personal period of mourning and bereavement. We have to learn to be patient with them—and their ignorance of the profundity of all this.

In our hour of need it can at first seem that there are not many people who can comprehend our bereavement. As a defensive posture we learn to readjust our relationships with others, including close family members. This can be extremely disappointing or even aggravating at times. We must also learn to be cautious and avoid hasty, angry over-reactions—which are more easily experienced now, but may be regretted later. Our sense of justified anger too often can override our common sense during this especially unstable time of our life. We are most vulnerable now, and we somehow still have to keep all of our best interests in perspective.

For many valid reasons, the mourning for a pet can be far more intense than for a human. This will be explained in more detail in the chapters that follow. The pain you are experiencing now is terrible, and can be very debilitating. You are actually mourning the death of your dearest friend, as well as a very close member of your immediate family—nothing less! It is interesting to note how many refer to their dear pets as their "furbabies." They actually are our best friends, lovers, and surrogate children—as well as our alter-egos. Mourning their unique loss is a time process, and understanding this will help you a great deal.

Death, in general, is a subject that most people in Western cultures are very uncomfortable with. Actually, many find it frightening, and avoid thinking about it. Discussion of the subject is awkward or even impossible. People don't know how to handle it without embarrassment, evasion, or pretense. They use euphemisms, which attempt to provide "sanitized" expressions for more specific terms and ideas. You may discover that the passing of your cherished companion pet is too difficult or distressing to discuss with people who are not completely sympathetic or able to deal with your loss.

Historically, Western tradition and religion have avoided the subject of pet death, leaving the full responsibility and burden solely up to the confused, lonely, and distraught mourner of a beloved animal. Up until very recently, each person had to suffer alone. Now we have become an acknowledged commonality within our ever-changing society, and our unique bereavement needs are being cared for—in greater degrees, every year. In an outstanding development, the Association for Pet Loss and Bereavement (APLB) was formed to serve all the needs of our special community. Visit their website: www.aplb.org.

Individual pastoral counseling in this context, if it can be found, may offer some help. Unfortunately, the death of companion animals is not dealt with by most of the world's major religions. Yet there are many who believe the concept of a soul includes any sentient being that is endowed with love. But this is too often met with skepticism and doubt. Only in the past few years has some theological adjustment been made to address the problems of pet death and bereavement. It is expected that in the future, official doctrines will adapt to our more contemporary needs. The spiritual requirements and considerations of modern society are constantly changing. This book presents a unique chapter, partly composed of brief articles by varied religious leaders. By offering a few different perspectives, it can help you gain a new outlook on this special problem.

Pets have become more significant, loved members of most households. Aside from veterinary care, a $21-billion annual business now caters to the needs and care of pets in the United States alone. All this economic pressure has its influence on us, through advertising, products on the shelves, new jobs in the industry, and so many other ways that affect our normal daily lives. Today, you see more pets than ever on television and in the movies. And they're showing up in greater frequency in contemporary literature and even songs. Why is this happening? America loves pets, and our changing lifestyles are making us better able to appreciate this. We are a nation of pets, and the grief suffered in their loss is a subject that is finally becoming much better understood, respected, and accepted.

It is no longer surprising to hear of people who are in deep grief over the death of a beloved pet. Unfortunately, their plight had traditionally been put aside as personal weakness and indulgence. But since this is a human story now being heard so often, others are getting a strong message from it. There are huge numbers of all kinds of pets in the United States alone. Aside from birds and other rarer kinds of animals, today there are over 120 million pet dogs and cats who are continually reproducing and dying. Literally, millions of us every year are affected by the death of a family pet, and they are all hurting, in varying degrees. Because of the enormous numbers of people involved so emotionally, bereavement for a beloved pet is becoming more accepted as a normal social experience. Now it is also much easier to find a support group or online chat room, with others who know from actual experience what this grief is all about.

Dynamic changes in contemporary civilization are causing the disappearance of the extended household, as well as a decrease in family size. Along with a very rapidly growing population, there are now many more single, divorced, and widowed people than ever before. This particular element of our social structure owns more pets than most others. Lonely people, in particular, are well aware of the wonderful love and therapeutic effects companion animals have in enriching and sustaining their lives.

In many ways, the beloved pet becomes a symbol of our own secret selves—an alter-ego, of sorts. It represents an innocence and grace we feel but cannot express to other humans. Without a pet, this important self-discovery may never be made. This is only one more reason, out of many, for the intensity of grief and bereavement for such a death. It feels as if the best part of our self has died with the pet, and we weep for that, as well. Another thing that affects us is that the pet is a loving soul, and we mourn it accordingly. We want to believe that it has gone to some other realm and that someday we will be there, to join again. Although nobody really knows the answer, too little is spoken about this, leaving us even more upset during our especially vulnerable time of need. Be wary, though. Unfortunately, there are some who would try to convince you that they can relay messages between you and your deceased loved one. Your grief and great susceptibility at this time can easily make you an unwitting victim.

Who has not experienced that special sense of excitement and greeting when we put the key in the lock and opened the door? Our coming home was always a major event to our pet. Over the years we had become so used to anticipating our special welcome—from a meow to a tail-thumping salute and kisses. Now the home is shockingly silent, and it feels terribly empty. But the pet's presence still seems to be everywhere. At this early stage it is not unusual to imagine for a brief second that we see glimpses of or hear fleeting sounds of our pet. That is a very normal thing, and most of us have experienced it. After this loss we still live in the echoes of the loving patterns that became our way of life. It takes time.

The loss of a pet also has another meaning for some. There are many heartbroken people who have literally lost their pets. Whether this was caused by their pets wandering off, unexpected happenings or circumstances, or even theft, these loving pet owners are thrown into a special crisis that is not comparable to anything else. Among other anxieties, they grieve and worry whether their pet will be sold to an experimental lab, or if it will be injured or killed by cars or other animals. It could also end up unidentified in a pound somewhere, where it would be euthanized, along with the millions of other poor strays in this country each year. A lost or missing pet is an especially horrible kind of loss, where there rarely is a happy ending. These loving pet owners are also in a state of mourning and will go through all the painful stages of bereavement you will learn about later—especially unresolved guilt. A special chapter on this unique kind of loss has been added for their benefit.

Often during pet bereavement, the people we rely on most fall short of our needs and expectations. At times, we are fortunate to find a caring, supportive new friend—usually another pet owner, who can share our unique feelings and responses. Such understanding is wonderful, but too rare. Up until now there have been far too few things published in any of the mass media on this subject. But all that is changing. This book will be your guide to that understanding.

Introduction

A few years ago my own dog, Edel Meister, died very unexpectedly. Despite my special training in human bereavement, my grief was intense and inconsolable. I was desolate for at least two weeks before I could make even a weak pretense at functioning normally again. Pet bereavement was little understood or respected then, except in a few small, isolated circles. I had to painfully crawl my way through my own intense grief and debility to get to a perspective on what this is all about. After much time and research, armed with this new knowledge, I resolved to write the book that I would have wanted for myself. It is dedicated as a loving, living testament to Edel Meister's cherished memory—and to all the other beloved pets in this world, throughout history. This is the best memorial I can give him—and share with you.

I am honored that readers of earlier editions of this book asked me to form a special organization for them. Out of this the Association for Pet Loss and Bereavement (APLB) was founded. And now there are many good people who volunteer with me there, to help new bereavers. They are also receiving a special personal sense of gratification that they are helping other bereaving pet owners who now feel all alone in their terrible grief. These wonderful workers' lives have become positive living memorials, honoring the memories of their own deceased pets. We are all made into better people by our beloved companion animals, and we are all in this same lifeboat, together.

This book will give you what you need to help yourself through the agonizing parts of your mourning. It is offered with compassion and care, in the trust that your loved one will inspire you to live on through the pain and grow, as mine did.

Wallace Sife, Ph.D.
Brooklyn, New York

Chapter I

The Human-Pet
Bond

Everything that lives, lives not alone nor for itself.

—William Blake

The human-pet bond is one that dates back to prehistoric times. Some early cave drawings depict dogs joining in the hunt, as well as many in the camp and around the fire, sharing the lives of our earliest ancestors. That initial bond was not an accident or rare occurrence, but rather a natural, deliberate interaction. It served both the basic needs of humans and these friendly cousins of the wolves. Humans and dogs benefited from mutual protection and companionship. In addition, this fortuitous union enhanced hunting success. Much later, dogs would be trained and specially bred for herding and many other practical purposes.

THE DOMESTICATION OF SOME ANIMALS

The first dogs were valued as friendly hunting adjuncts and reliable alarms, warning of intruders. Since human survival was a hand-to-mouth daily challenge, these semi-feral dogs were mostly left to fend for themselves, but were probably thrown bones and scraps of food (even as they are today in many undeveloped countries). Those who were the best companions and hunters were selectively bred, and in time this created the first breeds of true dogs—different from their

"Faithful and Constant Companions."

*Photo by W. Sife. Courtesy of
Hartsdale Canine Cemetery, Inc.*

In memory of a precious cat.

*Photo by W. Sife. Courtesy of
Abbey Glen Pet Memorial Park*

wolf ancestors. Much later, during biblical times, *pets* as we consider them now were still unheard of—aside from an occasionally favored livestock animal. Most likely, a family would take an adorable lamb or kid into the house and bring it up by hand, allowing the children to play with it. But in those unforgivingly hard times, this practice had to be temporary. Animals were raised for meat and milk, and even most of the favored ones eventually had to be slaughtered.

Times and people were much tougher then, and food was a family's first concern. Shelter, reproduction, and just staying alive were always primary, and anything else had much lower priority in each day's struggle for survival. This pet-keeping was still so temporary and occasional that there was not even a word to define it. The times were not yet ready for our present-day concept of a companion animal who did not first serve some other vital utility or purpose. Favored household animals had to be temporary indulgences—extravagances that generally did not fit into the normal long-term scheme of harsh, daily existence at that time.

We know almost nothing about the history of cats, until they were revered in ancient Egypt as quasi-religious figures. There they were sometimes killed and mummified as part of a rite we still do not fully understand. But cats were natural predators of mice and rats. They survived and increased, independently—especially well around farms and granaries, where they were welcomed and appreciated. They served a vital function in the growing agrarian development of mankind. The rats and mice they hunted were hated for devouring precious grain and other foods. This was particularly important during times of poor harvest, when there was a dangerously low supply for people to eat. Much later, in the Middle Ages, cats became even more valued when it was realized that rats and mice were the carriers of terrible diseases and epidemics.

A review of man's history shows that the actual concept and word "pet" first came into use in the Old Northern English and Scottish languages, at about 1000 A.D. It was used for any favored animal who was domesticated (or tamed) and treated with indulgence or fondness. Over the millennia this practice had gradually evolved and become much more common by that time. Our modern concept of a household pet was just developing. The coining of a new word was needed to help define it.

Nature has prescribed that very few animals have the personalities to be domesticated—and even fewer can be tamed. The first humans were hunter-gatherers. Eventually, when we began to emerge from the cave, we learned to take advantage of all the animals that could possibly be hunted, cultivated for food, or even scavenged.

For thousands of years, people captured and then selectively bred the many lines of livestock animals that have eventually become so familiar today. But as civilizations grew, dogs and cats—through their normal affectionate behavior—were firmly insinuating themselves into the homes and hearts of humans. Actually, the attraction was mutual and unavoidable. Since the social natures of cats and dogs are so different from most other animals, it was only natural that they adopted themselves into our lives. There is something deep within our human nature that loves this special relationship.

There are distinctively different kinds of temperaments in people. This is probably genetic in origin, and we can see a wide spectrum of types. There are evil people and social misfits of all sorts. Then there are the many who conform to the roles of society, but who have little love in them for others. They are not usually pet lovers. But the vast majority of people are basically good and loving. We have a normal need to give and receive love and to nurture. It seems that pets are our perfect adjuncts in life. History clearly shows us that as civilizations evolve, so does the role of household pet.

The transition to a pet-oriented society started when the focus was shifted from the favored domesticated farm animal to the tame but free-ranging dog or cat who lived with us, performing some service for the household. Cats are excellent mousers, and dogs are natural watchdogs and protectors—and loyal friends. This helped set the stage for our modern concept of family companion animals. We were only just beginning to discover the wonders of the human-pet bond.

When pockets of early civilizations first developed, wealthy men and leaders were the only people who could afford any luxuries. They enjoyed slaves, fine foods, clothes, jewels, and all the indulgences that most other people could only dream of. Dogs were selectively bred to serve specialized hunting functions or to display certain aesthetic appearances. Possessing these dogs became a matter of pride and vanity for their wealthy owners. At first, all cats were semi-feral—living in and around human dwelling places. But because of the inherent affectionate nature of humans, it was impossible for man and dog or cat to live under the same roof and not form a loving bond. It is as if our species were made for each other.

As civilizations advanced, the keeping of "pet" animals gradually became an established practice. The only exceptions to this today are found in extremely fundamental religious societies. It is interesting to note that even now these groups still do not have a vocabulary word for pet. Strict fundamentalists will not assimilate this relatively new practice into their lives because there were no biblical or other scriptural references to the modern-day concept of pets.

Gradually, pets became more commonly appreciated. Dogs were more utilized and kept for their companionship and loving, loyal natures. The history of our literature includes many references to beloved companion dogs. Even in Homer's *Odyssey*, the ancient Greek hero Odysseus returns home after twenty years and is joyfully welcomed by his faithful old dog, Argus. There were no literary references to cats until considerably later. We still don't know much about the special quasi-religious attitude and relationship the ancient Egyptians had for their felines. Only a few isolated mummified cats remain, and there is almost no hieroglyphic account for them.

By the middle of the eighteenth century, man's relationship with animals had already broadened quite a bit. The more developed civilizations and cultures were starting to keep pet dogs and cats for amusement, entertainment, and companionship—and not just for survival or religious purposes, as before. It is almost shocking to realize that this was only about 250 years ago. Increasing numbers of people were discovering the very rich source of love that these companion animals provide. Ever since the first few individuals were able to afford the luxury of pleasure and bonding with a household animal, we have never been the same. Gradually over the centuries, the numbers of household pets began to increase. Sailors even started bringing home tamed monkeys and talking parrots from exotic places. But the rest of us were beginning to realize that there were special benefits to our unique loving companionship with dogs and cats.

PETS FILL OUR NEED TO LOVE AND NURTURE

Most of us have a deep, natural need to love and be loved. This relationship is pure and unpolluted by any outside influences or conditions. But there are so many pitfalls and dangers in the process that we have learned to be cautious—indeed, too cautious.

Anyone who has ever loved a pet—regardless of the species—has known the very special magic that they give us. Some animals have an amazing capacity for loving us. This capacity to love is so profound that most of us are convinced that if there is such a thing as a soul, then they must possess this, as well. Many find great comfort that there must be pets in heaven.

Our natural role as steward is part of our basic human need to give love and to nurture—and to receive it. This is well illustrated by the innate tendency that children have to lovingly care for and integrate with their dolls and toy animals. Even some adults still enjoy the pleasure of owning such playthings. The inherent love of soft, cuddly, and furry things can be seen in the instinctive response of the human baby to them. This is in our nature. Dolls and toy animals have always been made into fantasy pals, and treated with great personal affection and attachment. As we grow up, this loving human instinct is usually transferred to more traditional objects of endearment. But we never really outgrow our natural tendency for stroking the fur of animals. It offers a sense of personal reassurance and comfort to many people.

The need to nurture is part of our innate makeup. It has helped to ensure the preservation of our species. In evolutionary terms, this is an essential instinct that grew as a result of our drive for survival. It is a basic part of our very nature, and it naturally carries over to our beloved companion animals. Pets are the perfect solution for our need to nurture and love when we are not too involved in the rearing of our own babies. And later, the pet animal becomes a unique companion for the young child, as well as the harried parent. It would seem as if nature had put certain animals on this earth to share their lives with us. Pets have become a basic part of our social evolution. A natural and symbiotic relationship has developed, greatly benefiting our mutual emotional and survival needs. Without pets our lives would be far less enjoyable and productive—and a lot lonelier.

The pleasures and benefits derived from keeping a companion animal are complex and many. They give us innocent dependence, companionship, and pure love—and are totally accepting and never judgmental. The unique emotional bonding between the pet and the owner strengthens for each. The result is a wonderful coupling that gives us added stability, purpose, and a sense of personal enrichment that defies description. People who do not have companion animals have no idea what they are missing.

The Human-Pet Bond

Each of us is capable of wonders. When we reach deep down into our very being, we can come up with some amazing things. And our beloved pets help us to achieve this.

The bond we develop with pets is as wonderful and rewarding as it is fascinating and practical. It is an active reaching out and sharing of life with another living being, who happens not to be human. This relationship offers us a chance to share and express our pure selves, without needing to defend our actions or feelings. Companion animals, as we have come to call them, give us our greatest opportunities to express love, without ever having to worry about being judged or rejected. They give us back a devotion that is unmatched by any other relationship, in a very private bond. Pets provide us with an oasis of unqualified love and acceptance in an otherwise demanding and critical world. Their obedience and respect give us an increased sense of self-worth that adds new meaning to our lives. In return, we assimilate them into positions of great personal value. Our bonds with them can be very profound and deep.

People can open up completely to pets, and receive an inner sense of joy and strength from them. It has often been noted that pets can be truer friends than others of our own species. They are never critical, and therefore allow us to blossom emotionally in ways that would not be possible with fellow humans, who tend to be competitive and judgmental. We make our companion animals our secret sharers, often with greater intimacy and trust than that which is often given to the people who are closest to us. Our bonds with beloved pets are in many ways stronger, purer, and far more intimate than with others of our own species. We feel loved and completely secure in sharing our secret souls with them. How often can this be safely done—even with a spouse? So when a dear pet's life ends, it really is very understandable and normal for us to grieve and suffer a unique bereavement. And then we have to learn how to cope with the physical breaking of that kinship. But the deeply personal, spiritual aspects of that bond remain unbroken, and stay with us.

Some pets are so innocent and transparent in their needs and feelings that we get to know and trust them better than most humans. And they feel the same about us. We touch and caress them freely and speak to them adoringly. And they respond with love and so many different kinds of reassurances that we crave and need.

TOUCHING AND PETTING

The physical act of fondling and cuddling is fundamental to our psycho-social stability and health. Unfortunately, our Western society still has leftover Victorian mores about people openly touching and caressing each other. This powerful primal need is satisfied in part by the loving, sensual contact we have with our pets. Petting and stroking is powerful medicine for us, contributing to our emotional (as well as physical) security and health. That is especially marvelous because it energizes a mutually beneficial response. The pet loves and benefits from it—and we ourselves are gratified and soothed, as well.

The pleasure of petting a companion animal has been proven to be of significant medical and psychological benefit to us: Blood pressure is reduced, heartbeat is improved, resistance to disease is heightened, and tension is eased—among other tangible benefits. As mentioned, this relationship has a dimension that transcends even the ties between people, as wonderful as they can be.

In this modern day of violence, superficiality, estrangement, and loneliness, the bond with a beloved pet can be a stabilizing and even sustaining force in our lives. But unfortunately, there are still many who would disparage this. That is something we have to learn to deal with and not allow to upset us. The bond is an important part of us, and it helps define who we actually are.

Sometimes these expressions and reflections of our very private selves are allowed to run out of proportion to what is safe or wise. There are many pet lovers who forsake some or much of their inter-human relationships in favor of the powerful sense of love and security their pets give them. There is potential danger, here. We can tend to insulate ourselves with our pets from the rest of the world's pains and insensitivity. It is too easy to build a safe emotional cocoon around us and the beloved pet, isolating us from the pain and unpleasantness that surrounds us. Most of us do this, though—in varying degrees.

But as comfortable and secure as it feels at the time, it can prove unhealthy in the long run. There are many people who live lives of quiet desperation and who become overly dependent on a pet for sup-portiveness in stressful social situations. Frequently, when there is a strong conflict between two family members, one of them will turn to the pet for comfort and love and for the sense of emotional security that is needed. This dependent relationship becomes very personal and secret. With time, it grows in magnitude and can even distort things, if it is not resolved.

LEARNING TO BE RESPONSIBLE TO OURSELVES

It is a wonderful experience to love and care for a pet. However, we must love ourselves as well, in order to survive and continue to lead productive lives. It is important not to lose awareness of our being an important part of the larger social structure around us. Aside from civic responsibility, we have a basic duty to ourselves—to change, grow, and prosper, and find our place within the community of humans. Lonely people who despair of finding love and being needed easily turn to pets for this. That is all well and good, but it should not become an escape or substitute, or offer an emotional buffer that isolates them from human companionship. With the inevitable death of the pet, this personal oasis evaporates. We too easily set ourselves up to be very vulnerable to the stark loneliness, grief, and bereavement that come when we lose a beloved pet.

Man is basically an emotional animal, and we need to be able to love and feel important to keep our balance and stability. The special challenges of living in an increasingly fast-paced, impersonal society compound our personal problems. Our private needs must be filled, regardless of how we do it. We have to find an outlet or substitute to serve this—and we normally seek it in another person, a pet, a hobby, or even our work. But too often, we do not have someone very dear to love or fully trust, and we are driven elsewhere to satisfy this insufficiency as best we can. There are also those who excessively immerse themselves in their work or hobbies, to sublimate a similar basic need for ego reinforcement, or to keep from feeling lonely. A large percentage of today's city dwellers is composed of people living alone and too isolated—and overly dependent on their beloved companion animals. Despite the natural tendency for denial, they are setting themselves up for disaster when the pet dies. There is a danger here for forming pathological attachments to pets without a healthy balance of human contact to offset this.

Insecurity often drives even the best of us, and some may feel that the only real love and respect they can get is from a pet. Forced by low self-esteem or personal vulnerability, there are many people who tend to become overly dependent on this sure relationship, within an otherwise uncaring, ever-threatening society. Personal happiness is often measured by the safe life and uncompromised bond we share with pets. Unfortunately, when these intimate companions die, that security is breached. The profound shock of being bereft in this manner can seem unbearable. We are catapulted into a state of shock that cannot easily be compared to anything else.

It is important to realize that we all carry "emotional baggage" with us, all the time. Because of the painful psychological nature of this, it has long ago been suppressed deep in our subconscious minds. We are no longer actively aware of it, but it is still there, buried in our emotional substructure. Excessive bereavement is almost always caused by these unconscious repressed memories and feelings. Since they are still in our subconscious we are not cognizant of them—or we may even angrily try to deny their existence. Much of the excessive pain we experience is set off by the death, but it comes from so deep within us that we feel sure it is only a part of the bereavement. This triggers an avalanche of long-suppressed pain, and it all comes down on us at this most personally vulnerable and confusing time. Trained professional therapists are needed at this time. We have to be able to recall and separate the different painful experiences in order to heal from them.

To a great many people their love for and from companion animals becomes the saving grace in their lives. Anyone who has ever bonded with a dear pet can easily understand this. Certainly, there is nothing wrong with adoring a faithful companion animal, despite what some bitter, self-proclaimed critics would say about that. People who are not pet lovers cannot really understand this special relationship. Pets give absolute love to their masters, regardless of how disapproved of or ignored they may be by the rest of the world. The lowliest and most downtrodden person is always lord and master (or lady) to an adoring pet. The unique bond that is established becomes a wonderfully empowering and enriching experience. This has always been understood by the privileged few. But there are many who can never understand our bereavement, and would even try to belittle it. That is actually their loss. Yet we are still vulnerable to their insensitivity and criticisms.

Today, a darling companion animal is considered a normal part of one's immediate family. In the case of a person who lives alone with a pet, the mutual bonding can become a complex and even more intimate relationship. However, death is the one thing we cannot really protect a pet from, and it is the one subject in life that we least understand. It scares most of us to extremes of avoidance. In Western society, we almost never contemplate or discuss it, and are continually attempting to disregard the unavoidable. But when death inevitably catches up with our pets, we are almost always shocked and unprepared. Compounding our grief, we are also often filled with irrational feelings of guilt or even anger because we couldn't delay or prevent its death.

Our culture contributes to avoidance in dealing with the discussion, philosophy, and ultimate reality of death. The subject is considered so disagreeable that many people feel it is impolite to even mention the word. They choose to use euphemisms instead. Death is perceived to be bad, the ultimate enemy—much too frightening and upsetting to confront directly. So we only allude to it indirectly, when we are finally forced to face it. Many people are very glad to leave the details to the professional thanatologists and clergy, and relieve themselves of fearful and unknown responsibilities and reactions. Unfortunately, this avoidance still leaves us very vulnerable.

In many ways, a pet can be very similar to a beloved and totally dependent child who never grows up. In such a relationship, our sense of bonding and responsibility becomes very complicated. One's secret self is intimately involved and is safely established in the relationship with the pet. In this modern world of fear and rushing about, and perceiving things through sound bites and superficialities, it is very natural and understandable that many people feel safer confiding their most sensitive feelings only to an adoring companion animal. It will never fail our love and trust—except to die.

When sensitive individuals lose a pet, their bereavement is frequently very different than for the loss of a human. It may at first seem remarkable, but many normal people can grieve more for a dear pet than for a close relative or friend—or sometimes even a spouse. Mourning for a pet is usually not comparable to any other kind of bereavement. We share a large part of our lives with pets, including some very private feelings which we would never allow ourselves to trust or communicate to another person. The relationship we develop with a pet defines the quality and style of our lives. We engender this, and ultimately become products of our creation. We love them as pets, as surrogate children, or as replacements for other people. We can dote on them, squandering our precious energies, resources, and time, or we can treat them as joyful companions in our own trek through life. That is our individual choice.

As we see, the bond between humans and pets has evolved dramatically, from biblical through modern times. Today, they are only rarely used as working animals, as in herding, sledding, or hunting. Now, a desire for the special company of a pet is all the justification we need. The most important function that animal companionship now serves is an emotional/psychological one. The pet's presence is comforting and full of love, restoring and reinforcing the ego, strength, and self-image of its master. Thus, our evolving human-pet bond has become a modern phenomenon—in an increasingly mechanical and dangerous world.

ACCEPTING THE LOSS

The human-pet bond is growing pervasive and strong in recent times, and we have come to a changing point in human behavior and awareness of the effects this has on us. Pet bereavement and its related concerns are emerging as a new, powerful social phenomenon of our Western culture. The fast growth and visibility of vast pet-related industries is also causing a new public awareness of this once little-understood and secret bond.

The sharing between people and pets offers many private and precious moments together. They are as unique as they are intensely personal and gratifying. Such mutual love is its own greatest justification for us. We find joy in our pets, as well as ourselves. Children have their security blankets; we have our pets.

We get much love and delight from them in life, and we grieve deeply for them when they die. Because of the unique enhancement they provide in our lives, they become a treasured part of us, forever. When a pet's life ends, more dies than just a beloved companion animal. Since we subliminally make them into living symbols of our own innocence and purest feelings, it can feel as if a treasured secret part of each of us also dies. But this can be reborn as we slowly pick up our shattered emotional pieces and move on. At this point in our healing, it is often natural to feel a need for a spiritual reunion with the pet. It is in our nature to want to believe that our souls will meet again—

and in a better way when we eventually follow them. This feeling stays with us for the rest of our lives, as a living tribute to the pet.

Pet lovers all talk so knowingly about the bond because we have such a deep emotional involvement with it. Animals who become our companions quickly turn into our best friends and confidants—constant supporters and even spiritual comrades. Therefore, we are really all committed experts on this subject.

The bond really is a very complex psychological relationship—and a challenge to define. The first word associations that may come to mind are *attachment, union, kinship, link, relationship, connection, commitment, loyalty, alliance, covenant.* Although many of these make good sense, they still really don't completely say what the bond is. That is because we are trying to define love, and that is so difficult. Perhaps it is not even possible. So instead of struggling with a definition, which has to be limited, at best, let's examine what the bond is, in terms of its affects on us, emotionally and psychologically.

But before we can do that, we first have to take note of the kinds of bonding relationships people have with their pets. There are three basic classifications: *weakly bonded, moderately bonded,* and *profoundly bonded.*

To some, the bond is not much more than a responsibility for physical care, such as food, hygiene, etc. For various personal reasons these people tolerate having pets around, but they do not really love them. Unfortunately, this is a commitment that is often breached. We see sad evidence of this all the time. These pet owners are weakly bonded—at best.

To others, a pet is a loving, pleasing *thing* to have around the house. It is a source of amusement and pleasure—but in too many cases the animal remains an "it" in the owner's mind. However, in this second category of owners there are still many who do love their pets. But that is a limited affection, and it primarily serves only their needs and more immediate satisfactions. When a pet dies in one of these families, there is sadness and maybe even some heartache, but that passes very quickly. These pet owners are moderately bonded.

And that leaves the last category of pet owners. Readers of this book are probably profoundly bonded. It seems characteristic that when we first meet our future companion animal we all react emotionally. Our earliest responses are spontaneous and loving—and nurturing.

None of us can be impassive to an adorable kitten or puppy (or any other baby animal). We experience a heartwarming sense of affection. And of course, that is enhanced by our rapidly growing deep interest and desire to provide the best possible care for this foundling.

Small pets are cute and endearing, and we can lovingly cuddle and hold them as we would a baby. Although our larger pets would certainly like this as well, it is not so practical. So we learn to admire their strength, character, and dedicated roles as our ever-vigilant and loyal protectors. What wonderful friends and outlets our pets are for us, regardless of their size or age!

In the cases of adopting older animals, we react protectively, wanting to take them in and lavish on them the love and care that is so abundant in our hearts—and which they need so desperately. In addition to being attractive pets, they are living personalities whom we learn to recognize and adore. We also appreciate their innocence and "I am who I am" straightforwardness—without any hint of self consciousness or doubt.

Since their ability to "speak" with us is so limited, we fine-tune our sensitivities to such a degree that we feel certain that we know almost everything about them—including their needs and emotions. When they try to tell us something, we feel so good figuring it out (or frustrated, when it is not understood). Psychologists are only just beginning to acknowledge the comforting, reassuring response in us that is actuated when we speak to pets. It is akin to the positive feedback that mothers experience when they sing and talk to their babies. And who among us has never felt the novel joy of interspecies communication and love? This aspect of the bond is something wonderful and special—and only we can really appreciate it.

It also must be acknowledged and understood that we bond more strongly with some pets than with others. This is normal. Even our children affect us this way. We love them all, but they hold different and special places in our hearts. Each is individual, and so distinctive, and we respond to them all in varying ways. That should not be something to invent guilt about later.

For a brief objective look at your own bonding, pay attention for just a few minutes to how you verbalize to your pet. That will tell you volumes that you may not have even considered previously. In many ways they are our non-human children. We don't speak to adult people with the same nuances. Then assess your own feelings during those intimate times when your pet looks you directly in the eyes, long and lovingly. Even without any verbal communication, this can feel intensely spiritual. We all sense something extraordinary and moving at such moments.

And for obvious reasons, very early on we start referring to the pet as *he* or *she*—and never *it*. The beloved and devoted animal becomes integrated as a fundamental member of the family. Indeed, some people don't like the term "pet owner" and will not even refer to any companion animal as a "pet."

Because of their complete dependency on us for every physical need, we develop a heightened sense of responsibility—committing ourselves to a personal determination that nothing will ever be overlooked. The pet responds to this, just as a baby would—naturally and with complete innocence and loving trust. Being responsive humans, we automatically react by developing an enhanced sense of commitment. Bonds like this grow even stronger with time. Actually, that kind of dedication creates ever-growing intimacy and emotional dependency in us. It is a prime factor in understanding this amazing rapport that has become such a basic part of who we are.

Each companion animal has a unique personality, and is full of innocent love and needs. Naturally, that brings out an overwhelming nurturing response in us, which never stops growing in our hearts. It is actually very much like having a new baby. Not only does this individual life and character thrive and develop—so does our relationship. This kind of love grows, and is ever-joyous and rewarding. And the bond becomes an essential part of us. Our everyday lives become completely involved and constructed around this unique union and dedication.

But this baby-like kinship is different, in that a pet does not grow up and leave us, as a child would. Companion animals are always dependent and constant, while still embodying total love and dedication to us. And who can be immune to that? It melts our hearts to be loved so absolutely, and without any judgmentalism. Even our closest human associates cannot be that innocent, pure, and dedicated.

This is only a brief account of the bond. It becomes a living and potent give-and-take emotional entity, with dynamics that shape and completely change our lives—during and even after the dear animal's life. It is a relationship that combines the elements of intimacy, love, companionship, spirituality, caregiving, and childlike dependency. And it is as profound as it is unique. Interestingly, the more we do for others the more needed we feel. And as that develops we become even more strongly bonded.

Many people are lonely and need to have pets to be their friends and companions. They are especially vulnerable, and it is too easy for them to be criticized for their personal problems and circumstances. But whatever their motivation—age, infirmity, loneliness, a sense of social inferiority—it makes no difference. The relationship with their companion animals is more than just beneficial or therapeutic. It is pure love. The pets don't judge them—and nobody else has any right to. The bond is essential medicine for all of us, regardless of our reasons or needs. Our human urgency for love and nurture is ideally satisfied by our intimacy with companion animals. The bond we form enriches us in unique and important ways. It consummates the relationship with a sense of security and love that is unlike anything else.

But death is so upsetting and confusing. How can we look for answers when we can't even comprehend the basic questions? All life is a kind of metaphor. But there is so much potential learning and growth to be gleaned from it. Each of us plays a role in this, with our beloved pets—not ever really understanding the larger picture.

So when a dear pet's life ends, it really is very understandable and normal for us to grieve and suffer a unique sense of bereavement. We have to learn how to cope with the *physical* breaking of the bond. After the initial stages of mourning, we come to realize that the deeply personal spiritual aspects of the bond still remain unbroken. And because of this we begin to understand that each pet's spirit is wonderful and symbolic to us. We learn more about love and ourselves, from coming to appreciate this. That is one of the many gifts that they leave us to discover. And with our longer lives we continue to evolve—enriched by the wonderful bond that lives on in us, forever.

SERVICE DOGS

Service dogs play a doubly important role in the lives of people with disabilities. In addition to being adored and respected pets, they physically help the owners perform. These wonderful animals give vital assistance and services that allow their owners to function again. What an amazing relationship this is! The bond here is especially profound. The owner's self-image and sense of identity is intimately involved with the dog. This is very different than with other pets. Sadly, when a service dog dies or becomes disabled itself, the owner must quickly replace it. There is no real time for mourning—and the grief here is exceptionally profound. Too few people understand this. The loss of a service pet goes far beyond the loss of a beloved pet. Unfortunately, there are still too few agencies or counselors available to provide knowing and compassionate therapy at such a terrible time.

CHAPTER 2

Responsibility

He prayeth well who loveth well both man and bird and beast.

—*Samuel Taylor Coleridge*

When we make that wonderful decision to have a pet, we create a complex set of responsibilities for ourselves. It is similar to the obligations of caring for a child. But in some ways, caring for a pet is even more difficult, since children grow up, become independent, and outlive us. Pets do not. They are completely reliant on us for everything, all of their lives. When they die, the special responsibilities we took on concerning them are gone—completely and dramatically. But suddenly, we are forced to take on new challenging obligations.

Our responsibilities now shift to providing a new kind of necessary care and consideration to ourselves—and the concerned people in our lives who seem unable to grasp the full extent of our plight. Paradoxically, we owe them something, too. (We will examine that later.) Sometimes our beloved pets give us a mission in life—after they leave us.

THE COMMITMENT OF PROVIDING CARE

The initial decision to have a pet requires acceptance of total obligation and responsibility. This includes caring for *every* aspect of the pet's life: health happiness, and well-being. We volunteer for a duty that soon becomes a passion, an act of love, and our new lifestyle. As our pets become more and more dear to us, this responsibility becomes routine, completely rearranging the basic patterns of our lives. We bond to our pets permanently and care and provide for them as we would for dependent children. They become an integral part of us.

As self-appointed stewards, we are totally and singly responsible for our pet's life and well-being. In a sense, we assume godlike roles. Our pets look to us with love and complete trust and confidence that we will provide and take care of everything. But despite our desire to arrange their lives in the best possible way, we cannot control the universe. We are unable to protect them from all possible dangers. Accidents and illnesses will befall them. When bad things happen, we may feel we have failed in our responsibility—with all its accompanying guilt. Our sense of failure is usually our own invention. Wisdom sometimes is temporarily affected by our human frailty. There will always be moments when our responsibility is redirected by a complexity of circumstances that can be truly beyond our control or understanding.

Sometimes our grief involves going through a period of anger at ourselves, and we challenge our previous actions. It is important to realize that whatever reasons we had were valid *at the time*. We can't judge our past actions or inactions using hindsight and insight we developed later. Hindsight should be used as a learning tool for the future—not as a way to create guilt about the past. It can be so easy to start obsessing about this. That cannot help, but it will hurt you. Nobody can possibly have all the right answers all the time. It is folly to regret not being all-wise.

During the precious lifetime of a pet, we must provide everything and assume a responsibility that cannot be taken casually. We have to deal with nutrition, medical care, toys, playmates, status, and quality of life—as well as anything else that may be of concern. There are also daily feedings, the water dish has to be checked regularly, visual checkups of the pet's appearance and health must be made each day, and the long list goes on. Strangely enough, this constant obligation strengthens our bond with our pets, and we actually become even more responsible and loving. Our personal investment has its rewards, too. It admits us into a private and very special world of mutual love and pleasure with our pets. The mutual bonding becomes a wonderful exchange of need and fulfillment between owner and pet. We involve our dear animal friends in a unique relationship that shares a much more personal side of us than we safely entrust to almost any human. Actually, they become our soul mates.

But, paradoxically, that can have its bad side, too. Because of a pet's innocent and complete dependency on us, we sometimes allow ourselves to become too emotionally dependent on her. We lose perspective on the relationship. And that can set us up for an emotional disaster later.

OUR RESPONSIBILITY TO OURSELVES

When we assume responsibility as stewards, we must also include stewardship of ourselves. Normally we don't think about that. We become too reliant on our pets—and that can be dangerous. There is no place for death in our love. When the pet eventually dies, as all must, the shock usually distorts our view of how we had handled things. Very often this can produce a vague but profound sense of intense personal failure and ill-defined guilt.

We are flung into bereavement and its stages. As ready as we may be intellectually, we are never really prepared emotionally for the death of a beloved pet. We all need as much help as we can get. At this time, we must draw on our own inner resources. But at such an emotional time, this insight is generally not available to us.

In the early stages of bereavement, it may be nearly impossible to accept that any good or healing will eventually come of this. It can be a normal response to even resent or reject any such suggestion—as though someone is attempting to offer inappropriate answers, trying to proffer a "bright side" when the whole world is dark. So many grieving people are afraid of letting go of their grief; they think it means letting go of the love and memories. But it really is releasing the sharp edge of the pain so we can go on with our lives. Our beloved pets become a permanent part of us and they stay forever in our hearts, enriching and blessing us.

The heartbreak we endure can be so tragic that we feel we need to suffer, without end. But it is absolutely essential to give ourselves permission to heal. Otherwise, we are spinning our wheels and will stay mired in our misery. At first, it is natural to want to cling to the pain. If we tried too soon to get rid if it, that would feel disloyal. Yes, that's irrational, but it's how we all process our loss.

Usually, we suffer from a terrible sense of guilt and failed responsibility. Justified or not, these feelings become an extremely private and personal matter that we tend to isolate from the rest of the world. Too often, even our closest friends and family can't grasp the depth and extent of our bereavement. So at this critical time of need, others close to us may seem to fail us because of their lack of understanding. If they are not pet lovers, or if they have a fear of death, their inability to respond in more supportive ways may seem insensitive—or even callous and judgmental. We owe it to them, as well as to ourselves, to try to maintain some degree of control during these very difficult times. Our passions can run strong, and our personal relationships with others can be strained or even broken when we are grieving for a beloved pet.

When bereaving the loss of a pet, we must open ourselves to a new awareness. That is where expert bereavement counseling and books like this one can be of enormous help. We are all made into better people by our beloved pets—at least they give us the potential for that. But what we actually do with this potential is another matter entirely.

As suggested earlier, when a beloved pet dies we lose a very close member of our immediate family—and a precious extension of ourselves. But the full responsibility we took on is not yet finished; we must now live on without the pet. That obligation to ourselves is one that we must be aware of and honor during this especially difficult time of grief. Healing our pain is a responsibility we owe to ourselves. If our loving companion animals could speak to us from beyond the grave that is exactly what they would ask us to do. And after a few days, if we are still unable or unwilling to give ourselves permission to grieve or heal, it is important to try to understand why. The emotional baggage we all carry can be disabling at times.

Our obligation to our pets lives on as we make ourselves receptive to transforming their memory into a positive, treasured part of ourselves—never to be lost. Some mourners temporarily fall apart emotionally, losing many aspects of personal control. This is a normal part of mourning and not necessarily a bad reaction. It will ease with time. But if it doesn't, then we owe it to ourselves to recognize that there are other major psychological burdens we all carry, and some of these may be impeding our healing. A pet bereavement counselor can't help with this, and the pain will not really be resolved unless proper therapy is sought.

Responsibility

Change is one of the many things in life that our beloved pets are here to help us with. Learning about this from them is only one of the many various gifts they leave behind for us. To ignore it would be such a shame as well as an additional loss—almost a slight to their loving memory. Our pets leave us gifts that take time to discover. When we finally are able to let go of the sharpest pain—and can smile again with living and loving memories and healing tears—things start getting better. Then we begin to discover some of these wonderful gifts that we couldn't identify while we were still in deep mourning. That is part of their legacy to us.

Most of us really don't know how to respond emotionally to death. However, using our innate common sense, we can find some guidelines from within. We, too, have animal intuition, just as our beloved pets do. Wouldn't it be a great testimony to them to try to learn from their way of dealing with loss? We should not deny ourselves the chance to call upon the pet's continuing presence in our hearts to improve our ongoing lives.

Even during mourning, our lives must go on—but in a new way. We are now enriched by the wonderful experience of having shared with and learned so much from our beloved companion animals. Each of us is capable of wonders. When we reach deep down into our very being, we all can come up with some amazing things. And our pets have helped us achieve this.

We have a hard time accepting emotionally that they have such shorter lives than we do. But if they outlived us, who would care for and love them when we die? And who would be there to honor their memories? Maybe this is the best way. It will always be very painful and tragic when a beloved pet dies. But that is what mourning is all about. Beloved pets are unique in our hearts. The love we have for them—and from them—makes it all so wonderful and worthwhile, despite the unavoidable heartache and tears.

Our dear ones bless us, just as we do them, and they enrich and prepare us for moving on in life. The loving memories become a permanent part of who we are, and they live on in our hearts. Our continuing and improving lives can be our best memorials to them.

Monument to a gallant soldier.
Photo by George Wirt. Courtesy of Bide-A-Wee, 1992

Memorial to a beloved ferret.

Photo by W. Sife. Courtesy of Abbey Glen Pet Memorial Park

SENIOR CITIZENS

Single senior citizens who have pets tend to be extremely affectionate with them. Although an older person's health and mobility may be deteriorating, the love for and from the pet is steadfast. A companion animal is there to share the unique loneliness and the changes in one's ability to do things. Very intelligent companion animals are able to comprehend these changes, and help their owners make accommodations.

As hearing, sight, and general physical condition diminish, the person's motivation to savor life sometimes weakens. Visitors, if any, usually become scarce, and life becomes a more closed-in experience with the pet. Who can fully comprehend the countless days and years that older pet owners must spend talking their lonely hearts out to their pets, and disclosing precious memories and dreams? The companion animal silently shares everything, and becomes a very dear and necessary part of the senior's life. Not so surprisingly, even younger single people can easily fall into this dependent way of life.

Eventually, when the pet itself shows signs of aging or deteriorating health, the senior is forced to rise to the occasion. These additional responsibilities can become a real problem to someone who is not functioning well himself. On the positive side, taking special care of a pet makes the older person feel even more vital, loved, and needed. However, when outside assistance becomes necessary, it may feel like a great personal tragedy for the senior. When someone relieves him of those duties, the wise old pet owner may feel that he has failed in a final responsibility to a beloved companion. Most of us have no idea how very sad this makes so many of our older people.

Usually, senior citizens have the wisdom that comes with many years of life experience. They have seen friends and family die, and they have learned to become more philosophical and tolerant of pain, loss, and loneliness. But deep bereavement and mourning is very common when they lose a pet. Death is so much closer and more meaningful to them, now.

Sadly, because of their isolation and pride, we too often don't really see their anguish. It is too comfortable to ignore them at such a time. Perhaps it is our own uneasiness with death that can result in fear or inability to offer real compassion and consolation to people who are nearing the ends of their own lives. It is too easy to lovingly lead them out into pasture and walk away, pretending (or hoping) to ourselves that we have helped. We need to remember that seniors form very special bonds with their pets. And they grieve more profoundly than most people realize—especially at this time when they are trying to make some sense of their own impending deaths. Regrettably, no studies have yet been conducted on this subject.

UNHEALTHY RELATIONSHIPS

A heightened sense of responsibility can be a wonderful aspect of raising a pet. But on the other hand, it can be taken to destructive extremes. Although commitment spans a wide spectrum of duties, its whole purpose should be justified by the mutual joys and pleasures of the pet's company and relationship. When we get too capricious or involved in the details of stewardship, we then lose the healthy perspective that is so important for the relationship.

Some relationships with pets can become pathological when the owner assumes a distorted sense of responsibility, vastly disproportionate to the animal's nature and needs. For example, we have seen many cases where pets are regularly dressed up in different costumes. In more extreme examples, they are given dolls or baby toys, and they are even pushed about in small carriages. This owner behavior gets a bit bizarre, and it denies an animal's true nature.

A strong argument can be made that the pet is actually being abused by not being permitted to live as an animal. Love is not a license to try to change a being's nature. In such instances, we must be concerned with an owner who may be losing a grip on things, or may be acting out unresolved nurturing needs and fantasies. This can become a serious problem and may require professional attention.

Case History

A married woman in her early fifties adopted an adorable puppy from the local animal shelter. She and her husband were well-off financially, and therefore they didn't have to work. Her husband thought her doting attention on the pet was cute, but he wondered if she didn't have other more important things to do. She explained that she had a sense of responsibility for the puppy's well-being.

The woman became very involved with training the little dog and talked to it as if it was a baby. Her need to be a nurturer again had a very powerful influence on her. She adored the pet, lavishing so much attention on it that it became very spoiled. This made her husband even more upset. He resented that her relationship with their grown children had never been strong, and now they rarely ever came to visit.

In addition to becoming a spoiled brat, the dog developed a habit of barking and chasing the vehicles that drove on the isolated street in front of their suburban home. After three years, the dog was struck by a car and severely injured, with the spine and ribs crushed. The veterinarian had to ask the woman's husband to insist that she allow euthanasia immediately. Although the dog was in intense pain, she still could not find the strength to do anything but weep in near hysterics. The husband finally gave his own permission, and the pet was mercifully euthanized.

The woman then withdrew into a severe depression, hating her husband for what he and the veterinarian had done. Their children came to visit and tried to help, but they were rejected. Although it may have been highly irrational, she felt that her responsibility to the pet had been usurped and that everyone was insensitive to her plight—or unwilling to understand.

The real problems, however, had little to do with the dog. Its death was only the trigger mechanism that released long repressed and powerful psychological issues that had never been addressed. She was experiencing an emotional breakdown of major proportions.

Counseling for problems that had to do only with pet bereavement could not help her; intense psychotherapy was needed. Not surprisingly, it turned out that she had suffered since childhood from deep feelings of inferiority and insecurity. Her parents had never let her do anything important by herself. She was never allowed the necessary sense of responsibility and fulfillment one must have to feel successful at anything. She felt that people were always correcting her, and she developed anxieties about sharing anything, including ideas. Her fear of being criticized or judged made her so vulnerable that she chose to take the offensive in all social situations. Actually, she was afraid of anything she was not able to control.

After her dog's death it took more than a year of intense analysis and therapy for her to become aware of her patterns of behavior. It turned out that she had wanted to successfully raise the puppy to make up for her perceived failure in rearing her own children. She really loved them, but was always in constant dread of failure and criticism. Being an only child herself, with insensitive and unresponsive parents, she had nobody to confide in. And she grew up alone, feeling inferior and insecure about nearly everything. When she got married, it was to a man who dominated her, and she even allowed her young children to take on this dominant role with her. Until her breakdown, she had no way to gain perspective on her self-destructive sense of inferiority and seemingly aggressive attitude toward others.

After more than a year of intensive psychotherapy, she was able to tentatively establish new relationships with her husband and children. She also realized that part of her responsibility to her dog should have included enjoyment and pleasure in their relationship, rather than worry and fear of criticism of the way she reared it. Of course, that applied to her children, as well. Her condition is very much improved, and she plans to get a new puppy soon.

CHAPTER 3

The
Grieving
Process

Your joy is your sorrow unmasked.

—Kahlil Gibran

"How long must I suffer like this?" is one of the first questions asked of bereavement counselors. This is a unique experience that can cause almost unbearable and unrelenting anguish It calls for as much help as possible. Generally, deep bereavement may last from a few days to several weeks, depending on many variables. There is no criterion for how long "normal" grieving takes for anyone. It is something that can never be predicted. People mourn much more intensely for someone on whom they were emotionally dependent. Of course, this includes pets. *You will grieve as much as you love.*

Some pet owners still fear that it is not socially acceptable to mourn for a pet as they would for a human. This causes enormous internal conflict and intimidation for them. They need compassion and supportiveness at this especially painful and vulnerable time. As a result, these isolated individuals suffer much more than they normally would. Additionally, they run the risk of suppressing these feelings to the point where it could impair the healing process.

A Prayer for Animals

Hear our humble Prayer, O God,
For our friends the animals,
especially for animals who are suffering;
for any that are hunted or lost or deserted or
frightened or hungry,
for all that must be put to death.
We entreat for them all Thy mercy and pity,
and for those who deal with them we ask
a heart of compassion
and gentle hands and kindly words.
Make us, ourselves, to be true friends to animals,
and so to share the blessings of the merciful.

—*Albert Schweitzer*

In a very real sense, the onset of this bereavement may be regarded as a type of separation anxiety. The well-established patterns of our lives are abruptly terminated by the death of a beloved pet. Suddenly, we are left alone and in a state of shock. The problems that arise can seem overwhelming, and this needs to be addressed properly and quickly.

UNDERSTANDING GRIEF AND MOURNING

Understanding the psychological responses and phases of grief and mourning that other people have gone through can help us when we go through this same process. This special knowledge can be used to help the grief-stricken mourner get through the worst of it and better understand what is happening.

Many people have a culturally induced fear of death and are frightened at being so controlled by this. As a result they are primed to cause real psychological harm to themselves when refusing to allow their true feelings to emerge. These profound feelings are real and need to be addressed, in order to heal and come to resolution.

We are products of our Western Civilization, in which death, dying, and anything to do with it is perceived as bad and to be avoided. Unfortunately, we are not conditioned to cope with the death of our deceased pets until after the fact. And even then our perceptions are distorted by that indoctrination. It scares us, and brings up hidden fears of our own mortality. And it can make the mourning period even worse.

The heartbreak we endure can be so tragic that at first many individuals feel the need to suffer, without end. It is absolutely essential to give ourselves permission to heal. Otherwise, we are "spinning our wheels" and will stay mired in our misery. If we are unable or unwilling to give ourselves that necessary permission to heal, it is important to try to understand what is causing this. As mentioned earlier, we all carry emotional baggage that can be overwhelming at times.

Mourning pain is normal and inevitable, but continuing misery is optional. Unfortunately, there is no easy way past this. We have to go through the worst of the pain and grief, in order to put it behind us. Then with healing tears we can help the loving memories come back. Mourning is all about pain and grief. That is the eternal way of all living things. It is something that is so hard to grasp and cope with— especially during the earlier stages of loss.

A tribute to one who will live on in memory.

*Photo by W. Sife. Courtesy of
Hartsdale Canine Cemetery, Inc.*

In memory of a cherished bunny.

*Photo by W. Sife. Courtesy of
Abbey Glen Pet Memorial Park*

That old adage about time being the healer can be very misleading. Time only dulls the sharp edge of new pain, and then gives us a better opportunity to heal ourselves of the worst of it. But some of the ache remains with us, forever. Yes, time does help with that transition. Yet it is not a cure; there is none for this. Happily, our beloved memories continue on with us, as they should.

Time does not erase the loving memories—or the sadness. It only makes them easier to live with by incorporating them into our continuing (and hopefully, improving) lives. You must go through the pain, in order to put the worst of it behind you. Otherwise you can't heal, and it will be so much worse for you.

While in the early stages of bereavement and profound grief, it may feel nearly impossible to accept that any good or healing will eventually come of this. It can be a normal response to even resent or reject any such suggestion—as though someone is trying to offer inappropriate answers, trying to proffer a "bright side" when the whole world is darkened.

Well-intentioned people try to get us to act cheery. But they don't realize that we must go through a period of mourning and bereavement. They don't want us to cry, but that is a necessary part of the healing process. We have to learn to be patient with them (as well as with ourselves). It helps to understand their ignorance and fear of the profundity of all this. At this time you also need to schedule yourself to be with good, supportive people—and distracting things. During mourning one doesn't feel like having any pleasure, but this is the general direction you have to lead yourself in. It is part of the healing process out of the pain. It is also helpful to reduce the number of visual reminders left around the house. They inhibit the bereaving person from adapting, and starting new routines and adjustments.

A second experience with death can be more painful than expected. That is because it can stir up repressed and deep-rooted psychological problems that were never resolved. Also, the staggering blow of a pet's death can easily trigger other issues that had been long dormant, just beneath the surface of consciousness. The experienced bereavement counselor should be able to point this out and help direct the client to professional psychological counseling that is specifically trained for this kind of problem.

Grievous mourning is always distinguished by specific reactions. It has been observed that human behavior during this time expresses itself in related phases or stages. This psychological reaction is an evolving process that requires time to complete the healing. However, there are things that the mourner can do to help this process along.

Talking about one's loss and feelings helps the recovery. Pouring out important thoughts and emotions and sharing them with compassionate people is a necessary step in this terrible passage through bereavement. It is important to vent these emotions—and it is okay to cry! In fact, it is necessary. Unfortunately, we often see extremes of these responses. On the other hand, many people who are in bereavement for a pet suppress this normal human expression of their heartbreak.

Repression invariably creates new problems, in addition to the loss already experienced. It will always take its terrible toll. Later. There are certain basic human emotions that must be released so we can grow past them. Some people need guidance learning this. However, there are those mourners who cannot or will not control their crying, and they unintentionally end up embarrassing or even imposing on anyone near them. Despite overriding grief, we still have social obligations when in the company of others. Fortunately, we usually have the ability to control these emotions when we are not alone.

The grief and confusion that follow the death of a cherished companion animal need to be better understood. When our beloved pets die, we can feel completely out of control—overwhelmed by jumbled feelings of loss and failure. This is almost always accompanied by a sense of deep personal guilt, confusion, and personal vulnerability.

Personal bereavement for a beloved pet very often is far more intense than is perceived by others. Of course, the degree of mourning and distress is determined by many individual factors, which may be impossible for them to grasp at this time. But the pain is so real that it must not be belittled or discounted by anyone, including the self-conscious mourner.

When we live with a dear person or pet for any extended part of our lives, we establish patterns in our lives and behavior. These become fixed routines and a living part of us and our personal sense of security. We are all creatures of habit. Everyone finds comfort in following the same general systemized ways in their daily lives. This is natural and normal. But when that person or pet dies, we are suddenly left with an enormous emptiness. Something basic and stable is ripped out of our lives and we are never quite prepared for it. It is a healthy and normal response to experience such intense personal grief at this time.

The Grieving Process

DIFFERENT REACTIONS TO GRIEF

In our society, males generally have a much more difficult time during any bereavement period. They have been conditioned by a lifetime of restrictive customs and cultural mores—and disciplined that it is not manly to cry, even in private. Fortunately, insight is improving into this unwise controlling of natural behavior.

Too often the "macho" image has to be presented, while their hearts are secretly breaking. In Western cultures, even men who have gone through training in "consciousness raising" tend to revert to their instinctive tendencies to maintain their traditional masculine image. It can be a very tough fight within one's self. Men are not supposed to cry or get too emotionally upset. It just doesn't fit the accepted image. Of course, that is nonsense and very self-defeating. Also, as mentioned earlier, the consequences of suppressing these intense feelings can surface later in many personally damaging ways.

It is interesting to note that although the population of male and female pet owners is about equal, far more women acknowledge their emotional need for support or even counseling. Men will keep their passionate feelings hidden as much as possible. With little means of venting their grief, they tend to find some solace by reading about the subject or observing and identifying with others who are grieving. That activity is safe and secret and does not reveal their perceived emotional "weakness" to anyone. Fortunately, the rapidly increasing public awareness of pet bereavement is making the male's expression of emotional distress a bit easier and more natural. But it still takes a lot more soul-searching for men in our culture to grieve as they often truly need to.

Sexual stereotyping is something we are gradually starting to do something about. Ours is an age of beginning enlightenment on many levels, as never before in history. We are all made into better people by our beloved pets, and offered an enhanced future. At least they give us the potential for that.

Depression is a normal human response that can be produced by particularly stressful circumstances. Intense bereavement will produce a whole spectrum of powerful emotions and psychological responses. It is a natural reaction to feel overwhelmed and depressed at this time. Indeed, there would be something very wrong if we did not react this way. We are normally depressed at the loss of anything we hold dear. This includes our habits, patterns of behavior, and even our possessions.

If a torn jacket, an unfavorable report, a smashed-up bike, or a dented car can depress us, certainly the loss of a beloved pet should do at least the same.

People who are prone to depression are at an even greater risk of being wiped out, emotionally, when a beloved pet dies. They need to address this and see their therapist right away. Unfortunately, not all psychotherapists are good at counseling in pet bereavement as well. It may be necessary for the mourner to see a petloss counselor at the same time. And it is critical to share what is learned with his or her therapist. Frequently, antidepressants are needed and helpful during this critical time. It is important to realize that they don't help the grief. All they can do is to make the patient less depressed and, hopefully, more receptive to the therapy. Hopefully, the repressed problems will not prevent gaining new and helpful perspectives on their bereavement.

THE STAGES OF GRIEF

Since the late 1960s, starting with Elizabeth Kubler-Ross, a few pioneering Western psychologists and sociologists began to make a science of studying the psychology of humans during bereavement. These investigating professionals observed that there are regular, predictable phases that all normal people must pass through during intense mourning, to get past their grief. This is nature's way of helping us to heal psychologically from such an emotional blow, and the process must run its slow course to be effective.

These phases or stages were then identified, listed, and studied intensively. It was quickly realized that they are universal to all humans raised in Western culture. After suffering the death of a beloved one, this process is a normal and predictable healing reaction of the mind, and it should not be interfered with. Mourners are counseled to face their grief and cope with it, however intense or debilitating it may be. One has to live through the pain to get past it. Because it is a normal response to avoid grief and suffering, this kind of psychological healing is especially difficult and requires time. Making a recovery that results in emotional stability is a gradual process and needs a great deal of patience.

The Grieving Process

People who resist or even suppress their transition through these stages always create more complex problems that will continue to distress them. It was learned that the only way to remedy the situation is to address the unresolved problems. This can be accomplished—even after many years of suffering, which could have been prevented.

These stages are characteristic and transitional, and they may manifest themselves simultaneously or in a different sequence than listed here. Although they usually do unfold in the order given, each will appear in due course and then fade away, if resolved. There is nothing to worry about if you perceive a shifting in the sequence. Nature has provided us with a natural beginning, middle, and end to all of this. Going with the painful flow will heal you.

The bereavement stages listed by Dr. Elizabeth Kubler-Ross were formulated to deal with human death. They have been modified and interpolated here to be specific to our experience in losing a pet. The reader should be aware that variations of the names and sequences for these stages have been suggested by some writers. But our specialized list is now universally accepted, and will be examined in detail, in the next six chapters:

Shock and Disbelief	Chapter 4
Anger, Alienation, and Distancing	Chapter 5
Denial	Chapter 6
Guilt	Chapter 7
Depression	Chapter 8
Resolution (Closure)	Chapter 9

Some counselors prefer naming grief as an additional stage. This is not used here because it is believed that the term is too general. Grieving is so personal that it cannot be clearly defined without becoming vague or generalized. Grief can be seen as our natural, overall emotional response while progressing through all phases of bereavement. Since all of us have such unique reactions and responses to death, it is necessary to examine each of these stages in some detail. The following chapters will guide you through this.

GRIEF IS A NATURAL RESPONSE

Intense grief is not an expression of extreme or abnormal behavior. Nor is it an indication of a neurosis or disorder. It is a natural response to sudden, overwhelming loss, and it runs a normal course within wide margins. It is considered normal as long as the grieving person is not in any danger of harming him- or herself or anyone else, and if it does not persist for an unnaturally long time. Support and compassion are what mourners need most while working their way through this heartache. This is the terrible emotional price that we have to be ready to pay. But despite the anguish, how can any of us say that the love and good we gave and got is not worth it all?

It needs to be noted here that unresolved other losses can be brought back to conscious awareness, after traumatic incidents—or even as a "side effect" of narcotics used in surgery. When in bereavement for a beloved pet, this can suddenly become additionally stressful.

People have so many differences in personality and the way that they are affected that it is not possible to predict how everyone will react through these stages. Thus, we have to deal with them as they arise. There are many factors that can affect us when dealing with our bereavement. These variables include: past experience with grief and/or death; individual personality differences and histories; degree and quality of social support; spiritual, religious, and ethnic background; cultural influences; age and gender; and of course, the special nature of the lost relationship. It has proven to be of great help to gain insights into these variables. The best ways to achieve better insight are through counseling, self-analysis, reading, and networking with others who have suffered this type of loss. Petloss support groups—whether attended in person or online—are excellent for this.

A beloved pet becomes part of the human companion. When the pet dies, it marks the tragic end of an era in that person's life. This death shockingly starts the forced close of one stage in the owner's life, and the beginning of the next. But each new one is based on the strengths and weaknesses of the last. Certainly the loving memory of the pet remains with us as we live and grow on. Each time a beloved pet dies it is like a painful metamorphosis in the life of the owner. The mourner should become wiser with age, and more seasoned with treasured memories and experiences.

Pain and experience are fundamental to personal growth and wisdom. But during mourning it is natural to want to cling to the pain. If we tried too soon to get rid if it, that would feel disloyal. Yes, that's irrational, but it is how we all process our loss.

Most people occasionally suffer to some degree from the "unworthy me" syndrome (some people more than others). But we must not let ourselves continue to play the victim in life. That is self-destructive, and it also prevents healing during intense bereavement. This demands a lot of introspection, which is also a good sign of healing. And, certainly, that is what our beloved pets would want most for us, now.

It must be mentioned here that there will always be some future emotional aftershocks, long past the period of bereavement. There will be times when we will suddenly and unexpectedly break down in tears for our beloved losses. This is normal, and to be expected. However well adjusted and healed we may be, our loving memories are always there within us. Such love is never forgotten or lost. Fortunately, the pain is not as debilitating as before. Gaining some resolution by going through the transitional phases of bereavement makes this possible.

Some survivors of great personal tragedy tend to be stoic in their behavior, especially when it comes to death. As mentioned, these people also may be inclined to suppress rather than accept their feelings, and will not willingly resolve their grief through mourning. And there are many who feel a need to experience their sense of guilt as self-punishment. Their real problems are not self-understood or perceived by others, and they are in great need of professional psychological counseling.

Ultimately, all life is change and growth. Otherwise, it wouldn't be worth living. It's a very hard lesson to learn, but a necessary one that our beloved pets can teach us. Yet it is nearly impossible to be philosophical or too rational when in deep grief. Our personal growth and evolution is another area covered by the messages they provide for us (if we are receptive to them).

Too many well-intentioned people enjoy playing the psychologist. But they can cause unintentional harm, sometimes even making the person who is grieving feel apologetic, defensive, or defective. With inappropriate intervention, those people often try to create the false impression that everything is really fine and that time is the only thing necessary for healing. This kind of misguided advice can cause the suppression of normal grief responses. And it will harm the process that must always be painfully worked through before resolution can be achieved. Despite their good hearts, they are untrained and unaware of potential problems that could be damaging.

Generally, it is unwise to intervene in anyone's mourning process. Offering impressive psychological terminology and explanations may tend to scare the already upset mourner, when he or she is not in a position to see things as they really are. Bereavers may be pressed into feeling that they are "losing it," although this intense behavior may actually be a normal expression for some individuals at the time.

Death is so upsetting and confusing. How can we look for answers when we can't even comprehend the basic questions? All life is a kind of metaphor. But there is so much potential learning and growth to be gleaned from it. Each of us plays a role in this, with our beloved pets—not ever really understanding the larger picture.

It will always be very painful and grievous when a beloved pet dies. Each one is unique in our hearts. But the love we have for them—and from them—makes it all so wonderful and worthwhile. One of the many gifts our beloved pets leave behind for us is a heightened awareness of our own mortality, and how to make our lives even more meaningful. Our best memorial is how we go on, enriched by their love.

Case History

One of my patients was a widow whose dog died four years before she came to me. When the woman's husband died a few years before the dog, she was shaken, but seemed to stand up well to the shock. She described the mourning period as brief and well-handled. To her it was very important to keep up appearances for the neighbors.

She tried very hard to put on a brave face. All her attention and love then focused on her dog, who reveled in this. As the years went on, the woman grew increasingly dependent on what the dog represented to her. It was made into a combination of surrogate roles—child, best friend, husband.

When the dog died a few years later, she was overwhelmed by inconsolable grief and even had to be hospitalized for a few days. After an intense period of mourning, which was never resolved, she tried to go about a normal way of life, but she couldn't without the dog. She would not get another pet, and as a result, her life became entirely devoted to the remembrance of her deceased dog. Her apartment was turned into a near–shrine, with pictures draped in black and the dog's toys and other memorabilia on prominent display. The pet's ashes and urn occupied the central focus of the living room.

The woman continued this way for a few more years in perpetual unresolved mourning and grief. She was finally referred to me. After analysis, it turned out that much of this abnormal behavior had been in response to other deep-rooted problems she had never faced or resolved. She suffered a deep sense of guilt for not having grieved for her husband as much as she felt she was supposed to. Afraid of letting any feelings get out of hand, she suppressed them. Thus, she could never complete or resolve the mourning process for her husband or for the dog.

Later, she admitted to another major complication. It turned out that early in her marriage she had a baby who died in an auto accident when he was only a year old. She had never forgiven herself or her husband for that, and it was a psychological time bomb just waiting to explode. She had been through two deaths that had affected her greatly, but only after the loss of her beloved dog did she react emotionally. That was the trigger mechanism that set everything off at once.

Her healing depended on dragging out old and very painful memories, and working on each of them. It was critical that she identify and resolve her suppressed feelings of worthlessness and guilt, which she had never been able to admit to herself. Her therapy was long and difficult, taking a few years, but there is a happy ending to the story. She now is living a normal life after having wasted so many precious years. And she is beginning to socialize again, although shy about meeting men. Two cats now live with her as her loving companions and constant support.

Case History

A young man in his mid-twenties called me, explaining on the telephone that his dog had died about a week before and he was much more upset than he should be. He tried to appear in control, but it was clear that he was extremely upset. Not surprisingly, he readily accepted the suggestion to come in for a private session.

He was a rookie cop in the New York City Police Department, married for about three years. His father had also been a cop and was a hard, insensitive man who never allowed him or his brothers to cry. They were told that was only for girls. His dog, a fourteen-year-old Golden Retriever, had been with him since his teens and was almost like a sibling to him. It became old, weak, and half-blind, and it had fallen down a flight of stairs, severely injuring itself. He had to have the beloved pet immediately euthanized. "I thought I was losing it," he told me, describing his heartache.

His young wife was sympathetic, but she could not share his profound bereavement. She was in the last month of her first pregnancy and had other things that concerned her more. He had nobody close who could really understand and had no way to identify and express his anguish. At work he was "one of the boys," trying to make and live up to a reputation of being a tough cop—a "real male." His friends at the precinct were all very "macho." And he was always trying to gain the approval of his veteran partner, an older man who hated signs of weakness of any kind.

He didn't dare expose his feelings of grief and mourning for the dog, feeling certain they would either poke fun at him or think him a wimp, undeserving of their camaraderie or respect. But he realized that something terrible was going on, deep in his head and heart. Even during work he was in a state of emotional distress and tension. He thought about going to a departmental psychologist, but feared the embarrassment he thought that could instigate. He knew that he needed some sort of help, and he had no close friends who could share and commiserate with him in his mourning. In addition, his pastor had discounted and minimized his bereavement for a dog, saying that the grief would go away by itself, soon.

In two sessions he was able to have a good overview of what the bereavement process was like, especially for him. We also discussed his need to hide his feelings, especially when his manhood felt threatened by their exposure. Although these few consultations were not enough to cure all his problems, they established a better sense of understanding and self-assurance. We explored ways he could share his feelings with others who had already experienced the same grief. We also discussed the effect that "macho" attitude had on him and how he could learn to address that in the future. Then, he was able to face his grief and pass through the period of mourning with less emotional chaos. "This was the foothold I needed," he said and decided to start private psychotherapy to help work on other personal problems, as well. "Everything is connected," he said.

CHAPTER 4

Shock and Disbelief

O aching time! O moments big as years!

—John Keats

Shock and a sense of disbelief are the first responses to the death of a beloved pet. This very normal reaction may last from a few hours to several days. This is a time of emotional overload, and initially we usually can't even begin to grasp the full reality of the situation. Our mind is stunned by powerful psychological reactions that can devastate whatever feeble emotional strengths we still have. We respond at this initial stage with a physical or mental numbness that is often overwhelming. We may block out lingering, disturbing images and information related to the death, as if they never happened. During this overwhelming time it is also possible to lose our sense of logic or perspective.

Bereavement counselors are very familiar with the question, "Is he/she really dead?" The question is often repeated over and over, despite the fact that the client has already received specific information or proof of the pet's death. Disbelief and *temporary* rejection of reality are normal mental defenses. This is so common that it is even reflected in an everyday utterance: We are all familiar with the expression that begins, "I can't believe . . . ." At least in other contexts, though, the speaker is able to accept the reality.

BENEATH THIS
STONE
IS BURIED THE
BEAUTIFUL YOUNG
LION GOLDFLECK
WHOSE DEATH WAS
SINCERELY MOURNED
BY HIS MISTRESS
PRINCESS
LWOFF PARLAGHY
NEW YORK 1912

Epitaph for a beautiful young lion.

Photo by W. Sife. Courtesy of
Hartsdale Canine Cemetery, Inc.

RESPONDING TO A SHOCK

In extreme instances, the mind may respond to a shock by becoming completely oblivious to the situation. It may actually refuse to accept any input that supports the traumatic news. It is as if a person is hypnotized and instructed to totally overlook certain information. This response of numbness after the initial shock and impact of the death is the brain's way of protecting itself from having to handle too much, too soon. It shields us from an unbearable overload to the mind that can be caused by grievous news.

The mind has fantastic defenses. For example, there is a similarity between extreme examples of shock and disbelief and some forms of amnesia. In some cases of childhood abuse, the person's memories of the offense are completely suppressed and blocked out. Rarely does the abused person spontaneously recall the offense, and the person could be middle-aged or older before even beginning to remember anything of what really happened.

The mind also plays similar tricks on people who suffer from multiple personality disorder. Because they cannot handle stress, almost any sudden shock or strain will shift them into an invented safe personality who can deal with such a situation. Staggering under the initial shock, the mind shifts realities as a way of buying time to be able to live with a situation that is otherwise unbearable.

Shock is sometimes the first sign of a post-traumatic stress syndrome, such as intense bereavement. When the initial shock and disbelief wear off, an overwhelming torrent of other strong emotional responses will follow. At first, this flood of emotion can be full of distortions and misperceptions. But time will help with the healing, and we must be patient with ourselves despite how abstract that idea may seem to be at the moment. These strange and unpleasant reactions are part of the mourning process, and will normally run their course and fade.

Powerful emotions and intense reactions can prevail for a while. They are normally accompanied by an all-pervading sense of distress, violation, and utter helplessness. Of course, the intensity and duration of these feelings depend on many personal factors. But we need to keep in mind that we are dealing with the sudden impact of human tragedy—something for which we can never be fully prepared.

We tend to heal slower from bereavement than we would from other adversities. That is because we may also be going through separation anxiety over a radical change that has come about so abruptly. In this particular situation, normal patterns of daily living are disrupted and we have no other routines that can carry us through. Sometimes we need the structure of going to work or being seriously involved in some other activity. These can provide the necessary means to keep us going while our inner emotional resources have a chance to rebuild themselves.

We plunge into the depths of our misery and suffer intensely—although to varying degrees. Because of this extreme response, it is not uncommon for people in deep bereavement to wonder about their sanity. But we must realize that there is an important difference between this normal, temporary agony, which will pass, and one that may not ease within a plausible period of time.

In bereavement, a reasonable amount of shock and disbelief are normal responses. These reactions fade and pass fairly quickly, although some of the heartache will remain forever. We all experience this to some degree. The intensity of shock and disbelief is an accurate measure of the emotional distress we will encounter in the bereavement stages that are yet to follow.

The heartbreak we endure often can be so tragic that at first we feel we need to suffer, without end. But it is absolutely essential to eventually give ourselves permission to heal. The "letting go" is only of the debilitating misery—not the love and memories. Our beloved pets become a permanent part of us and stay forever in our hearts, enriching and blessing us. If we are unable or unwilling to give ourselves that permission to get over the worst of the grief, it is important to try to learn why we are reacting that way.

In the early stages of bereavement it may be nearly impossible to accept that any good or healing will eventually come out of this. It can be a normal response to even resent or reject any such suggestion—as though someone is trying to offer inappropriate answers. But that is the grief speaking. Soon enough, the healing will begin—if it is not interfered with.

Eventually, some of your mourning will be accompanied by occasional smiles and loving memories, instead of devastating pain. Then you will know that you are healing. But that takes time, and many more healing tears. There is no easy or painless way out of grief.

ACUTE GRIEF

Acute grief—also called exaggerated grief—is not a normal mourning response. This kind of overreaction is not difficult to identify. Some of its many symptoms are desolation, overwhelming misery, and a terrible agony of the soul. There is often a short loss of rationality involved. Suicidal ideation (but not an attempt) is fairly common. Fortunately, in most cases that is only a passing passion. We often see persistent irritability and sleeplessness, or even their opposites—extreme withdrawal and fatigue. Other signs may be excessive anger, antisocial behavior, or persistent nightmares. Sometimes one will experience hallucinations, such as hearing or seeing glimpses of the deceased pet. These "sightings" are nothing to worry about, if they are not persistent or too upsetting.

Often, this kind of acute stress syndrome is glossed over as something that will eventually go away by itself. It does eventually, if it is confronted and dealt with. But, unfortunately, if it is repressed it will probably fester for the rest of the person's life. There must be a release.

Acute or exaggerated grief is usually experienced by people who are least able to cope with it, and are already emotionally injured and are suffering from other major stresses in their lives. The weight of bereavement can become the proverbial straw that breaks the camel's back for them. Professional help is needed.

Case History

A single woman in her early thirties went on a month-long vacation to Europe. She left her dog at a reputable and expensive boarding kennel. When she returned, she was informed that he had died of sudden heart failure about a week after her departure. Since there had been no way of contacting her, the body was cremated and the ashes kept for her return.

She became furious at the news and refused to accept it as the truth. She was certain that there must be a conspiracy, and felt that her dog must still be alive somewhere. Talks with the veterinarians who tried to save the dog and the managers of the kennel and crematorium only intensified her anger and disbelief. She tried, in vain, to call the police in on the matter. Then she tried to retain a lawyer, who attempted to advise her that she was denying what was, in fact, the reality of the situation. This only further distressed her to the point where she could not go back to work until she received what she deemed to be satisfaction.

A close friend persuaded her to come into therapy just for an initial meeting. Fortunately, we were able to strike up a rapport with one another. Follow-up sessions established that she now felt totally responsible and guilty for having been away and unreachable at this critical time.

We discussed the reasons for her shock and denial, and the truth began to seep in. But it was too painful for her to bear, and she went into a deep depression. It became necessary for a psycho-pharmacologist to prescribe specific drug therapy, to be used in conjunction with her psychotherapy sessions.

Fortunately, she was able to return to work in about two weeks, and she slowly recovered afterward. Prior to that much-needed vacation, other stresses she could not confront had been tearing her apart emotionally. The death of her beloved dog was the trigger mechanism that set her off into shock and extreme denial. She now understands this and is working toward a resolution in regular psychotherapy sessions. Her prognosis is good.

A prayer in bronze.

*Photo by W. Sife. Courtesy of
Matthews International Corporation*

CHAPTER 5

Anger, Alienation, and Distancing

Freeze, freeze, thou bitter sky,
thou dost not bite so nigh
as benefits forgot:
Though thou the waters warp,
thy sting is not so sharp
as friend remembered not.

—William Shakespeare

Sometimes our suffering makes us want to lash out at someone—anyone. The anger stage of bereavement is a temporary response to an overwhelming sense of frustration and outrage. It can take many forms, but it is always easily recognizable. We are ingenious at creating impassioned justifications for redirecting the rage within us. At this time it is very difficult to cope rationally with disappointing or distressing people and situations. Under these circumstances, we may vent this anger in all directions, almost at random.

ACTING OUT ANGER

From a safe state of total responsibility for and control of the pet's life, we are suddenly plunged into a condition of helplessness and despair. We agonize that, somehow, this death should not have happened, and

God, fate, or something we depended on has betrayed us. The absolute nature of death leaves us no bargaining chips. We are totally helpless. This is in stark contrast to the freedom we had in making all decisions before the pet's life was snatched away from us. Suddenly, we have been made powerless and robbed of our love and joy.

This can be unbearably frustrating. It is a normal, temporary response to react with passion when we are suddenly checkmated like this. Most of us have trouble expressing anger at others because we are not effective in using it. But when we are suddenly immersed in the passions of bereavement, even the mildest personalities can react with rage. We are confused, hurt, and angry at everything and everyone— including ourselves.

At such an unstable time, we may transform any remotely involved person or organization into a scapegoat. Because of the veterinarian's dominant role in the pet's life and death, the hospital and medical staff are usually the easiest and therefore the first to be blamed. They may be completely without guilt, but at this time we are in a blind passion to dump our anger on someone or something—anything! When we are in this early stage of grief, we lose some sense of perspective and logic. Normally, this does not last too long.

When a beloved pet dies, what we possessed and adored is torn from us. We are suddenly bereft, and feel distraught that we have nothing left to hold on to. This is so distressing, frustrating, and final that part of our shocked mind craves some means of escape. Anger is tangible and powerful—and, amazingly, is perfectly suited to fill this temporary need. We can feel anger, and almost taste it. It is so real! And because the anger is about the deceased pet, we don't want to let go of it. Of course, this is not the rational part of our mind at work. But something deep in our human psychology needs to cling to this only remaining representative of the pet. So we use the anger as an emotional substitute. It is still too hard to comprehend the total physical loss, and part of our mind still wants to deny the death, so we hang on to anything that can offer us some relief or temporary alternative.

When we are in this state of grief, people or situations that could be interpreted to be even remotely culpable will be blamed, however irrational this may seem at another time. Frustration and rage, aggravated by a violent sense of loss, can distort our reasoning and even our sense of right and wrong. In our passionate need to assign blame during this phase of the mourning process, tiny incidents that would normally have been overlooked can be misunderstood and exaggerated. Too often we feel we are completely alone and are not understood or properly respected, and we are prone to overreact.

Anger can express itself in amazing forms. It is turned inward just as easily as outward. In frustration at somehow not being able to prevent this death, it is a normal human response to blame ourselves for all kinds of imagined weaknesses and faults. Being forewarned, though, can sometimes take the sharp edge off this response. The control and security we had taken entirely for granted is suddenly gone, and it is not unusual to feel anger and even remorse at our own survival after the pet's death. This frequently leads to depression or even temporary suicidal ideation. We need validation, rather than rebuttal or rejection from others.

Lashing out is not likely to produce a sympathetic response. It becomes an irrational exercise in frustration, pain, and personal rage, as we are trying to cope with our fury at being rendered so powerless as to be cheated by death. Sometimes we are so angry at ourselves that we actually create social situations that become intolerable to others, however inoffensive or undeserving of that they actually may have been.

At this time many mourners develop very disturbing feelings of guilt. It is interesting to note that overreactions and inappropriate anger can come from an unconscious need to be punished. This response is not uncommon, but it can be self-destructive. We cruelly punish ourselves by unnecessarily burning bridges behind us. This irrational action is similar to temper tantrums in children. The overwhelming emotional pain and distress at this time is never justification for our own bad behavior or self-injury.

This kind of unreasonable anger and outrage is always temporary—even if it doesn't seem so at the time. The pain of mourning is normal and inevitable, but continuing misery is optional. However, it may take a little time to get this into perspective. For your own sake, you must eventually get control of this malfunctioning expression of your passion and loss. How long can you sustain and justify such an emotional drain on yourself, when it may not even be really clear what or who is at fault—if anyone? We must be able to give ourselves permission to heal. If we can't, then there are other personal issues hiding underneath these more apparent feelings. They need to be confronted, with the help of a good therapist.

Some degree of irrational but all-pervading self-blame is always present in this stage of bereavement. And that just adds to the confusion and distress. Suppressed anger will always become a self-destructive force. It needs to be understood and vented, to let it go. But of course, this anger is an intensely personal, subjective response. Confronting it is very difficult and it requires you to be absolutely candid with yourself. You and your pain deserve better treatment than keeping anger submerged and unresolved. But first, you must make it more objective and approachable.

ANGER MANAGEMENT

If this is a major problem then it is urgent to work with a professionally trained specialist. This section outlines a very effective method to try to help yourself get control of your anger. It should take at least a few sittings for you to finish this exercise and find it useful. Do not try to do it all at one session. You need time to think things over and gradually add to the lists you are making.

You are going to make two lists under the general heading "Anger." Number each item in the list individually. Leave plenty of space between each item for later additions.

1. On one page write down the names of the people you feel *very* angry with. Do not include yourself.

2. Make a second list of the names of people you feel have upset you in lesser ways during your bereavement. (They may be the next victims of your anger.)

3. After you have finished these lists, go back and fill in the reasons why you feel each person is "guilty."

4. Make a third list of the names of institutions, situations, or anything else you feel is even remotely responsible for causing you unnecessary pain in your bereavement.

5. Make a final list. Head it "Me." Make notes on any reasons you feel angry with yourself.

Put these lists away for at least a few hours before adding to them or reading them again. Work on this for a few days. When you finally feel there is nothing more to add, then rewrite all the lists, neatly organizing any added ideas. This will help you a great deal, and you will see why. Amazingly, this exercise can give you greater objectivity and stability. And your anger will not be as generalized or upsetting as before. Being more clearly focused, you can deal with your anger more effectively.

A CLEAR PERSPECTIVE

There is no question that you are deeply hurt and that your terrible loss might have been more clearly understood by people who should know better. Yes, there are always going to be some insensitive ones who upset you with their callousness or stupid comments about your bereavement. But are *they* really the bad people in your life? Perhaps there is something in their own lives that prevented them from understanding what you now face. Are they unable to cope with your problems because they are reacting to their own? Getting so involved and angry can actually make their inadequacies your new problem. Get your perspectives straight.

Sometimes when we hurt most, we want to strike out at family members and others who are closest, especially if they failed to help us when we needed them most. A secret cry for love and understanding can turn into a confused sense of "justifiable rage" and a sense of righteous indignation. This can be the most damaging kind of anger.

We can become very narrow-minded and selfish during bereavement. It is too easy to become judgmental of others—and inappropriately act out our anger at this time. That is something we hate when it is inflicted on us, and it would be hypocritical now to inflict it on others.

Is it possible that your anger is disproportionate and unfair? What might this be really about? Could it possibly be directed at yourself? Maybe it was bad luck or the wrong time. Maybe you blame the establishment, your parents, or your spouse—or even God. There are so many situations that can affect our lives. Respond as candidly and as frankly as you can to this hard self-examination. Are you overreacting? Think about that for a moment. This is a sign that something else is likely troubling you unconsciously. When we are angry, it is easy to mistakenly identify problems or responses. And it can be nearly impossible to think clearly—especially when we feel alone and not understood.

Of course, we will always be vulnerable to the insensitivity and criticisms of the few who enjoy being judgmental. They have to be handled differently. But for the majority of people, ask yourself: Are you really just looking for any "peg" to hang your anger on? When will you be willing (or ready) to be more tolerant? Was the veterinarian really at fault, or is that a construction of your temporary emotional need to blame someone or something?

Try acting out your anger with your therapist (if you have one) or a close friend. If you are fortunate enough to be in a support group, try this with them: Bring in the list you made of people who have hurt you. Ask someone whom you feel understands how much and why you are hurt play your part—while you play the part of the offending person. One at a time, act out the reasoning and possible excuses of each person on your list and discuss this with the others present, until you feel you have gotten some satisfaction. Consider any possible excuses the people on the list might have to offer—even if you think they really are at fault. Listen to what the others are saying, but be fair. There is a lot to be learned about yourself and your needs from this kind of objectivity. It will help ease your pain, too. And that will be a wonderful living testament to your beloved pet. Honor the memory with good things—not bad ones.

RELATING TO OTHERS

Friends, family, colleagues, religion: Where do they fit into all this? Were there any true attempts by any of them to help you? Were your expectations realistic, knowing their capacity as you do? Or were you actually hoping, rather than expecting? Did you feel they invaded your privacy? Maybe you really didn't want to let them touch your secret vulnerability and grief. Did you seem demanding or imposing? Are you really able to explain and share your pain? If not, how could you blame others for not crossing the impossible barrier you may have set up? We sometimes don't consider these things until it's too late and we have damaged relationships.

Rash actions are easily justified at the moment, but they are almost always regretted. We cannot ever truly take back something we have said—often to our enormous sorrow. In our passion, we can all too easily lose perspective of what is good or bad for us, and end up being self-destructive when we are really trying desperately to help ourselves. A moment's outburst—however good it may feel at that instant—is not worth the potential loss of support and love. Loving a pet and later grieving its death should not justify self-punishment and destructive behavior. There is too much good and love we have learned from our pets and incorporated into our lives to toss away in a moment of anger.

It is easy to be caught off-balance by those who seem rash and judgmental about our grief. Who among us has not heard the comment that we shouldn't be so upset because, "It was only a cat (or dog)?" Or perhaps you've been told that your pain would be gone if you just got another pet right away. What do such people really know about you and your relationship with your dear pet? How dare they be so insensitive and critical!

Actually, some of these people may be trying to make what they think is a legitimate point, from their limited perspective. We can call them stupid, but does that make them bad? They just cannot seem to accept the concept of deep bereavement for a pet, and thus come up very short of our needs and expectations at this terrible time. It hurts even more during this grief, when our reserve of emotional strength is especially low. Some well-intentioned people try to get us to act cheery. But they don't realize that we must go through a period of mourning and bereavement. We have to learn to be patient with them, too, and their ignorance of the profundity of our experience.

GENUINELY BAD PEOPLE

Unfortunately, there are also people in this world who enjoy being cruel. Just look at any day's news, and you will find reports of horror and evil. There are some genuinely bad people in the world. You may already have met some of them; they find pleasure in trying to inflict more pain on you. They prey on the most vulnerable victims they can find, and anyone who is grieving for a pet is a target for them.

An angry response to this sort of social misfit is well-deserved. But spending too much time on such people is really a waste of your vital energy. Actually, your reaction probably won't bother them at all. In fact, they thrive on the emotional responses they provoke in others. You have more important things that require your focus. Scorn these people and walk away from them. They hate that.

But don't be in too great a haste to judge everyone who disappoints you. You may have missed some very important information about some of them. It can be too easy at this very painful stage to tar them all with the same brush. There are also many good people, but not all have the understanding or capacity to respond the way we might want them to. As mentioned earlier, at this time our normal reaction to such frustration is to become hurt and angry with those closest to us. And in rare instances there may even be sufficient reason to validate our alienation—making us feel that we never want to see or have anything to do with that person again. When we are irrational or petulant, though, we tend to take dramatic steps that are most often regretted later. But then it may be too late. Being too quick on the draw is usually dangerous and final.

OUR RESPONSES TO OTHERS

We are in great distress and vulnerable at a time like this. And we tend to seek any outlet we can find for all our powerful emotions. It becomes too easy to justify vilifying someone who hurts and disappoints us. But we must not go on burning our bridges. Some of the personal relationships that are strained at this very difficult time still have real value and positive significance in our lives. It can be self-defeating to turn on these people. But it is still a normal reflex to want to show our anger and punish them.

Distancing ourselves from a person or situation is sometimes the best way to handle anger and disappointment—and the potential damage we can do to a relationship. Sometimes we later learn that a particular person is better kept at a distance, but that can be a better choice than outright alienation. This allows for possible rebuilding and healing later.

Permanently alienating or distancing ourselves from someone, however, may not serve our real and long-term purposes. Also, in turn, they may not forgive us. This could be a foolish, preventable loss. Self-pity during intense bereavement can push us to do some damaging things that we may regret later. Knowing about this now can help prevent these kinds of losses.

Some of the people who anger us may see pets as possessions, childish playthings, or frivolous wastes of time and expense. Or they might be very upset and threatened by the hidden meanings of death, which they refuse to confront with us. They may become agitated and short with us for lavishing all of our sensitivity on a pet's death, when it is too frightening for them to contemplate the thought of death at all. The intensity of your feelings may be intimidating to them, with their inadequate grasp of the subject. Their defensive behavior may seem to be rude, uncaring, or even hostile. But maybe this was because they felt you were being pushy and overly demanding. During intense bereavement we can easily reach out in desperation and overreact. When support is not provided by someone we hoped would be there for us, this reaction is natural. In responding to keen disappointment, it is too easy to be impatient and react with critical, disturbed, and powerfully negative emotions.

There are also people who are close to us but may not offer any response at all to our grief. The resulting silence or absence of a meaningful statement can be too easily misperceived as an unspoken critical comment. Very often, people do this because they just do not know how to reply. Death is a frightening thing. They may be unable to discuss the subject without feeling greatly threatened. If you love and respect them, despite your own breaking heart and need for support, don't push! They are human, too. At this time your need for understanding and support can be dire. But despite that, you still have to keep reasonable expectations of others.

TYPES OF RESPONSES

You can make three basic types of responses to a perceived assault on your grief. The first is to strike back quickly, with bitterness and immediate anger. As mentioned earlier, in some rare cases this may be well-deserved. The second response is to be caught so far off-guard that you don't know what to say. Your confused or embarrassed response may give the impression that you are not really contradicting or disagreeing with the person. And that can make you even angrier later. Sometimes a person in authority, such as a supervisor, may have you at this disadvantage if you are not ready to handle the remarks.

The third and most effective response is to be prepared. You can look a reasonable but insensitive person right in the eye and say something like, "You don't have a pet and can't possibly understand what kind of love and understanding there was for me. How can you judge my grief? That hurts and offends me. If you have any respect for me, please be more tolerant when such deep, personal feelings are involved!" Often that person may actually make an unexpected turnaround and begin to grasp what you are going through. Being prepared will help you better deal with others who are not responding as you wish they would. It can also assist you in clearly identifying those who *really* are not good people for you to be around.

Consider your alternatives. How can you more efficiently handle an insensitive reaction—*for your own sake?* The answer above is just one example of a non-threatening response to the challenges that may confront you. It is very important not to force anyone into a corner. This non-threatening approach can maintain the respect you might otherwise lose. And it can keep you in control of the situation. The unexpected logic of your reply might elicit an insight that the person could not have otherwise reached. But whether or not it does, it probably will help to save a valuable relationship. And finally, it may prevent additional unnecessary suffering for yourself.

At this very vulnerable and reactive time, it can be difficult to remain cool and not react to perceived hurts and insensitivity all around us. It is encouraging to realize that this emotional turmoil is a normal response to grief. It will pass more easily if we express our hurt feelings to caring and sympathetic listeners. Friends and pet support groups are the best medicine at this time.

Anger is a highly personalized, emotional response to a perceived offense or violation. It has many legitimate uses as well as abuses. But what valid purpose can it serve in memorializing a beloved life that has been snatched away? Can we be angry at death or the reality of loss? Should we be angry at ourselves for not being able to outmaneuver death? And must we be angry at the professionals who could not save our pet's life? Fortunately, this fury is temporary and it will pass.

TAKING LEGAL ACTION

There are situations where anger is legitimate and well-deserved. Sometimes other people are directly involved with a pet's death or suffering. Veterinary malpractice can be one of these situations. This is very rare, but it does happen. Too often the vet and staff are blameless, but they are in the wrong place at the wrong time to receive the unfair broadsides of our pent-up anger. But sometimes terrible things happen while the pet is at the vet, or is being boarded, or in the care of petsitters—and the list can go on. The very important thing we must bear in mind is that although we may have legal cause for action against someone, we need to keep that separated from our bereavement.

Most lawyers don't want to take these kinds of cases, because the clients tend to be overemotional and unwilling to compromise. And even if you could win a judgment, the financial compensation usually is far less than your incurred legal expenses. Remember, the law is out-dated and still considers pets to be property.

In these extreme cases we crave retribution of some kind, but the world is not always fair. At one time or another nearly everyone has been the victim of some type of personal outrage. This can range from minor and soon-forgotten incidents to major traumatic experiences that are ruthlessly inflicted on us. The sense of outrage and impotence we feel is profound. It is an onslaught of personal hurt, insult, and anger that craves immediate satisfaction.

Meanwhile, in pursuing legal action the anger and craved retribu-tion will stagnate the healing process. We can too easily get stuck in the legal process, while being consumed by our fury. Watch out for this. It can become an obsession, ruining our lives and complicating the pain of bereavement.

What do we do when there is no real redress for our grievances? Somehow, we must allow ourselves to recover from the onslaughts and tragedies we experience. The sense of outrage and violation is a very powerful provocation that can too easily obscure everything else, if we let it. We must regain control of ourselves. It is time to lick our wounds and go on with our lives. Of course, this is easy to advise and so terribly hard to do.

This kind of outrage can also generate a terrible sense of personal failure and self-disapproval. Each of us has to draw some final line between healthy and self-destructive behavior. Are we still being our pet's advocate by fighting for redress of our own grievances? When faced with such a situation, we must ask ourselves *why we are clinging so desperately to our anger and outrage?* Ultimately, the personal cost to ourselves is always too great.

By determining to overcome this kind of emotional havoc, each individual can make a very personal resolution not to be a victim of malefactors any longer. We are above that, and despite the offenses, we are actually stronger and better people now. It is time to continue with the positive aspects of our personal growth.

Mourning is a recognition and overall recovery process. Eventually, we must accept the new reality of life without the beloved pet. We have reached the bottom. Since death knows no bargaining, we have to come to terms with ourselves, our anger, and our loss. There is no other sound way.

Case History

A 17-year-old young man was referred to me when he started experiencing strong feelings of anger and alienation with many people close to him after the death of his beloved dog. The dog was 14, and the two had grown up together as extremely close pals—almost siblings. It needed to have a tumor removed, and although the vet had explained the potential dangers of general anesthesia for older dogs, the boy felt it was necessary. He also opted to have its teeth cleaned while it was under. Unfortunately, the dog died on the operating table.

The young man was devastated and went through shock, disbelief, and fury at the veterinarian and her technicians—trying unsuccessfully to find fault with anything they might have done. In need of compassion, he turned to the people closest to him, but his adored married sister made no extra effort to console him. In his grief, he swore he would never speak with her again. He was co-captain of his high school track team, and the coach he had worshipped belittled his grief and told him that he was "acting like a baby" and that "it's time to become a man." In addition to these keen disappointments, his girlfriend suggested that he just get another dog.

The young man was in an intense emotional crisis and was angry and hurt. He felt alone and very bitter toward the people closest to him, whom he had most relied on. He was referred to me by his concerned parents, who could not reason with him.

Fortunately, this young man was bright and open to new ideas. He had not believed his dog would die and was unwilling to accept his own feelings of guilt. In therapy, he tried to consider the people who had so bitterly disappointed him, and he admitted that his sister had her own troubles. He recalled that she had experienced problems dealing with the death of her father-in-law, and couldn't even go to the funeral. As much as she loved her brother, she could not handle the death of his dog, and she avoided discussing it with him.

He had to learn to accept that his coach was not the sensitive man he had idealized—which was so hard to do. But he did not act on his immediate impulse to quit the team. The next semester he won a statewide competition, with the guidance of this same person. And he had to learn the hard way that his girlfriend was not really his soul mate. They actually had little in common. It was ironic, but the insensitive coach was right in insisting the boy had to become a man. Of course, there were other, more caring and acceptable ways he should have expressed that.

It was a difficult year for the young man, but in just a few sessions he was able to understand why these people were not able to be there for him during his bereavement. He was forced to do a lot of growing up, unfortunately at the especially terrible time of his loss. But after working to understand his feelings of anger and alienation, he was able to get through the period of mourning and social realignment within just a few weeks. Growing up always has its painful moments, and his grief and mourning were aggravated by these other emotional disappointments.

Learning about the different stages of mourning helped him greatly. It became his means for gaining a perspective on his feelings of alienation and distancing. His healing was quite rapid, but of course he was never the same—which he seemed to regret at first. He would have liked another dog, but he was going to an out-of-town college the next year and wisely decided to get one at another time in the future.

A faithful companion.   *Photo by W. Sife. Courtesy of Hamilton Pet Meadow,*
                              Memorial Park and Crematory

CHAPTER 6

Denial and Disbelief

Parting is all we know of heaven and all we need of hell.

—*Emily Dickinson*

D enial and disbelief accompany the shock of first learning about a beloved pet's death. This is usually one of the earliest and briefest stages of mourning. The two terms are often mistaken for one another, but they actually refer to two distinctly different responses. Disbelief is a conscious doubt or unwillingness to accept a fact. But, under duress, we do painfully acknowledge it, even though we don't like it or want to believe. We also feel dazed and stunned. It is still too hard to process the shocking information, and the truth needs time to sink in. This is a common early response, and it is normal to feel this way.

Denial is not the same. It is a psychological reaction to something that we unconsciously find too painful or uncomfortable to bear—and the mind refuses to accept its reality. Amazingly, we can deny even the most obvious facts, if they are too upsetting. They just don't exist for us; we simply refuse to acknowledge that the pet is dead. There is a powerful need to believe that this has not *really* happened.

THE FANTASY OF DENIAL

Denial is related to fantasy and a passionate hope for wish-fulfillment. When we are overwhelmed by the terrible finality of a pet's death, at first we are strongly tempted to deny its reality. There is a natural tendency to want to believe that it was all a bad dream or some kind of

"One Small Furry Friend" bronze plaque.

Photo by W. Sife. Courtesy of Matthews International Corporation

"Come to me."

Photo by W. Sife. Courtesy of Abbey Glen Pet Memorial Park

terrible hallucination, and that our pet is not really dead. We passionately hope it might all be okay again. This protective fantasy removes us from a little of the pain we are experiencing. But gradually the grim reality will set in. The life of the pet is over, gone, ended! The pain is with us now.

As mentioned, denial is usually a brief stage, and fortunately it is over quickly. But when it is acute or prolonged, there is little that most people can do to ease it for anyone else. The person in acute or prolonged denial needs professional help.

We live in what can be considered a euphemistic society, in that we tend to prefer indirect references to unpleasant words or concepts, and avoid certain aspects of reality. Euphemisms also enable us to try to redesign the truth a bit. This opens a wide door for escape from hard reality. The fantasy of denial may seem like an extreme psychological reaction, but in fact we make some use of this all the time. A euphemism is a mild or vague word or phrase that we substitute for a blunt or harsher one. For example, we seldom say the word "death" outright, preferring euphemisms such as "passed away" or "went to heaven." Unfortunately, this is just another means of trying to disguise and avoid the full acceptance of existence.

In our culture we are also nurtured and conditioned to believe that "wishing might make it so." The classic play *Peter Pan* illustrates this: If we all clap our hands at the right moment, Tinkerbell will live again. And cartoon characters are never killed or hurt, despite fantastic calamities. The fairy tales and other stories we knew as children were filled with plots in which good people were sometimes given a second chance to escape from death or harm. Magic and romantic reverie were at the core of our early emotional development. That stays with us all of our lives as a delightful retention of childhood experience and innocence.

The human brain registers and retains everything it experiences. However, during times of extreme stress the psyche may delete an emotional trauma from our outer level of awareness. This is the mind's equivalent of an emergency fuse or circuit breaker. That is why denial is considered an escape mechanism. This self-protective impulse is so strong that if there is no safe memory or idea, the mind will immediately create one. We may suspend our judgment for the moment and think that if we wish or pray hard enough, maybe, just maybe, our beloved pet will be okay—or even come back to life. We also tend toward superstitious actions. For example, most people feel that they should not alter their regular routines, fearing that this may change their luck and make things worse. As a benign example, consider which shoe you put on first—left or right. This is a perfect example of quasi-superstitions habituation—without an apparent reason. It is illogical, yet so many people do it. But of course, wishing and superstition really can't bring our pet back. Only our love can do that—but in a different way.

Death is not the only reality we seek to deny. As adults we are often confronted with shocking everyday circumstances beyond our control. We have learned many ways to avoid accepting such situations, but there are times when we can do nothing about them. In times of adversity we may feel like pawns, moved around mercilessly in some vast cosmic chess game. Sadly, some people grow to accept this as their deserved fate, and they go through life living the "unworthy me" syndrome. Others perceive themselves as the constant victim of others—as well as of circumstances. These are also distortions of reality.

The innocent child within each of us naturally craves a happy ending. Thoughts about death are so carefully avoided that we can never be really prepared. But it does come to all living things, despite our fantasies and most fervent prayers. Once death has taken over, it is too late. Most of us are never ready for this grim reality.

Sometimes we need to regress to a childlike state of make-believe. As in fairy tales, we often indulge in magical thinking. Oh, how we want to believe! For example, if we put out the food dish, maybe somehow our pet will come back to eat. This is a lovely reverie, but it is not real. We have to let go.

Psychological defense mechanisms such as denial play a very important part in maintaining our mental stability. Denial serves our immediate need to delay the full emotional impact of a reality that is too upsetting. It temporarily limits the damage this trauma can produce by putting us in a sort of painless limbo. Normally, denial in bereavement lasts only a short while. Other realities quickly close in, forcing us to confront and accept the facts of the death and our private loss. As painful as it is, we are going through the necessary stages of the grieving and healing process.

The death is real, and we are being carried onward in the stream of life. The pet has died, time is passing, and we must go on. We have to stop clinging to passionate memories and fantasies, and learn to some-how incorporate them as love-filled components of our new lives.

BARGAINING WITH GOD

When we understand some of the fantastic things the human mind is capable of, it is not really surprising to learn that there is another form of denial. This is called delayed denial, and it is more like a fantasy or dream. Delayed denial comes later, usually after the body of the pet has been provided for and all our other immediate responsibilities have been met. It seems to crop up when we are alone, smothered by grief, frustration, rage, and a sense of helplessness. The pet's presence is still very strong, and we still somehow expect a greeting at the door when we come home. The apartment or house is now too empty. It doesn't seem real.

At this stage, occasional mild hallucinations are not uncommon. We may sometimes think we heard or saw a fleeting glimpse of the pet. This can be thrilling to some people and upsetting to others. It is almost as if reality has gone through some sort of time warp. And, despite our logic, we still fervently wish that things might somehow revert to the way they were. Maybe the pet really isn't dead—or doesn't have to stay that way. Maybe if we try to make some deal with God, our pet will come back again.

At this stage in bereavement we are emotionally primed for what is called bargaining. If we know the death is coming, sometimes we even do this even before it actually happens. We need to be aware that bargaining doesn't ever work. We are living now, after the terrible fact. And a fact it remains. All our tears and wishing cannot wash it out or change it.

Despite the reality, in this stage it is very normal to grasp at any-thing that could possibly bring back our beloved pet. During intense grief, logic does not influence all of our thinking and feeling. Why not turn to intensive prayer and renunciation of certain very personal aspects of our lives? Wouldn't God see how earnest and genuine we are and possibly make some sort of exception for our pet? We have been raised to believe that miracles have occurred, so why not now?

Distraught people can be ingenious in their sincerity and ardor. Some mourners who are stuck in their grief will set up a whole new lifestyle—one that calls for dramatic change, sacrifice, and self-denial.

This is presumably for our edification and the appeasement of God, to bring about that beseeched miracle.

Some degree of bargaining is almost always considered by grieving pet owners. But of course, it is never successful. Unfortunately, such conduct can also be harmful, for several reasons: It doesn't work; it reinforces a deep sense of guilt; it disrupts one's life; and it tries to sidestep reality. Failure to achieve the miracle also often precipitates a state of prolonged depression and immobilization. As mentioned earlier, extreme depression is almost always caused by other deep, underlying problems that have never been resolved and desperately need to be addressed. The loss of the beloved pet is not the real issue, but only the precipitating event. This is pathological behavior and it desperately needs professional help.

MESSAGES FROM BEYOND

Most people would love to believe in magic. We all have seen magic shows where amazing things happen. Admittedly, what we are really seeing is illusion and sleight-of-hand entertainment. But there are always examples that appear so real we can't explain them. That leads many people to wonder why couldn't there be some kind of magic that may work for them in their terrible need. The more we become educated about the ways of the world, the more we begin to realize how little we really know or understand. It may be possible that there *really are* magical wonders awaiting us, if only we knew how to evoke them. The entire history of civilization is filled with examples of this search. The existence of real magic has never been proved, and by the same argument, it has never been completely disproved. In our pain, need, and vulnerability we are ready to believe almost anything.

One of the things some mourners end up believing is that there are special people who can communicate with their dead pets and bring back messages. This is a social phenomenon that had its beginnings only recently, when grieving during petloss became much more open and common. These so-called animal communicators capitalize on the grief and vulnerability of their clients, offering tailored answers that they know these distraught people desperately want to hear.

The same thing was extremely popular a century ago, during the heyday of what was called spiritualism. Mediums convinced many people that they could communicate with dead loved ones. But these mediums were eventually exposed as fraud, as widespread trickery and deceit was always discovered behind it. The interest in spiritualism faded away.

Beware of people who claim they can give you messages from beyond the grave. Many of these "animal communicators" are good, compassionate people who really want to help others, and they actually believe in their "powers.' They are very persuasive to vulnerable mourners who yearn to believe them. But be careful. Most of these "pet" messages indicate a human perspective and awareness of things that a pet could not possibly possess—even from beyond. We would all love to believe that communicating with the dead—human or animal—is possible. But while so many, many claims can be disproved, none has ever been confirmed. This is an example of people wanting so hard for something to be real that they actually begin to believe it.

VIEWING THE BODY

This deep desire for a message from beyond is complicated by the fact that many pet owners were not present when the pet died. They fantasize about it still being alive, somehow. People who were away at the time have an especially difficult time accepting the immediate reality. They must endure the shock of having to be informed somewhat impersonally about something so intensely personal. This appalling end to such a very close relationship is announced by a stranger, who can feel like an unwelcome third party to this very intimate relationship. That seems wrong, somehow—almost as if the relationship has been defiled. The terrible message is often received with anger and rejection, along with resentment for the messenger.

Most veterinarians have become aware of this situation through experience and common sense. Today, veterinary colleges and teaching hospitals are finally starting to offer sensitivity training to their students. They have found that it is important to have pet owners actually see the body, if they can. This visual confirmation helps in acceptance. The newly grieving pet owner is then best served by having some private time, alone, with the body, if possible.

This is also true for the other pets (if any) in the home. Some surviving companion animals grieve the loss of their deceased friends. The pet seems to have just disappeared, and the remaining animals may react very emotionally. But animals don't fear death as we do (notwithstanding their strong survival instincts). If it is at all possible, always arrange to have surviving pets view and smell the body. They may sometimes appear upset, but will then also accept the loss much easier. But don't feel disappointed if they seem to mostly ignore the body. That is not what is really happening. Animals deal with death in their own way. There is so much that they can teach us, if we are receptive.

While animals instinctively accept death as something natural, seeing a pet's body can be overwhelming for some people, and they need to maintain some emotional distance. They fear their own responses in particular, and death in general. Seeing the body of your deceased pet is a terrible confrontation with death, and most people don't really know how to handle it safely or even comfortably. Because we have been taught by convention to avoid talking or thinking about death, we are conditioned to fear it. As a result, there are many people who cannot be present for the euthanasia procedure or to view the body. Yet, they are emotionally torn by the need to be with the body, even for a short while. Too often they later suffer a heavy sense of guilt for not having been able to be there for their pet.

We understand, intellectually, that death comes to all things. But our conditioned fear and avoidance of this ultimate reality gives us some excuse, up to a point, for denial and bargaining. When we are faced with death, however, we can discover that we instinctively know a lot more about it than we realized. That awareness also scares some people.

RESPONDING TO DENIAL

Some expression of denial is one of the most common defense mechanisms observed in bereavement. We all feel it, even if slightly or momentarily. Denial is expressed in a very wide variety of ways, and several studies have been made of it. One fascinating variation is selective memory. This is much more common than is realized. We have all known people who do not remember unpleasant or bad things in their lives. They have restructured their reality to be much more acceptable and painless. When done in limited or minor ways, selective memory can be relatively harmless. But if it is carried to extremes, it becomes pathological and requires professional help.

Generally, the best way to respond to moderate denial in others is to accept it until they are ready to face reality on their own—unless there is psychological risk involved. If they feel pushed, or if the denial is criticized too harshly or suddenly, there is a chance of triggering other underlying psychological problems. A defense mechanism is justifiable, even valuable, when it serves as a temporary "Band-aid" to protect us from immediate and overwhelming problems. But it should not last too long—only long enough for reality and natural healing to set in. If the response is excessive or prolonged, then of course, this needs to be examined further.

Defense mechanisms are created by the human mind when it needs to hide from some very painful reality. Accepting the full truth is extremely difficult and always heartbreaking—and sometimes unbearable. Effective therapy is also painful, because it must confront the problems we want to escape from. Because of all the powerful psychological factors at play here, it will take some people much longer than others to go through this stage of bereavement. We need to be tolerant and patient with them during this particularly difficult time. Fortunately, in most cases denial will gradually be transformed into other less destructive expressions of grief, and it will eventually fade away.

Case History

A retired widow in her late 50s was referred to counseling because of her acute denial concerning the death of her beloved dog. She had suffered an intense bereavement for her husband about five years earlier, and had found much comfort in the dog's loving presence. The relationship between the woman and her 11-year-old pet had always been close, but it became very dependent, as well. She doted on the dog to the point that her close friends felt it was becoming a spoiled brat. The situation became so obvious and obnoxious that she was criticized by nearly everyone. Her response was to escape into a lonely life without company. She rarely saw people any longer, and secluded herself and her adored dog from the world.

Then, inevitably, the pet died. There was nothing the veterinarian could do to prevent it. The dog was about 16 years old and its heart just gave out in its sleep. Although she was fortunate that her dog died peacefully, the personal tragedy overwhelmed her.

After an elaborate funeral and burial, she decorated her apartment with every possible reminder of her beloved pet. Pictures and toys were prominently displayed, with black and purple crepe placed everywhere to declare her bereavement. Very few friends and family visited her at first. About three days into this bereavement, she started praying fervently for the dog's return. She lived in the belief that a "simple miracle" would happen, that reality would somehow be reversed for her. Everything else in her life was put on hold as she waited for the pet's return. Nothing could dissuade her from this passion.

Friends and family tried to show her the error of her thinking. This only made the situation worse, and she refused to let them into the apartment any longer. Fortunately, a friend she still listened to was able to persuade her to seek professional help to ease her terrible grief.

We worked on her unresolved bereavement for her husband and her great fear of death. It was important not to stress her irrational feelings of denial, though. In time she began to accept the painful reality on her own, and the denial ceased—slowly at first. Most of the visual reminders of her pet were removed from the apartment, with only one small, shrinelike area remaining. After about six months of psychotherapy she was ready to start her life over again. She has begun to socialize again with family and friends. After a lot of new painful insight she has reconstructed her entire life, for the better.

CHAPTER 7

Guilt

*All of the animals except man know that the
principal business of life is to enjoy it.*

—Samuel Butler

uilt is a psychological invention based on insecurity or a negative self-evaluation. It is a normal response when we feel as if we have failed some duty or obligation. This can vary from a mild uneasiness to a powerful sense of self-blame and needed punishment. Interestingly, it is closely related to the emotion of anger. During bereavement it is based on what the bereaver perceives as a failure in responsibility in not preventing the death of the beloved pet. Guilt is one of the most commonly experienced responses in the human emotional repertoire. This is a normal stage in bereavement. But sometimes we get stuck there, and it prevents healing, until it is resolved.

It is worth noting that guilt is not limited to people, although it is a human contrivance. We sometimes can see it when training or scolding our pets for violating an expected behavior. Pets, however, would not feel guilt on their own. That is an emotional response we imposed and trained into them, with our unending list of rules and regulations. Not surprisingly, guilt as we know it has not been observed in the wild. If seen in the right perspective, there is so much we can learn from our animal friends, if we are aware and receptive to it.

The unloved are loved.

*Photo by W. Sife. Courtesy of
Hartsdale Canine Cemetery, Inc.*

In memory of a beloved horse.

*Photo by W. Sife. Courtesy of
Abbey Glen Pet Memorial Park*

GUILT AND BEREAVEMENT

We need to consider the feelings of guilt and failed obligation that almost always crop up during intense bereavement for a pet. Whenever we accept the responsibility of being the lifetime steward of a companion animal, we also take on a moral obligation to be absolutely reliable. This sense of duty concerns every possible aspect of the pet's life, health, happiness, and well-being. It becomes a powerful self-obligation that remains with us, even during the bereavement. Sometimes this guilt can be distorted into a vicious cycle that seems at the time to have no good way to end.

Usually, there is no place for death in our loving scheme of things. It scares and mystifies us, so we naturally avoid thinking about it whenever possible. When death eventually does come, the shock can be followed by a strong feeling of inadequate responsibility. In effect, we sense we have failed in some way to fulfill that duty—that we are actually responsible for letting the pet die. And we are very good at inventing rationalizations to support that concept. This self-depredation is part of the normal emotional response during the early stages of bereavement. It is usually unfounded, and not based in logic or reason.

We are completely responsible for so many things in our pets' lives. This includes nutrition, medicines, medical care, grooming, toys, playmates, sexual status, and quality of life—and the list goes on. The bonding that results is two-way, with the human becoming emotionally dependent on the pet, as well. In our pain we are prone to creating guilt. During the intense emotions of bereavement we tend to create a powerful sense that somehow we have failed to be in total control. We were unable to be perfect in completely protecting the pet from all possible dangers—especially death. In a sense, we assume godlike roles to our pets. But of course, we are still fallible. We have limits, despite our most fervent desires. And we have to learn to accept this and be forgiving to ourselves.

RELINQUISHING CONTROL

Responsibility is not solely measured by action or inaction. It is affected by a vast complexity of circumstances that are beyond our control or comprehension. Despite that reality, we respond with powerful emotions that suggest we should have somehow been able to alter or even prevent the contributing factors in the pet's death. We feel a terrible sense of guilt in losing this imagined control.

During the early stages of mourning, anger, grief, and guilt can overwhelm us. These feelings easily distort most attempts at objective thinking. Such irrational pain can be the result of our becoming obsessed with what "might have been," had we only done something that could have prevented some aspect of the tragedy. Some counselors refer to this as the "Should've-Could've-If Only" stage. At some time or other, we have all experienced at least some small degree of this expression of guilt and penitence. We are filled with feelings of remorse and failure. And we ponder over how this fate could have been avoided "if only" we had done something else. This kind of guilty thinking can load our minds to the point of bursting. We begin to feel as if we had not been sufficiently responsible to the pet. But it is foolish to regret not being all-wise. Nobody can have all the right answers, all the time.

We are human, so we long for many things—including those which we cannot fully comprehend. And we can criticize ourselves unmercifully after a pet's death. But we need to remember that if we did take action, whatever was done for those circumstances was right—however sad the result. Whatever reasons we had at the time were valid to us, then. As suggested earlier, we can't judge our past actions or inactions by using hindsight and thoughts we developed later. Hindsight should be used as a learning tool for the future—not as a means to create guilt about the past. It can be so easy to start obsessing about this. If you hang on to that kind of irrational thinking, it will be painful as well as damaging. We are all imperfect. But if we are loving and good, our pets know this—and we should, also.

Death has always been a mystery, and despite all our impassioned senses of guilt and responsibility, its comprehension will remain elusive. Western civilization treats death as though it is an evil thing, an enemy to be feared and avoided. But that is very foolish, indeed. Since we cannot blame death for the loss, we tend to blame ourselves—or others. We are predisposed to feel that the death resulted from a loss of control on our part. We had complete responsibility but it was snatched away. Oddly enough, by assigning blame, even to ourselves, we are unconsciously able to create a sense of still holding on to the pet. Guilt is like anger; we experience it strongly. And that can play a temporary role as something to desperately hang on to—in lieu of the pet. Again we see a strange process of the mind, under extraordinary stress. But in the long run we have to let it go.

Actually, that presumed complete control never existed. Maybe you could have done things differently, but isn't that true about everything? The faulty logic used is really an exercise in negative fantasy. Deep down in our anguish its purpose is to give us an excuse to blame or punish ourselves. Strong guilt feelings are traumatic. They offer something we can grasp and feel when trying to cope with death. They also can indirectly give us a false sense of still having some control at this time. Yet things are way out of control. Maybe it is time for a reality check.

Case History

There was the case of a woman who had to have her cat declawed. It was subject to temper tantrums and had destroyed furniture and scratched her badly. This seemed the most sensible thing to do at the time. It made life bearable with an otherwise angry and destructive pet. The owner was a person of great responsibility, and she had a deep affection for the cat, despite its bad behavior. It was well understood that without declawing she would have had to give the cat up—or worse. However, this logic later gave way to irrational feelings.

About two years later, the cat died from feline leukemia. The woman shifted her chaotic, bewildering grief into feelings of guilt. Somehow, she began to blame herself for making the little remaining time in her pet's life less than it could have been because she interfered and caused some temporary pain and confusion. Forgetting all the valid reasons, she was now obsessed with the thought that she was guilty of having made a bad decision to declaw the cat, ruining its happiness and quality of life.

Therapy had to show her that the logic was as faulty as the emotion behind it was intense. As expected, it turned out that there were earlier emotional traumas in her life that had conditioned her to feel that she was a failure, and would always remain one. She was able to identify that bad feeling as one she had had since childhood—that she deserved to be punished, but didn't know what for. This made her a prime candidate for inventing all sorts of guilt and self-punishment—for anything she had been involved with throughout her unhappy life. With therapy and guidance she soon saw that the death of her cat was only the spark. It ignited a powder keg of underlying repressed emotions and feelings that she desperately needed to work on and resolve.

As already mentioned, when one is experiencing grief, rational thinking sometimes gets thrust aside. Sometimes feelings of guilt can be completely unfounded. People in deep bereavement for a pet often express a neurotic need to perceive themselves as failures. Deep down, some individuals even feel that any kind of guilt and pain are part of a deserved self-punishment for who or what they are. A sense of guilt and low self-esteem becomes a way of life for these people. It is absolutely essential to be able to give ourselves permission to heal. Otherwise, we are "spinning our wheels" and will stay mired in our misery.

It is interesting to note that some individuals go so far in this as to blame it all on the misunderstood concept of "original sin." If man is inherently sinful, then they feel it explains and even seems to condone their feeling guilty about everything. They sometimes find consolation in this contrition of the self. Unfortunately, that is also often used as justification for self-denial, mediocrity, or even failure. When a beloved pet dies, these people are the most prone to suffer exaggerated and prolonged guilt.

The death of a beloved pet is often sensed as a ripping away of one's control and responsibility. If an individual cannot fully accept the perception of guilt, then he or she may need to pass it on. At this time of distraction and grief it is easy to assign fault to someone else. This shift is a variation of one of the most common human psychological responses—passing the buck. Counselors in petloss and bereavement deal with this all the time.

Turn-of-the-century memorial.

Photo by George Wirt.
Courtesy of Bide-A-Wee, 1992

AFTERTHOUGHT

Guilt can also be a product of afterthought. It is more easily created in the mind of one who is already suffering and vulnerable. This serves no other real purpose but to hurt the one who invents it. The real question each individual should ask is, "Why do I need to feel guilty?" It is normal to ponder about responsibility and possible alternatives that we might have taken, but it is very unhealthy to obsess on this. Mistakes can be made, yet that is the way humans operate. Nobody is perfect or exempt, and it is very important to realize this, especially when trying to be faultless for our beloved pets. But we have to be self-forgiving. There is no alternative other than prolonged misery and self-deprecation. Certainly, that is no fitting memorial to a beloved pet. Our continuing lives should be as better people, because of our cherished companion animals.

Guilt is often a warping of afterthought and reflection. Pet bereavement frequently is beset with such dilemmas. These uncertainties also often concern euthanasia and other unresolved thoughts about what we might have handled better. If only we had second sight! But we do not. We are human and flawed, but blessed with love and a sense of the ideal. Each expression of guilt needs to be examined separately to determine the reason it was created. The greater the love for a pet, the greater the possibility that feelings of guilt will somehow find a way of intruding themselves.

But death has slammed the door of life in our face before we could grasp its full significance. When we try to comprehend this, so many new problems and questions seem to arise. This can be so emotionally overwhelming that we become especially vulnerable—in many ways.

Anger can also be directed at religion for not being able or willing to help at this terrible time. The bereaver may be unable to find consolation for the guilt and other questions he or she is so desperately seeking answers to. Unfortunately, there are still precious few clergy in most Western religions who would even try to help in pet bereavement (see chapter 16). Do our beloved pets have souls? Is there a heaven for pets? Will we ever see them again? And we are flooded with feelings and questions about why such an innocent, good, trusting, loving animal must die. Without an afterlife it just doesn't seem fair. Because religion does not seem to be there for some bereavers, they may be even more prone to turn back on themselves and imagine some kind of failed personal responsibility.

It is easy to believe that most pets are better than many humans. They are living examples of authentic love, loyalty, innocence, and trust. Guilt and the many other problems of humanity do not corrupt the purity of their spirit. So, why doesn't organized religion offer us help in understanding the souls of animals? It seems very reasonable that pets should have the promise of some heaven, too. Do we rejoin after death? Where does the bereft heart turn? To whom? To what? In trying to better understand our sense of failed responsibility, we need time and support from others—especially those who should be sensitive to our spiritual needs and responses.

Eventually, we have to find that final measure of strength within ourselves. Yes, we tend to lose our perspective when there is death, but we do have some redeeming graces. Our pets loved us despite all our frailties. What was the good they sensed in us? It must have been real then—and it must still be real. That important recognition should help wash away some of the stubborn self-blame we cling to. Guilt soils the beauty of the memory, and it should be healed.

RESPONSIBILITY TO OURSELVES

Responsibility must now be shifted to include taking care of one's self. Be the wonderful person that your pet saw in you. Let yourself mourn constructively, by accepting the death and preserving the loving memories. This is your duty now. If your pet could send you a message, it would tell you to take better care of yourself, since he or she is not there any longer to protect you. Think about that.

Case History

The problems of another patient can illustrate this type of grief. Here we have the case of a young woman in her late thirties who lovingly housed two stray kittens until she could find a home for them. This took about two weeks to accomplish and gave her great pleasure. But her real pet, an older cat, felt jealous and became stressed during this period.

A few months later, this older cat suddenly came down with a previously undiagnosed congestive heart problem. The pet died just three weeks later, despite every possible attempt at medical assistance.

The young woman could not overcome her grief. She felt guilty about being "selfish" and not showing enough love to her cat when it "must have been feeling jealous." She began to recall how her pet misbehaved and was punished when the kittens were being temporarily housed and cared for. She imagined that this surely must have negatively affected her pet's quality of life, somehow contributing to the heart disease and early death. Although she strongly felt this, she did not really believe it. She was conflicted and vulnerable, and a deep sense of personal guilt had free rein over her. Fortunately, she sought professional counseling and soon was shown how to help herself out of this terrible state of mind. Then she still grieved her loss, but without the guilt.

ACCIDENTS AND LEARNING TO FORGIVE

Bad things sometimes happen to good people and their pets. Accidents can be terrible, and will dramatically affect our lives. But because these traumatic happenings are completely unintentional, we call them accidents to set them apart. Those traumatic happenings are just that—accidents. Your life and energy can be wasted, immersing yourself and drowning in guilt. Yet that is a normal, deeply personal, initial response. We are not perfect. Since we are human, we also will make mistakes. If they are not viciously intended, don't we deserve forgiveness and some compassion as well? Certainly! However, that must come from deep within one's self. And it takes time and many tears. Pain is inevitable. But continuing and unremitting misery is an option. After accidents we sometimes create an exaggerated sense of guilt. And the reasons for that need to be considered. Talking it out with trusted friends or a counselor is always a good step—and sometimes absolutely necessary.

Even carelessness, as avoidable as it is, should be seen in this light. There are accounts of all kinds, such as that of the puppy on an outdoor tether who was attacked by a free-ranging stronger animal. There was a sweet kitten who was carried off by a hawk in front of the horrified pet's owner. One of the most bizarre of these events happened when a man's dog accompanied him fishing at a pond just outside his home in Florida. An alligator seemed to appear out of nowhere. It sneaked up and seized the dog in those terrible jaws, dragging the startled pet into and under the water, while the man shouted and watched helplessly. Another woman discovered, in shock and horror, that she had backed her car over her beloved dog, fatally injuring him. There are so many kinds of accidents that happen to our pets. All of these awful events resulted in terrible feelings of guilt for the owners. Each one felt he or she could have prevented the death by being more diligent. They all believed their perceived carelessness caused the deaths, and they condemned and unfairly punished themselves with guilt.

Yes, they were guilty—in varying ways. But how long should they have to suffer such heartbreak? When should it ease or stop? How can they ever give themselves forgiveness? Heartbreaking accidents will happen, but we cannot be on guard all the time. Death can even be caused by the normal use of anesthetic during a routine operation. Indeed, there are risks we haven't ever thought about. It is impossible to prevent all accidents. All we can do is try to improve the odds of survival. We live with danger all the time. A normal street crossing is a potential hazard for us. One could even be killed by a falling meteorite. Who can say there should or could have been preventive action? But if a beloved pet were killed that way, you can be sure the owner would be inventing guilt feelings about it.

We do not really know how to deal with our own guilt—especially when it is deserved. There are times when the human mind does some powerful damage to itself. Where does one realistically draw the line on self-punishment? Both we and our beloved pets stray from perfection, and this needs to be realized and accepted. That amazing, loving bond between a human and pet is so wonderful that any transgression is quickly forgiven. It is absolved by that great mutual love. In these special cases we have to be able to eventually give some of that to ourselves.

There are times when we must punish our beloved pets, just as we do our children. This is the way they have to be shown how to behave. Isn't a well-trained, well-behaved pet a happier one? Unquestionably, the training process is necessary—with all its occasional upsets and losses of patience. During bereavement, some people think back to the training period and seek justification for their guilt. Even something as necessary and benign as kind punishment is used at this time to justify their confusion and pain. They need to feel guilty.

In our role as steward of a pet, we have assumed such total responsibility that we are psychologically unprepared for the sudden closing down of that duty. After a lifetime of self-accountability, we still feel deeply responsible. The patterns we have established over such a long period of time remain, and the resulting emotional conflict with reality can be very upsetting. As already discussed, we may become obsessed, pondering whether destiny is preventable and if we might have effectively intervened. But how much control do we really have over our fates? Perhaps it is hubris to feel that we can fully determine the fate of our beloved pets. Some philosophers claim that everything that happens is natural and had to happen exactly as it did.

Sometimes we are so distracted by other things that we can be really at fault. In that case, our guilt is valid, and it has to be carefully examined and lived through. Life must go on for us, yet how do we do that after being such an active player in the pet's life and later demise? This is so hard. Each person brings into play all the previous accumulated problems in his/her life. (This is the emotional baggage we referred to earlier.) But self-forgiveness is absolutely necessary. Yet how? Who can really judge anyone else, at a horrible time like this? And how do we eventually come around to giving back to ourselves forgiveness and sufficient motivation to go on with our torn lives?

Somehow, we have to reach deep within ourselves and come up with the saving grace of self-love. We must be able to forgive ourselves and ease up on the guilt—merited or not. The terrible memory will be with us always—but so will the love and wonderful remembrances. If your pet were to sit in judgment over you, surely there would be forgiveness. There is no greater love and absolution than from our pets. Our continuing lives should be influenced by all they have taught us. But sometimes it takes time and a great many tears for us to learn this.

Guilty feelings are an invented response to a sense of failed responsibility. We each have such varied and unique complexities of personality that no generalization about our reactions can ever satisfy all. But by examining this normal human guilt response we can more effectively help ourselves cope with it—especially at this particularly grievous time in our lives. Pet lovers have very good hearts and generous spirits. Without hesitation, we lovingly give all for our beloved companions. And isn't that exactly what they would want us to do for ourselves at this time?

Our beloved pets bless us with their love. They did this during their lives, and they continue to bless us, now.

"Sleeping" and at one with nature.

Photo by W. Sife. Courtesy of Hartsdale Canine Cemetery, Inc.

Memorial to the adored pets of Vern and Irene Castle.
Photo by W. Sife. Courtesy of Hartsdale Canine Cemetery, Inc.

CHAPTER 8

Depression

*There is no greater sorrow than to recall
a time of happiness in misery.*

—Dante

Doctors speak of diseases in terms of their mortality and morbidity. The mortality of a condition is a reference to its ability to end life, whereas morbidity measures a condition's degree of misery and pain. Today, a strong case of the flu has a very low mortality index, but its morbidity is quite high. The same can be said of the depression aspect of the mourning process. Fortunately for many, it can be brief, but quite morbid while it lasts.

Most people in deep bereavement experience feelings of depression throughout the entire mourning process. Even though this is frequently referred to as one of the stages of grieving, because of the timing it is not technically a stage or a phase. When in deep mourning our emotional strength seems to give out, and things may feel as if they are crushing down on us. All we seem to care about is the pet's death and our own misery. A sense of numbness and indifference creeps over everything else, and we don't seem to care. Life feels overwhelming and very heartbreaking. It is normal to be depressed during intense mourning, but if that becomes prolonged or is too intense, then the depression needs to be treated by a properly trained professional. Most pet bereavement counselors are not qualified for this.

SYMPTOMS OF DEPRESSION

Psychologists classify depression as a syndrome characterized by several different symptoms, such as a markedly lowered mood, difficulty in thinking, and unusual physical fatigue. There may be signs of anxiety, obsessive thought, appetite loss, and difficulty with normal sleep patterns. All of this is dominated by an overwhelming attitude of gloom, dejection, and despair. Things do not seem to matter much, and those suffering may feel ambivalent about nearly everything. Generally, they prefer to be alone to stew in the juices of their sorrow.

There is an old adage that says, "Misery loves company." But that does not generally hold true for depressed people. They prefer their suffering alone, and in silence. Depression can develop to any degree of intensity, but it is not a cause of alarm unless it poses an actual danger to the individual. That almost always could be predicted by one's emotional health prior to the tragedy. Actually, depression can temporarily dull some of the great pain. This offers some necessary escape or relief from the overwhelming intensity. However, normal depression is usually relatively minor, despite the intense degree of emotional torment involved. Typically, the worst of it should pass in a few days or so.

FEELING SELF-DESTRUCTIVE

Suicidal feelings are much more common at this time than is generally believed. Fortunately, suicide is most often contemplated and not attempted. But severe depression can create a serious potential danger. Persistent or intense self-destructive thoughts are not unheard of during bereavement for a pet. If you think this is getting out of control, you should be counseled by a qualified practitioner of mental health. There is no stigma or shame in asking for help.

Only a small percentage of depressed mourners consider suicide. These feelings are almost always produced by well-defined, long histories of emotional upset and disturbance. The grief of bereavement is only the trigger mechanism for these thoughts, not the cause. Normally, the typical depression that is related to mourning is nothing to get alarmed about. As awful as that is to go through, it is not dangerous.

It can be said that depression is probably the most normal of all responses to the death of a pet. But we become upset in differing degrees at the loss of anything we hold dear. This includes our habits and patterns of behavior, as well as our possessions. Even the owner of a dented car, a torn jacket, or a broken toy can become depressed. Certainly the death of a beloved pet is a more than sufficient cause for depression. It is a very normal human reaction. But as we all know, even a moderate depression can produce a high level of upset and distress.

WITHDRAWAL

During this aspect of mourning, we tend to withdraw from the rest of the world. People and incidents don't affect us as they normally would. We may become disconsolate and listless, concerned only with the pet we have lost and the misery we are drowning in. Not only do we not feel good about anything, we don't want to feel better. Our sense of self-worth is at its lowest, and we really don't seem to care much about anything.

This condition dulls even our powerful guilt responses, as well as pangs of conscience and shock. We become quiet, dull, listless, melancholy, and ambivalent about things in general. Nothing seems to motivate depressed mourners as they withdraw into themselves. Fortunately, this improves with time. Normally, deep depression lasts not more than a few days to a week. If it persists, with little or no sign of improvement, then it should be dealt with, as suggested earlier.

At this time it seems as if there is nothing left in the world to ever smile about again. We are in a retreating, self-protective state of mind during this stage. Our sorrow for ourselves and our pets acts like a barrier between us and the rest of the world. It may be nearly impossible to accept that any good or healing will eventually come of this. During this period it can be a normal response to even resent or reject any such suggestion, as though someone is trying to offer inappropriate answers, trying to proffer a "bright side" when the whole world is darkened. Well-intentioned people will try to get us to act cheery. They get upset, seeing us like this. But they don't realize that we must go through a very personal period of mourning and bereavement. However, if the depression is intense, their concern may be justified.

Depression can make it seem as if it takes all of our best efforts to just endure. Even gentle, caring friends who want to help may seem pushy and invasive to the depressed person who needs more time to be alone and feel miserable. We may feel at this time that our thoughts for the deceased pet are too personal and intense to even try to share with anyone else. We need some time and privacy to recover from depression.

Sometimes when we are so miserable, we have to make a conscious effort to accomplish even small things that have become great obstacles—like getting out of bed, opening the blinds, and even brushing our teeth. These can feel like major acts of courage and great accomplishments at this time.

During this phase, we may even seem to "lose" ourselves for a while. We are involved in a total and disproportionate focus on the beloved, deceased companion. Also, we may be distraught because religious and philosophical teachings don't assure us of an afterlife for this pet, and we are unsure whether we will ever meet again after death. It can be additionally depressing because there are no answers when we need them most. We may feel at this time that life has little or no value. The future seems to have no meaning or importance. These are normal symptoms of depression, and they will pass. We constantly hear about time being one of the best healers. Although that can seem abstract or even intrusive to the bereaver, later one always learns it turns out to be true.

A HEALING STAGE

Mourners need communication with others, validation of their feelings, loving consideration, and time to be alone. Only in cases of abnormal depression will those in bereavement be unable to take even some small action to help themselves. Most of us will pass quickly enough through this seemingly unending period. It helps greatly to be able to talk out our story with some sympathetic person or persons. Close friends and support groups are probably the best help during this, the saddest part of the mourning process.

Surprisingly, depression as a major part of bereavement does serve a good purpose. It diminishes the intensity of emotions and gives us time to live with and assimilate the grim, new reality. We meditate and ponder on the pet's death and begin to lay the foundation for a new spiritual strength and perspective that we could not have had before. It is all part of the amazing healing process that nature has provided for us. We have to go through the worst of the pain in order to put most of it behind us.

When the depression passes, we are much closer than before to the resolution stage of the mourning. Things are beginning to look upward now. The worst part is over. For the first time since the death, it is possible to sense the easing of pain and to see some light at the end of the tunnel.

Ultimately, all life is change and growth. Otherwise, it wouldn't be worth living. This is a very hard lesson to learn, but a necessary one that our beloved pets can teach us. Yet it is nearly impossible to be philosophical when still in deep grief and depression.

Case History

An attractive, single woman in her late thirties had a history of being lonely and moderately forlorn. She owned a large, two-year-old male dog on whom she relied as her protector and closest companion. There was strong therapeutic value in this, but it was compromised by her becoming somewhat reclusive. She had given up on marriage or ever finding a suitable boyfriend. She lived with her beloved dog in a sort of emotional cocoon, safely isolated from everyone else.

The young dog died quite suddenly and unexpectedly from a respiratory ailment with cardiac complications. Almost immediately, the woman went into shock and deep depression. She felt panicky, abandoned, mildly suicidal, and terribly alone. Her job performance suffered, and the rest of her time was spent crying alone at home. She believed that nothing could ever make her smile again, and she said she wanted to die. Fortunately, her alert and compassionate neighbor noted some of these danger signs and finally persuaded her to come for counseling.

After a few sessions of sharing her heartache and utter dejection, we were able to plan some constructive direction in her thinking. Focus was placed on her family and friendly relationships. After getting into serious therapy and analysis of her more formative years, she was able to get some insight into many of the disappointments and problems she had experienced as a child and why she was always so emotionally insecure and lonely. That insight helped her come out of the clinical depression that her dog's death had triggered.

Her history revealed many years of low self-esteem and weak ego strength. She had always felt somewhat inferior and alone. Her alcoholic father was deceased, and her elderly mother, with whom she never had a close relationship, lived halfway across the country. Her only sibling, a brother, abused her as a child and she had been estranged from him for many years.

In a few sessions, her bereavement was able to progress to a reasonable resolution. Then we were able to go on in detail to analyze her underlying feelings of inadequacy. She became aware of the powerful symbolism her dog had and her reasons for shyness and low self-esteem.

She is in long-term therapy, but is now leading a happier and much more active life. She is still a bit defensive and laughs about her "pet rock" that needs no sustenance or care and can't die. Frequent, short travel vacations have begun to help give her a new base to improve her ego strength. Her social life is much improved and is growing even healthier. Now her dream is to meet a good man, settle down, and raise a small family, with a dog. The prognosis is excellent, as constructive therapy continues.

Dedicated to the memory of the
unknown canine soldier.

*Photo by W. Sife. Courtesy of
Hartsdale Canine Cemetery, Inc.*

CHAPTER 9

Resolution (Closure)

Our deeds still travel with us from afar.
And what we have been makes us what we are.

—George Eliot (Mary Ann Evans)

There is a time to have and to hold, and a time to let go. We will know sorrow just as we do joy. This final phase of mourning is the time of spiritual healing. Because we have gone through all the other developmental stages in preparation for this, we can finally release most of the pain without diminishing the beloved memory. Resolution is the knitting up of open wounds, but there will always be a secret scar and some pain. It is the taking of a brave step forward, and putting things into new harmony. Finally, we are able to allow the focus of emotion and attention to shift, permitting us to continue with our life's growth. This is when the pain changes from an immobilizing force to precious remembrance. This is the time of self-regeneration and healing. This is the time of closure.

This term "closure" is a good one when used by psychologists to refer to resolution of a problem. But experience teaches us that it is not the best word for use in dealing with anyone in deep bereavement. It is obviously derived from the word "close"—and that association can be intolerable at this time. We have noticed a tendency to resist this by clinging even harder to the pain and grief—out of fear of closing some kind of door on the love and memories. That term may also imply that the counselor using it is not fully in touch with what you are really going through. Although this word is widely accepted and universally used, for our purposes it needs to be replaced. Bereavement counseling is a relatively new field, and we are just beginning to realize that some traditional terminology is not appropriate here. The bereaver must not feel threatened by an arbitrary word that seems to compromise his/her personal value system and bereavement. For our purposes, we will use the more fitting term *resolution*.

After the terrible ordeal of mourning, the time has finally come when we can stop clutching teary memories and start to incorporate them as loving components of our new lives. Things must go on, but we never let go of the love that is still so cherished. It becomes a part of us, a deeply personal passion, never to be lost. What we do with that and how we may choose to memorialize the loss will vary with each individual. Actually, our ongoing lives can be our best memorials to our beloved pets.

Completing the painful passage through the bereavement process will in no way degrade one's intensely personal love for a deceased pet. This is the time in each mourner's life when we can start functioning fully again. At this point of transition, each of us has become different from before. Now, left without the pet's physical presence, we are enriched with a new dimension of its love. And that is very healing. In reaching this stage, we learn to incorporate that loving memory into the wiser and better person we have become because of this. The love and memories live on and forever enrich us.

A DIFFICULT CONCEPT

Death is the inevitable and only destination of every life. It is that simple. We so easily accept the concept of birth and living, but we become upset and troubled by thinking about the end of life. Because it is so completely mysterious to us, this subject becomes too disturbing to confront when not absolutely necessary. Most of our experiences with the ending of life are rationalized or blocked out. We try to pretend it away. And we try to deny that death is always around the corner, in every life. We like to make believe that it can be controlled by modern medicine, when it may be only postponed, at best. And sometimes that is not for the best.

During the mourning process, we can become obsessed with a sense of anguish and personal tragedy. We are ever so unprepared for death. Even the word "death" provokes general discomfort. As a natural result, we have created many word substitutes and euphemisms. We even tend to think in euphemistic ways, avoiding direct confrontation with the subject. People don't generally discuss this topic. And it is usually extremely uncomfortable to even hear others talk about it. Thus, when a beloved pet dies we can be unready and frightened, as well as completely overwhelmed by that grim finality.

CHANGING ATTITUDES

Western culture needs to make some adjustments to its attitude toward death. Fortunately, it is beginning to show some changes. The introduction of some Eastern philosophy has enlightened large numbers of seekers, in many ways. As we work our way toward improving knowledge, we begin to realize that death is neither bad, nor is it our enemy. It is a natural part of the life sequence. We also can be upset by the idea that at life's end, there may be nothing else afterward. Since we celebrate a birth as a beginning of an unknown life, we should celebrate death as the logical end to a beautiful life that gave us a very special love. The funeral and mourning should incorporate the sadness and loss, while also commemorating and honoring that life. If nothing but tears and grief are there, then something very important has been left out.

It is interesting to note that primitive or underdeveloped civilizations accept death much more easily and rationally than we do. That is not because they are less sensitive or intelligent. Simply, they have not yet been culturally deceived into believing that nature can be controlled so completely. All of civilization's complications and powers cannot revoke death. All the scientific and technological command and dominion that we have attained over other things is useless here. We can no longer continue to pretend that death does not follow naturally and is not inevitable. If we close our eyes, it doesn't go away. This is like the proverbial image of an ostrich hiding its head in a hole in the ground to avoid danger. Time and death will always catch up with us, even if we try to ignore the fact. Death should not be characterized as something unfathomable, supernatural, or bad. All living things must die. Unfortunately, we have been conditioned to illogically feel that we have gained such mastery and control over life that death is a mistake, or an accident, and can be constrained. Death is a natural event, and it will go on forever, for all living things. This can seem simplistic, but during intense bereavement we tend to lose perspective on it.

We love cut flowers and enjoy their beauty. But when they wilt and die, it is time to put them aside. There is no sadness in that. The life of a beloved pet, or anything else, is really very similar. We are enriched and deeply affected by the years of the pet's love and companionship. But this profound relationship has reached down to the core of our existence and helped change our sense of identity. Although it is hard to put aside the physical being, we keep the love and joy within us. We have to learn to accept that there is a natural limit to each lifetime. If an individual can add religious significance and consolation to this outlook, all the better. To see only sad things in a death is to lose perspective and fail in our respect. It diminishes the value of that life. That is not the way we want it.

We are discovering that even stars and galaxies are born and die in turn. Somehow, in the grand scheme of all things, everything is related. All of the ancient stars that have exploded have created newer elements that spread out to help form even newer stars and galaxies. And these in turn have done the same, all the way down the line for over fourteen billion years. Amazingly, that has evolved and created all the present physical matter in our cosmos. Our bodies are actually made of what was once stardust. Everything is. The constant cycle of life and death is the rule of all things. Everything in nature has a beginning and an end. Understanding that, it is unreasonable to see death as the enemy—to be feared and hated. Somehow, each of us has to develop a healthier and broader outlook on the meanings and values of life. That is why the wisdom of the East still has so much to teach us. We are all part of nature, and we need to develop a more natural outlook on all things, especially our own lives and those of our dear ones.

Mourning for a beloved pet has always been kept very private and secret, as a means of self-protection from criticism. But now we have reached a point in our cultural evolution where this humane expression is finally being let out from under wraps. People are beginning to talk more freely about the effect of a pet's death upon them. Our personal vulnerability and stigmas of shame are being reduced and removed. Others are increasingly being made aware of the vast numbers of us who have experienced this type of grief. We are no longer looked upon as social oddities. There is some encouragement in this growing social change. It enables us to no longer feel as restricted in expressing our heartfelt feelings and emotions for a pet's death.

A STEP-BY-STEP PROCESS

The entire mourning process, with all its stages, is a painful living-through situation in which we are unconsciously preparing ourselves, step-by-step, to let go of what we held so dear. But the expression "letting go" can be misleading. It does not mean that we forget the beloved, or stop having loving memories. It is the letting go of our debilitating pain and anguish. This "closure" or resolution only comes to us gradually, along with the acceptance of the grim reality and its effects on us. It is achieved when thoughts of a beloved pet no longer occupy the forefront of our minds. It enables us to remember and feel all the love, without the shock and grief caused by a pet's death. When we are able to reach a sense of this, we can begin to pick up and go on with our lives. During the early stages of bereavement, this may seem selfish. But at that point we may still feel an irrational need to suffer. It can seem to us that if we stopped hurting, we would stop loving—and that thought is intolerable. Later, we will finally see that it is not true. Our special love has transformed itself into a permanent part of our new self.

To help reach a sense of closure, the following time-tested method is suggested:

- **Make a list**—Itemize particular times and situations that still give you special pain and trouble in your bereavement. Continue expanding this list over several days. Later, read it over and look for some common denominators. What repeated themes are there? To help put this into better perspective, it is best to discuss your list and themes with someone you trust and respect.

- **Don't berate yourself for not feeling as much pain as you first did**—Sometimes we tend to be anxious about what may feel like too rapid or even too slow a recovery. The healing process makes us stronger and better, but it involves pain, time, and self-respect. And it takes lots of patience.

TIME AND CHANGES

It is often said that time heals all wounds. Superficially, this statement is correct, but it is trite and incomplete. A better statement would explain that what really heals us is learning to live with wounds. This

A beloved raccoon.   *Photo by W. Sife. Courtesy of Hamilton Pet Meadow,*
                           Memorial Park and Crematory

requires time to achieve and complete. What we achieve is a beautiful memory, filled with loving sentiments that live on in us. That is the best memorial possible.

With the passage of time, we don't ever lose that special love for a beloved life that has ended. However, we do learn to be less and less overwhelmed by the death. We learn to let go of the shock and pain, but not the cherished loving memories and associations. And we go on living, with this change in us. Unfortunately, part of life is suffering, and we have to learn this the hard way. There is no choice.

The process of gradually picking ourselves up to continue with our lives is upsetting, yet necessary. But, somehow, this is accomplished in time. Mostly, the hard part is done at the subconscious level of awareness and healing. Gradually, the shock diminishes, and we are able to go on. But there will be unexpected moments in all of our lives, far into the future, when we will suddenly break down in tears, for our beloved ones. This is normal, and to be expected. Our love lives on with us.

There are some who react to the death of their beloved pets as if they have become different and better people. Indeed, they have changed. We all have. Others may feel a spiritual dedication to the pet's living memory and redirect their lives accordingly. We move on and move up on the staircase of experience, ever changing and improving as we go. With each step we are more aware, and hopefully wiser. The experience of living with a beloved pet is an enriching one—one that benefits us forever. It adds a special endearing memory and strength to us, now and for the rest of our lives.

We always become products of our former experiences. After discovering the beauty and wonder of that special, loving life, we owe it to its living memory to heal and grow again. We must go on. Certainly, that is what your pet would want for you, if you are to be able to put its feelings into thought.

At this state of resolution and closure, it is heartwarming to be able to realize that your new life alone, without the deceased pet, can become a living memorial. Your improved outlook and ongoing life is the ultimate testimony to that love.

CHAPTER 10

Other
Kinds
of Loss

≈

That grim abduction still eluded me, until too late,
with pitiless events in nature's normalcy called fate.
Dispossessing profanation, so irrevocable,
wrests my unremitting grief to wretchedness and wait.

—Modern Rubaiyat, Wallace Sife

Most people think about the loss of a pet in terms concerning its death. But there is another kind of loss that we should all be made aware of because it can happen to nearly any one of us. This other horrible experience is bereavement for a pet resulting from its disappearance. One hears of all sorts of shocked and grieving owners, advertising desperately for the return of their beloved companion animals. Sometimes very large rewards are offered, even by poor families, to hopefully bring that cherished pet back. But there really is no measure for a beloved pet, other than love. We tend to take our pet's security for granted, and the grief is terrible when that pet is suddenly gone.

Many pet owners find it necessary to seek bereavement counseling when their animals disappear. Some of these pets probably strayed away and confronted the perils of traffic, predators, vicious dogs, or any number of things. Their owners are in all stages of grief and mourning, despite the fact that there was no direct indication of death. Many seem to be even worse off than those who have recently deceased pets. The people whose pets disappear are in a unique category of bereavement because they can still cling to a golden spark of hope that their beloved animals are still alive and may yet return home. But they know that the probability drops to near zero as time passes. Sadly, they may never know that their pet is dead. If they at least knew that, then some of the worry would be over. And that knowledge might ease the terrible anxiety. Now, however, the awful grip of uncertainty, guilt, and suspense dominates every waking moment—and even their dreams.

WHEN A PET DISAPPEARS

There are so many ways a pet can disappear. This usually happens in a flash, when we drop our vigilance for just a brief moment. And that is all it takes. A bird, even with clipped flight feathers, may flutter out a just-opened door or a window opened only a crack. There is no such thing as having been only a little careless when a pet disappears. It is a matter of all or nothing. Dogs and cats get out of the house, stray, and become lost. If they are lucky they become members of feral groups, living on garbage and anything else they can find to eat. Or they can be picked up by people who then keep them as their new pets. There are dangers such as vicious feral animals—and wild ones that are natural predators in some parts of the country. And there are contemptible humans who delight in trying to drive over any animal they see alone on the road. Many strays are captured by animal control officers and sent off and are eventually euthanized. And then there are the professional suppliers to the experimental labs. These are despicable human predators who are always on the prowl for *any* dog or cat they can find. And they are very accomplished at capturing these unwitting pets. It is worse than a jungle out there!

Pets are frequently stolen out of yards and cars, and for just a few dollars they are sold for experiments and testing—with no questions asked. None survive the ordeal. There is no animal more vile than an evil human. The unrelenting guilt and grief that owners of missing pets go through as they try to endure this unresolvable experience is like no other kind of bereavement.

When a pet disappears, some of the stages of bereavement are intensified and distorted—always underscored by uncertainty and an overwhelming sense of failed responsibility. Unfortunately, there can be no real finish for this unique grief. Closure or resolution could come with either the return of the pet or certain knowledge of its death. But that rarely ever happens. The initial stage of shock is even slightly different. There still may be hope, however dim it is. Usually, there is no disbelief because of the circumstances. Here the guilt is often justified. Almost all of the anger is directed at oneself for being so negligent. In the case of known petnapping, anger is also directed at the thief and others in general who would deliberately do this to your pet. This kind of loss becomes a terrible exercise in rage, dire frustration, and emotional catastrophe.

Anger quickly turns into guilt. It is loaded with passionate fantasies of "should have," "could have," and "if only." But it is too late. That is when a variation of the denial stage kicks into gear, and fantasy becomes fervent hope. We offer up all sorts of prayers to try to bargain or plead with God for the return of the pet. This phase can be even more painful for an owner when the pet disappears, rather than for one whose pet dies. But sometimes we are very lucky. On rare occasions lost pets are returned, and strays come home.

PREVENTABLE LOSSES

There are so many ways a beloved pet can be taken from us that it is important to consider them—hopefully before they have the opportunity to happen. Most often this kind of loss is preventable, as contrasted to death, which is inevitable. A very important lesson can be learned in the following pages, and it can decrease the probability of this type of loss. Constant watchfulness and vigilance are required in the care of our pets. That is part of the commitment we make as stewards.

Cats can be very efficient at escaping or getting lost. Everyone hears about their climbing up trees and then becoming too fearful to come down. Sometimes local fire departments will not come to the rescue, claiming they are too busy at the moment with higher priority calls. Cases of lost cats have been reported as a result of this kind of situation. It had been presumed that they would eventually come down, despite their fright. That, however, could take many hours, and most people can't just wait there. They mistakenly expected their cats to eventually come down on their own and return home. So much can happen at a time like this. There are also many cases of cats who escaped out of a momentarily opened door—or disappeared out a partially opened window.

Dogs are frequently reported missing because of other careless conditions or practices that their owners engaged in. Most of these losses arise from preventable circumstances. Some dogs are regularly allowed to freely roam their neighborhood. Their owners have many different, inexcusable justifications for having permitted this.

Beloved pets disappear and are never seen again. Was it because of thieves who routinely sell them to labs, or strangers taking them in as their new pets? Or was there some kind of terrible accident? These bereaving pet owners will probably never know. And they will most likely have to live with this grim uncertainty for the rest of their lives.

The same missing pet complaint also arises from situations where dogs are routinely tied up outside stores, while their owners are inside shopping. Again, the excuses and justifications are easy to come by, but the pet is lost. There are several possibilities here, and they are all dire—and they don't really matter. Now it's too late to defend against this! Sadly, there are many recorded instances of concerned people who tried to warn the owners, but who were routinely told to mind their own business. This is another tragic irony of preventable loss.

Stealing a dog or cat from a yard or a car is the most common type of petnapping. No one ever thinks that such a thing will happen, but it does—and it can be prevented so easily. This does not mean that one should confine the dog in a car with the windows shut to prevent criminal opening of the locks. Too many deaths by heat prostration happen every year because of that. A pet left in a car in the sun can die in as little as twelve minutes, or it may be left with permanent brain damage in much less time. Although it can be inconvenient, the owner must consider the possibilities and work this problem out before the danger or possible theft has a chance to happen. The professional petnapper is very adept at luring and baiting most animals, in all kinds of situations. Don't rely on your pet being too smart or protective to be fooled. Some go willingly, after being offered a tasty tidbit. Professional dognappers often use a captive bitch in heat to easily lure male dogs away. Even the best-trained ones are taken this way.

Sometimes people are forced to give up their pets because many landlords and other housing authorities do not allow pets. Tenants who do not know this, or who disregard that clause in their leases, are almost always required to finally give up their beloved pets. It is important to be enlightened that there are federal laws that prevent this, if it can be demonstrated that the pet is important to the emotional health and welfare of the tenant. Landlords know about this and will not challenge it in court, as they *always* lose.

There are also cases when people lose their companion animals while on a trip, and they can only stay for a limited time to search for them. The resulting grief immediately changes their lives, and the emotional scars can last forever. These are also very commonplace occurrences that too often could have been avoided by some careful, advance planning.

Loss Due to Divorce

Divorce is another situation that can cause the loss of a pet. As necessary as the break-up of a family may be, most often both parties always suffer. But somebody has to lose the pet. One partner takes it, along with other agreed upon possessions and goods. The tragedy is compounded—the winning ex-spouse really does not love the pet as much as the other. It is too often used as a means to get back at the other person—and the animal's best interests are traded off with other angry or competitive settlements of property. Whoever loses custody of the pet suffers other feelings of outrage, as well. This kind of loss is always complicated by additional problems that result from the broken marriage and the final unpleasant compromises and settlements. But at least in this kind of loss there is some solace in knowing that the pet is alive and well—not missing. Its basic safety and well-being are most likely not in any danger. There are many cases on record in which visiting rights and alternate days of care are written into the final agreement. But be cautioned because sometimes the pet suffers from this. In bad marriages there are many variables of spite and revenge that are inflicted on pets—as well as children.

In cases of domestic violence, when a woman finally gets up the courage to relocate to a shelter, other problems can complicate matters. Pets are not allowed in such places, and they often have to be left behind with the abusive husband. Such women deeply suffer the loss of their pets, and they also worry that their companion animals may be deliberately mistreated, in retaliation. That fear is often well-founded. There have been too many incidents recorded in which the brutal person beat, tortured, or even killed a pet that was dear to the woman. Sometimes the pet's safety is used as a hostage situation. It is all part of a very sick and abusive way of exercising control. Judges have only recently started taking a more realistic attitude about this.

WHEN A PET IS REMOVED

There are always a few dogs that are more frightening than others to neighbors. At times these pets have to be removed by law because of their biting, excessive noise, or just because they are of a breed and temperament that some communities unreasonably fear. Most people who train their dogs for protection or to attack others are almost asking for action to be taken against them and their pets (who were innocently turned into "monsters"). When these dogs are taken away, even these selfish owners may suffer their own kind of private grief. Regardless of who or what we are, we all see and feel things in our own perspectives.

There is a very surprising high rate of dogbite incidents on record. Amazingly, even sweet little dogs can bite people (especially children) they perceive to be threatening them. Whether provoked or not, these otherwise good pets are frequently removed from the home by animal control personnel. Too often they are euthanized, and not returned to their distraught owners. This is another example of preventable loss—as well as the avoidable pain and suffering inflicted by the bite. And then there are also probably going to be legal problems, as well.

There are many other instances in which pets are forcibly taken from homes by animal control personnel. This is often initiated by complaints of inhumane crowding and inadequate treatment. This is frequently accompanied by all sorts of disagreeable noises and smells. Too often these animal abusers are out of touch with reality, on several different levels. They may well be of limited mental competence, but all too often they are just very foolish and extremely self-indulgent. In their narrow perspective, they love their hordes of animals and don't seem to realize that they are doing them actual harm. These lonely and self-isolated people also go through the painful stages of bereavement for their seized pets. Everyone sees his own problems as no one else can. We all have our private sorrows and wretched reactions in bereavement. As pet lovers and humanists, we must keep our objectivity and awareness that all grief should merit some compassion, regardless of the circumstances.

Human sickness and disability are other common reasons for having to remove people's pets. When some people no longer have the ability to care for them, the pets must be picked up and sent somewhere. Unfortunately, most often they go off to shelters to be euthanized. These owners are usually very loving, but they are too infirm or unable to continue their responsibilities as stewards of their pets. In addition to an agonizing sense of loss and bereavement, their misfortunes often cause other problems. All this becomes even more complicated by a terrible sense of failure and utter loneliness without their beloved companion animals. As a result, they often suffer further emotional spiritual, and physical collapse. Pets can be our psychological and spiritual life preservers in seas that would quickly drown us.

Occasionally, utility animals, trained to assist people with disabilities, are stolen. Their unfortunate owners, already at such a tremendous disadvantage, then have to grieve about the possible terrible fate of these beloved companion animals. They bond much more powerfully and depend entirely on their animals for even a small sense of independence and self-esteem. The loss of these pets can sometimes be too much to bear, especially for older or extremely handicapped people. One woman who had been confined to a lifetime in a wheelchair died of grief after her trained assistance dog was stolen. She loved her dog dearly, and the bonding had been very intense. For nearly three years that dog had been her dearest friend, and it also personified her strength to go on with her tortured daily existence. The horrors of what might have befallen her adored companion animal were too much to contend with. The unbearable uncertainty and loneliness caused her to suffer a fatal heart attack. Elderly and disabled people are always much more vulnerable to the loss of their pets—whatever the causes.

Too often these very highly trained guide and service dogs are taken and then sold to experimental labs, as just additional bodies, along with surplus anonymous shelter animals, and stolen family pets. Unfortunately, there are still a few shelters that sell off their surplus of unadoptable animals, and advertise themselves as no-kill shelters. What a cruel deception that is! It has been documented that some labs remove all identification when they buy animals. Cases have been verified in which even ID tattoos and implanted chips had been surgically removed or made unreadable. These institutions and the fiends who supply them with animals are some of the vilest elements in our society. They continue to thrive under existing laws that protect and encourage them to continue. They are modern-day vampires. Aside from the horrors inflicted on these pets, the lives of the good people who love them are broken and can never be the same. They never know the fate of their lost companions—and these labs are their worst fear. Even death is preferred to this appalling fate for them.

We occasionally hear of pet snakes and small reptiles escaping from their confines and disappearing. Sometimes they show up days later in the most unlikely of places, still in their homes. But too often they are just gone, never to be found again. Although they can survive for long periods without food, they may all too easily have crawled into hidden spaces and died there. The temperature may have dropped, causing them to lose energy and become fatally entrapped. Most people are surprised that the owners of snakes and reptiles can get so extremely upset emotionally. The most common reaction of others to this kind of loss is that a cold-blooded animal doesn't show love and affection as other pets do, and it couldn't possibly be as loved as a more common pet is. But this seemingly logical response doesn't hold true. It is based on exactly the same kind of prejudice that we have been fighting all these years, in expressing bereavement for dogs and cats. Who is to be anyone else's judge when it comes to loving and feeling grief? The spirit and hope that we want for ourselves in "coming out of the closet" with our own grief in pet bereavement is exactly the same for the owners of less understood or liked species of animals. There can be no exceptions or attitudes of superiority or scorn here. The tendency to give snake and other reptile owners short shrift should send us a shocking message about how close we are to being guilty of what we condemn in other, less sensitive individuals. As pet lovers, we must respect all pets, as well as their owners' feelings of bereavement. This is a matter of simple love, understanding, and tolerance. The regard we want is the same that we must give. Sitting in judgment of other people's feelings and grief is the very problem that others have plagued us with. What right has anyone to decide if another person's grief is justified? So if the beloved pet is a lizard or even a goldfish or rat, we must respect the owner's feelings. Someone is grieving deeply, which is all that should really matter. We are animal lovers, and God bless all of us.

PETS FREE TO GOOD HOME

Some desperate families, unable to keep their pets, take out "Free to Good Home" ads. Many of these animals are then taken from their homes with false promises of a new, good life. Too often they are then unscrupulously sold by licensed U.S. Department of Agriculture (USDA) "B" dealers to research facilities that pay hundreds of dollars for each healthy, gentle dog or cat. Stolen pets are occasionally recovered from "legitimate" research institutions across the nation, but that is far too infrequent.

Last Chance For Animals, a wonderful nonprofit organization in California, is actively pursuing ways to combat this national abuse, including U.S. Congressional action. Through ambitious, vigorous campaigns, it continues to stop pet theft and the profit it offers some individuals. At this time they are the only organization to apprehend, bring to trial, convict, and send to prison licensed "B" dealers, who are selling stolen companion animals to experimental laboratories. To help in the mission to eliminate this kind of vile activity, or if you have any information about pet theft in your area, call Last Chance For Animals at (800) 271-6096 or (888) 88-ANIMALS.

RESPONSES TO A PET'S DISAPPEARANCE

The loss of a pet is a terrible experience, but perhaps there is nothing worse than loss through disappearance. The responses are different, and as already indicated, the grieving stages are often distorted and unending. The only escape from the haunting, unresolvable heartbreak of this experience is by conscious repression of the feelings and bad memories. Of course, that is not a healthy way to reconcile a problem, but in this exceptional circumstance, it seems to be the only release from endless anguish.

Deliberately repressed feelings always lead to unconsciously suppressed complications. They can fester within us all our lives unless psychotherapy is employed. The bereavement one suffers for a missing pet can be even worse than the grief we would go through in responding to its death. This is like an open sore that doesn't really heal. There is a direct comparison here to the emotional reactions of families of combat personnel who are reported "missing in action," with no trace of them ever found. How do their families find closure or resolution with this? It is exactly the same.

Truth is often stranger than fiction. Countless daily dramas are being played out in amazing variations on all themes, including the losses of beloved pets. One graphic example of this is illustrated in the unusual and completely unexpected tragic experience of one family.

Case History

A young father of two children was dying of cancer. Shortly before his death, he gathered his small family around his hospital bed and told them he wanted them to get a German Shepherd Dog to love, and who could be their protector when he was gone. He did not discuss this in advance with his wife, and the idea came as quite a surprise. It was something the family had never thought about before, but in the grief of their bereavement, they accepted this as his last wish—which had to be honored.

The young mother got a Shepherd puppy but didn't know the first thing about dogs or their training. She was overwhelmed by her bereavement and had to be all things for her two children, at the same time. The frisky pup quickly grew into a large, slightly spoiled, affectionate young dog, and it was adored as their surrogate protector—a symbol of perceived replacement for the deceased father.

The children were not too careful about keeping him on his leash in the yard, and after about a year, the dog disappeared. Then, along with all the usual problems and heartache of losing a pet this way, unexpected additional complications suddenly arose. In addition to their grief for the missing dog, they now suffered an unexpected secondary bereavement for the father. With the disappearance of the pet he wanted to represent him by watching over them, in their minds he seemed to die and leave them again. They were completely overwhelmed by this double blow and had to go into intensive family and individual therapy. Despite their eventual healing and recovery, some emotional scars will always remain in each of them.

Other Kinds of Loss

When we lose beloved pets, we always lose what also had been treasured as secret reflections of ourselves. When conditions prevent our ever being able to find some reasonable resolution, healing can't be completed. Although time seems to relieve all wounds, this kind of unresolved grief creates suppressed problems that may continue to disturb us for the rest of our lives. While therapy can treat this quite successfully, nothing short of amnesia can remove the memory of this special kind of loss. So we must do something positive about learning to live with it. But regardless of the kind of loss, many years later, we often can experience a sudden and unexpected emotional breakdown—and the tears and painful memories come back, for a short while. This is normal, and to be expected.

We all have different kinds of personal regrets and feelings of misgivings in our lives, but they belong in the past. Now it is our primary responsibility and duty to ourselves to put aside whatever emotional baggage we are left with and move on. Yes, it is easy to give this advice, and so hard to follow it! But personal growth must never stop. We owe that to ourselves, as well as to all who love us. And that also must include our beloved missing pets. In a sense, they are never completely lost, as they will always still be in our hearts.

The Association for Pet Loss and Bereavement (APLB) has several links to wonderful organizations that are dedicated to helping owners of lost and missing pets. Go to www.aplb.org and click on the Links page to see a list of helpful links. Also, go to any of the major online search engines, such as Google, and look up "missing pets."

"My little pal."

Photo by W. Sife. Courtesy of Hamilton Pet Meadow, Memorial Park and Crematory

CHAPTER 11

Another

Pet?

A friend is a present you give yourself.

—*Robert Louis Stevenson*

There are many good people whose personalities are ideal for owning a pet. The relationship they create with their companion animals is one of great mutual love and trust. Pets and humans lead an enhanced, happy life together in a marvelous, symbiotic relationship. Each partner gives and gets in deeply personal ways that are amazingly beneficial. Such a bonding can be enriching beyond description. Unfortunately, many of those who are not pet lovers don't seem to understand this.

There will be a time during the initial bereavement period when pet people start thinking about getting another one. It is almost a sure thing that they will want another one, some day. But when? Although this may not be a major problem, sometimes there are circumstances that make the decision very difficult.

ARE YOU READY?

Timing is everything when considering whether to get another pet. You must be ready for the new relationship, or both you and that pet may suffer because of some underlying resentment. At this time we may feel willing, but are hesitant or even fearful. This could easily feel

"Good-bye My Loves."

*Photo by W. Sife. Courtesy of
Hartsdale Canine Cemetery, Inc.*

Mariposa and Rose Marie.
*Photo by W. Sife.
Courtesy of Hartsdale
Canine Cemetery, Inc.*

like betrayal to the deceased pet, even though it really isn't. Indeed, resentment or even rejection of the new one may follow if the replacement is made too soon. Most people need to be alone for a while with their memories. We all need to mourn in our own, very personal and private way. And remember that children are people, too. If they are not too young, let them in on the underlying thinking and the decision-making process, as well.

A new pet can stimulate a healthy improvement of your lifestyle. But you have to be ready. After a period of bereavement and depression, a new start can be very beneficial. Another side benefit is that this new pet opens a means to meeting new people. We become exposed to social situations when walking a dog, buying pet food in the store, attending membership meetings at a pet club, and so on. Regular walks with dogs also provide us with much-needed exercise. We get out of the house and break the grip of isolation and depression. However, being forced prematurely into a new pet relationship is another problem, and one that can be very upsetting.

Advice is cheap, easy to get, and usually well-intended. But in the emotionally charged subject of resolving your personal bereavement, no one else can really know your feelings about bringing a new companion animal into your life. Even you may not be sure of your own readiness. It is important that you never let anyone try to talk you into getting another pet. The decision has to come from deep within yourself, and the timing has to feel right to you.

Sometimes people who have lost their pets may be more ready emotionally than they had at first realized. The following exercise will help you to make your own decision on this issue. It will offer an objective demonstration of whether you are ready to have a new pet.

1. Visit an animal shelter. Do this just to look around, not to adopt at this time! You must be firm with yourself about this resolve. Watch out, though. Temptation can be strong for the moment, and very hard to resist. Hasty, impulsive decisions may be very much regretted later.

2. Write down your feelings after this visit, and read them again at another time. Share them with a trusted friend. What new feelings are you beginning to have now after the visit? Did you retain a strong memory of any particular one? Sometimes, being exposed to these needy souls, we

unconsciously help ourselves break out of the most maudlin part of bereavement. Feeling pity and love for homeless, lovable animals in this kind of situation can stimulate a quicker resolution to our bereavement. It can change our perspectives in a positive way, without pain or argument. And it is not betrayal.

We tend to forget the difficulties in rearing a pet. Do you remember how long it takes for one to adjust to its new home? And do you recall how long it took for you to adapt too, with all the work, frustration, annoyance, anger, time, and expense involved? If you are really ready, your experience might well make the training period easier. You will find out soon enough.

3. Write down some more notes. Our deceased pets are now out of pain. Most people believe they are now on a higher plane, where they have become one again with the cosmos—or if you prefer, with God. There is only wisdom and love there. (See "All Pets Go to Heaven" at the end of chapter 16). With this in mind, write down what your beloved pet must be thinking—concerning how bad you feel. Write down some of the things that come to mind— what you feel he/she would now tell you about getting another companion to love you. Our beloved deceased pets are our personal "angels" now. They want the best for us.

Children who want an "immediate replacement" should have it explained to them that there is no such thing. Each animal is unique, especially in personality. A pet is not a toy, and a new one cannot be used as a substitute. If they are above the age of four or five, children should experience some mourning first. Don't try to protect them from this because doing so may cause unnoticed emotional damage that can last them through the rest of their own lives.

Bereaved pet owners feel that their loved one could never be replaced. This is correct. We really don't want a replacement. That pet was uniquely important. The pet's remembrance becomes a symbolic link to the past and our own ongoing evolution. The thought of getting another companion animal at this time may at first feel like disloyalty. During the earlier stages of bereavement, before resolution, that feeling can be especially strong. But later this does change, and the pain eases, as well.

Getting another pet would mean companionship again. This new addition would love to be your new friend and would be "someone" to care for. Being responsible for a dependent animal's life again is a good experience. Death should not scare us away from new life. But keep in mind that any new pet will have its own personality. Although your new relationship with it may turn out to be wonderful, it will be different from before. It has to be. Some people get new pets and then try to train them to be copies of the one who died. That is always a big mistake. First of all, it can't be done. And it is actually disrespectful to that pet, as well as your relationship with it.

It is very important to realize that a beloved companion animal can't be "replaced." Some mistaken people try this with others of the same breed, sex and markings, and it never works out the way they planned. That is just sheer foolishness. Appearance does not make the pet, and it can never substitute for individuality. The very special relationship and bonding that existed with the old pet was so unique that its loving memory lives on within us. There can be no replacement of that.

Sometimes we may fantasize about cloning our beloved deceased pets. Unfortunately, there are too many misconceptions about what cloning really is and what it can achieve. Most people don't know that cloning does not produce perfect or even identical living specimens. Although in time this will surely improve to some degree, the actual rate of seemingly healthy cloned animal babies is astonishingly low. We are also just beginning to be told that those few surviving laboratory specimens are too often flawed. And at best, the successful clone is only a physical replica. In no way does cloning reproduce personality or temperament. Each is unique. Even identical twins have different personalities. One could always search for and find an almost identical copy of our deceased pet. But as mentioned above, that is highly inadvisable. This is looking for a substitute and does not allow for full acceptance and respect of the pet's death. It will also hinder successful healing from the loss.

When I conduct group support sessions, I usually allow my dog to be present. She senses the grief and goes around the circle of bereavers, stopping to love and be loved by each one in turn for a few minutes. It is amazing and gratifying to see the therapy a little loving animal can give to people in deep mourning for their own pets. She has been hugged, kissed, whispered to, and cried over. Almost without exception, I have been told by patients how helpful this exposure was in easing their grief and assisting them to determine their levels of readiness for a new pet.

We can touch and caress our pets. This is so good for us for many reasons. It decreases loneliness and depression, and has been proven to be wonderful medicine. Our general health improves by being with them and interacting as we do. They lower blood pressure, relax our bodies and minds, help improve our resistance to disease, and give us love, loyalty, amusement, and other pleasures. It has been clinically proven that pets can even lengthen the duration of one's life by improving its quality.

Do you have a strong fear of having to go through another pet's death and mourning experience? If so, would you be able to handle such a loss and bereavement again? The answer is probably yes. But you should not opt for bringing another one into your life until you have worked through your present grief and early phases of mourning. Keep in mind that no one else can tell you when you are ready. If you feel indecisive about getting another pet, don't do it yet! You can be ready only when and if this ambivalence is replaced by more positive feelings about yourself and a new animal-friend. Only you will be able to sense when the time is right. Stay with your "gut feelings." Trust your instincts; they have much truth underlying them.

Generally, it is not advisable to rush into getting another pet. But sometimes, under extraordinary circumstances, getting one soon is the right thing to do. Some people have a strong need to be able to love a pet again. On the other hand, sometimes well-intentioned people may try to show their love and concern by giving a replacement pet to a bereaved owner. This caring but foolish act can create a major problem. In effect, it forces mourners to accept an immediate substitute (which cannot be done) long before they may have been able to work through their basic grief and resolve it. Because we love animals, we will feel concerned for a little orphan, reflexively responding to its needs. Giving someone a replacement pet can be especially cruel if done at the wrong time. It really is forcing one's will upon another person who is still in mourning, and may not yet be ready to make a reasonable commitment. No one can make such a covenant for that person.

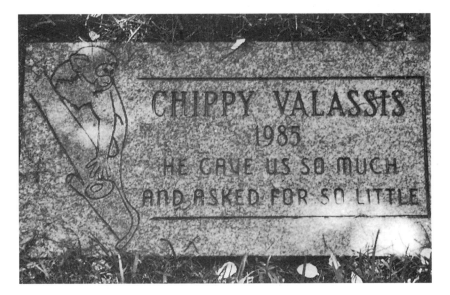

Testimony to a dear monkey.

Photo by W. Sife. Courtesy of
Abbey Glen Pet Memorial Park

A monument at Bide-A-
Wee for former President
Nixon's dog, Checkers.
Photo by George Wirt.
Courtesy of Bide-A-Wee

THINGS TO KEEP IN MIND

When you finally do decide to open up your life to another companion animal, there are a few things that should be kept in mind. If you like the same breed and color, that's fine, but do not try to remake the new animal into a replica of your deceased pet. As mentioned earlier, this cannot be done. The initial period of adjustment teaches you, as well as the pet, about each other. Make a new relationship and build it on mutual trust, love, and respect. This will be your new friend. Get toys that do not remind you of your deceased pet's playthings. Give this newcomer a chance to be wonderful, too, on its own merits. It deserves this respect and love. You might love to tell your new pet bedtime stories of the dear one who has passed on. This can be a wonderful part of the new bonding process. And it is so good for you, as well.

Some older people feel they should not get another companion animal, just in case they become too ill or infirm to continue to care for it. They fear developing a strong bond and then becoming unable to live up to the responsibility. They may worry about dying or becoming disabled before the pet dies, which could become very complicated. It also would traumatize the pet. If they live alone, that adds to the potential problems. But if they can make arrangements to have someone visit and play with a new pet, then this person would probably provide a safe and happy home for it, if that ever becomes necessary.

Or instead of their getting another companion animal, it may be better to visit with friends and neighbors who have a pet. Most often these people would be happy if an older friend enjoyed and played with their pets, within certain limits. Discuss this with them. Perhaps occasional pet sitting or walking their pets may help fill the need to enjoy a companion animal's company. It could be something like being a grandparent—with all of the pleasure and little of the responsibility.

Pet people are special. We have so much love to give—and get. But we get confused what to do about this when a beloved one dies. Many of us need to go on loving others, as well. Sometimes it is an excellent idea to get another companion animal before the first one dies. It may make good sense to bring home a baby friend for the older one, as well as for yourself. If the older animal accepts this (and most will), the quality of its remaining life will be much improved. This will also have psychological benefits for you. Now there will be "someone" who can intimately share the loss of the older pet when the time comes. Also, you will not be left alone. There will be another sweet companion animal to love and care for, and help buffer some of the sorrow. But arrange to have the surviving pet see and smell the deceased one before having it buried or cremated. That will help with acceptance and understanding of its later disappearance from the household.

Remember, it is inevitable that a new pet will make many mistakes and possibly cause some annoyance as well as damage to your property. Perhaps you forgot this. But, in punishing it, you must never vent your possible anger for the previous one's death—even if innocently provoked by this youngster. This is another loving life and a completely different set of responsibilities for you.

An unusual example illustrates an interesting problem, concerning getting a new pet.

Case History

A married man in his late sixties lost his beloved dog after fourteen wonderful years of close companionship. After a few weeks, he still was deeply depressed and heartbroken and came for bereavement counseling. He was unable to get through the shock and denial stages.

Suddenly, his well-intentioned daughter, who did not even live with him, took it upon herself to get him another dog. She did this without his knowledge or permission. It was the same breed and color as the deceased pet. She tried to get him a replacement copy.

He was stunned, deeply resentful, and furious at this intrusion into his bereavement and personal life. But because she left it for him while he was not home, he couldn't outright refuse the endearing puppy. As a result, he was gruff and indifferent to it, but felt this was an emergency and he was forced to temporarily care for it. That first day there were pitched battles between him and his family. Torn apart emotionally, he made a second appointment for counseling. But he felt obligated to take care of the helpless puppy until he could regain some composure.

Several days later, the controlling daughter visited and found her father on the couch, with the puppy delightedly crawling all over him, with licks aplenty and tail wagging madly. He was still confused and angry, and hated to admit that the puppy was good for him. But that was too obvious. He conceded this in the next session, which was his last one.

This might have had a far different and tragic ending under other unforeseeable circumstances. The daughter had been lovingly motivated, but could have caused a monster of a problem. She was very foolish, but lucky. In this case, the arbitrary replacement of a pet was a good thing.

A Contrasting Case History

A woman in her late twenties had a very close relationship with her 12-year old dog, who had been killed in a tragic accident. Her childless marriage had been rocky since its start, about four years prior. She suffered intense bereavement for her dog, and lapsed into deep depression. Her husband became impatient and bullied her into going for bereavement counseling.

While she was away from home attending her first session, he went out and bought her a nearly identical puppy. When she returned home and was confronted by this, she grew so hysterical that her husband became frightened for her for the first time. She absolutely refused to have anything to do with the puppy and wouldn't even look at it. She retreated into a state of morbid isolation and acute depression and required immediate professional attention. Of course, the new dog had to be returned right away.

She was aware that she had a history of emotional instability, and tended to become hysterical when threatened or overwhelmed by demands on her. She felt this incident had been triggered by her husband's betrayal of her feelings and oppressive domination. There had been little mutual respect in the marriage, and she was unable to fight back effectively.

Her bereavement counseling turned into intense psychotherapy sessions. She soon realized that her deceased dog represented the only real love and security she had left. The pet's death had created a terrifying sense of helplessness and fear of being alone. And it aggravated her feelings of inferiority to her husband and others. Losing control was her only emergency escape. It proved effective this time only in that the husband returned the puppy and stopped pressuring her to do and see things his way. But he kept implying that she was too ineffectual to be of any value to herself under stress.

Obviously, this is much more complicated than a simple example of pet replacement, and we will not go into the other psychological and marriage problems. But this does illustrate, rather graphically, that making a decision for another person to get another pet can create very complex consequences. In this case, the arbitrary presentation of a replacement pet proved disastrous.

"All of God's Little Ones."

Photo by W. Sife. Courtesy of
Hartsdale Canine Cemetery, Inc.

Memorial tree, with individual
leaf inscriptions.

Photo by W. Sife. Courtesy of
Abbey Glen Pet Memorial Park

CHAPTER 12

Children

and the

Death of

a Pet

There is only one smartest dog in the world,
and every child has it.

—Anonymous

Bereavement in children too often has been trivialized or given inadequate attention. We are so involved with our own adult world of complexities and learned associations that we tend to lose some perspective on how and why children feel bereavement for a pet. We too often presume that it is advisable to shelter them from this "grown-up" experience, which we find to be very upsetting. In nearly all examples, that is absolutely the wrong approach. If they are old enough to reason, then they sense very accurately when they are being left out of important discussions about things. The death of a child's beloved pet matters a great deal in his or her young life. How this is handled now will remain with the child for the rest of his or her life.

HELPING THEM UNDERSTAND

It would be a great service to our children if we would step out of the restrictive mold of our traditional response to death. We have a strong obligation to them to begin their experience and knowledge of death in a constructive manner that is not as evasive and euphemistic as that which we grew up and live with. Each child, depending on the individual level of development, should be allowed to experience his or her own natural feelings of bereavement without being overprotected. We hate to see them cry, but they need to process the loss and mourn, also.

Children do not respond to death as adults do, unless they have been taught by example to behave this way. They always look to us for their role model, how to deal with this. But their normal reactions are much more natural, curious, and varied. There are several important factors affecting their diverse responses to bereavement. They are very intuitive, and are likely to sense when things about a pet's death are being kept from them. Sometimes this even becomes a sore spot for anger and resentment when they are older. Their age and maturity must be carefully considered when trying to work things out.

The following age categorizations are generalizations that are rather accurate. But each child is unique, and may not fit exactly into this kind of grouping. There are always variables that the watchful parent should be aware of. It is advisable to read all the developmental aspects listed below, to get a better perspective.

2- TO 3-YEAR-OLDS

Two- to three-year-olds do not have the life experiences to give them an understanding of death. They should be told the pet has died and will not return — but that that is okay. It is important that they be reassured that they did not do or say anything to cause the death. Children at this age may not understand what death really means, but they will sense and copy your emotions. Note that it is good to cry and show your own feelings of grief, but these must be controlled, and perceived as a normal response to the loss of a loved one. Extra reassurance and maintaining routine will help the child. Children at this age will usually accept a new pet very easily.

4- TO 6-YEAR-OLDS

Children of this age group usually have some understanding of death but may not understand the permanence of it. They may even think the pet is asleep or continuing to eat, breathe, and play. They may also feel that past anger towards their pet—or some perceived "bad behavior"—was responsible for its death. Manifestations of grief may include bowel or bladder disturbances as well as a change in playing, eating, and sleeping habits. Allow the child to express feelings and concerns through frequent, brief discussions. Give extra reassurance. Drawing pictures and writing stories about their loss may be helpful. Include the child in any funeral arrangements.

7- TO 9-YEAR-OLDS

Children in this age group know that death is irreversible. They do not normally think this might happen to them, but they may be concerned about the death of their parents. They are very curious and may ask questions that appear morbid. These questions are natural and are best answered frankly and honestly. Children this age may manifest their grief in many ways, such as school problems, anti-social behavior, somatic or physical concerns, aggression, and withdrawal or clinging behavior. As with younger children, it is important that they be reassured that they did not do or say anything that caused the death.

10- TO 11-YEAR-OLDS

Children in this age group are usually able to understand that death is natural, inevitable, and happens to all living things. They often react to death in a manner very similar to adults, using their parents' attitude as a model. A pet's death can trigger memories of previous losses of any kind, and this should always be open for discussion.

ADOLESCENTS

This generalized age group reacts similarly to adults. However, the typical adolescent's range of expression can range from apparent total lack of concern to hyper-emotional. One day they want to be treated like an adult, the next day they need to be reassured like a young child. They should be allowed to grieve in their own way with no time frame. Peer approval is also very important. If friends are supportive, it is much easier for them to deal with a loss. Also, always keep in mind that an adolescent is trying to find his or her own true feelings, and may often conflict with a parent on how to express feelings and grief at this time. It is important to avoid antagonisms over this.

YOUNG ADULTS

Although young adults can hardly be called children, the loss of a pet in this age group may be particularly hard. They may also have feelings of guilt for abandoning their pets when leaving home for college, work, or marriage. There may been a very close relationship with that pet since early childhood. Among other pressures experienced upon the departure from home, this can add additional stress. Due to geographical distances, they are often unable to return to the family home to say goodbye to the pet or to participate in family rituals associated with the loss.

WHAT IS SAFE TO TELL CHILDREN?

Here we are very concerned with their ability to handle the major stress of facing death, especially for the first time. Our overly protective tendencies too often will prevent them from meeting this experience on their own terms. Because of our fearful preoccupations with death, we too easily overlook the simplicity of a child's levels of awareness and needs or responses to a pet's demise.

It is a natural instinct to protect children from facing stressful things, in general, and death in particular. Parents try carefully and, at times, excessively to ease or prevent their children's tears. Too often, young people are not permitted to attend funerals, wakes, burials, or even memorial services. Nor are they allowed to visit anyone who may be dying. Children are shielded and not expected to be able to extend sympathy to others in bereavement. But how then can they learn this for themselves, for later in their lives when other loved ones inevitably die? Because of unnatural protection and interference, they have only minimal and indirect contact with death. They lack the firsthand experience that teaches a realistic understanding of death and bereavement.

Parents cannot really conceal their feelings from children, because children are much too intuitive and perceptive. But because of our attempts to exclude them from stressful events in our lives, children can respond in ways we do not expect. Feeling left out, they may secretly feel shame and guilt at not being worthy of our trust. They know when they are not included in what should be a natural family sharing of things, bad or good. Around age five this begins to matter a great deal. Of course, this age of readiness varies.

The general subject of death is not unknown to children. They watch movies and television, and they hear reports from their schoolmates and friends. There is little that would really surprise them. In some ways, they are a great deal more sophisticated than we were at their age. It might astonish most parents how much children perceive. Depending on their age and experience, they are also somewhat aware of the taboo surrounding death and discussion about it. And when they are excluded, they may feel guilty, feeling that somehow the death is their fault. Perhaps they feel that they have been "bad" again and don't really remember how or why—as is so often the case with children.

But children are very pliant and can accept nearly anything if it is presented in ways they can comprehend and believe. Any questions they may ask about a pet's death should be answered as honestly and simply as possible. Too often parents become very awkward or overprotective when it comes to discussing death, so they oversimplify, use trite euphemisms, or even lie to the child. "The dog is visiting someone, way out in the country, but it will be back later." "The dog is in the hospital, but it will be back soon." "The pet went on a trip." These are examples of some of the evasions and lies that will slap back in everyone's face, sooner or later. Parents hope that the child will quickly forget and not challenge the idea. But children easily sense a betrayal of their trust, which can permanently damage their image of a parent. That often is repressed, and it surfaces later in life as deep resentment and disappointment.

Parents will have even more trouble explaining death if they themselves have a problem with it. Children are very sensitive to this. Fortunately, they are resilient and accepting, and they perceive only as far as their limited understanding permits, at that time. Things that are complicated to us are frequently glossed over with no problem at all by them. They should never be lied to about things concerning the pet's death (but on very rare occasions, there can be justifiable exceptions to this). Try to explain to them what happened at a level that they can comprehend without undo distress. Expect tears, but remember this is an important and necessary part of their own bereavement process. And always keep in mind they will pattern their responses to yours. It is good that that they generally find resolution much more quickly and easily than their parents.

For many possible reasons, children may not have yet adjusted to the prior death of a significant person in their lives. When this happens, there was no resolution. The child is actually in a state of arrested mourning. That is most likely the result of having been overprotected to a point where any later reference to death can really be even more upsetting or frightening. Very often the household with a beloved pet presents an emotional time bomb to children with already repressed and unresolved loss. They will frequently create a fantasy world with the pet, constructing a personalized environment of love and security. If the pet should die or go missing before the child can resolve any earlier problems, a new level of stress will result. This also may remain suppressed, or it may be suddenly expressed as secondary anger and grief, worsened by the first loss. Sudden behavioral problems always indicate there is something significant that is deeply disturbing a child.

EXPLAINING A DEATH

How do you explain a pet's death to children? A good start is to find out what they think it means. Use that level of perception as your basis to start sketching out your answers. Don't try to explain fully. Most people can't do so, anyway. You will be even more frustrated if you try, and children will sense this. That might also diminish their future trust in your ability to help them.

Even if you work very hard at preparing a complicated or thorough explanation of the pet's death, it easily could be beyond the comprehension level of the individual child's developmental readiness. Streamline your ideas, but not to the point of oversimplifying them or making them seem trivial to the child. Ask questions, and customize what you say, based on what you learn from the level of the answers you get. Ideas that could be upsetting to adults are often glossed over by the youngster. To better understand how the child is responding, get some feedback at regular intervals. Ask him or her what is confusing or upsetting about the pet's death. Work on that at the child's level, not yours.

Younger Children Are Not So Interested in Adult Detail or Logic

After a long and complicated painful explanation, the child may say something like this: "Oh, all I wanted to know is if Fluffy is in heaven." This demonstrates that explanations beyond a child's level and ability to understand may be lost on him or her. But don't misread this by being too simplistic in your approach. Such treatment may be deeply resented on a subconscious level of awareness. There are so many complicated reasons or explanations for things. But we must try to adjust our discussions about death to each individual's perceptions. Younger children are not so interested in adult detail or logic. They mostly seek easy, satisfying answers that address their current level of inquiry and awareness.

Try discussing pet death with your child. If it is at all possible, do this well in advance of the actual event. Most parents are surprised at the level of the child's awareness, openness, and willingness to discuss this, even if it may be very elementary. Such a discussion, of course, depends upon the child's emotional development and maturity. Even if the child doesn't seem to comprehend your strong feelings on the subject, this experience will provide a lesson in respecting emotions in others. You are always a powerful role model to your child in everything you do and say.

There are also many excellent and heartwarming illustrated books for children on the death of a beloved pet. Get some of these and read to them. It will be good medicine for both of you. The Association for Pet Loss and Bereavement (APLB) website (www.aplb.org) has a bibliography on petloss that includes a special section on books just for children.

In our culture, some bereavement problems result from the awkwardness or inability of others to respond to those in mourning. This happens because they generally don't know any better. An awareness of death probably had been withheld from them. Any experience or guidance in bereavement sensitivity probably had been denied them as children. Now, as adults, they can become defensive, impatient, or even critical of anyone bereaving for such a "trivial" matter as a pet.

HOW DO CHILDREN ACCEPT DEATH?

Children do not accept death as adults do. They perceive concepts more at their surface values. They easily presume things, and tend to blame themselves for bad events that happen to the people and pets they love. It is not unusual for children to feel that somehow they were naughty and that God or someone is punishing the pet now, for their behavior.

Children may tend to suppress their guilt, fears, and negative feelings because they do not know how to talk about them. Sometimes these escape from the subconscious and are expressed in upsetting dreams. Nightmares come from the repression of frightening ideas. They emerge with great force during sleep—the time when restraints are gone. It is wise to avoid any possibly lurid or morbid details that concern the pet's death (or death in general). Alarming ideas may turn into misperceptions that could upset the child for the rest of his or her life.

Sometimes we are shocked by responses we never expected. It is important to never attempt to trivialize a child's grief as a means to ease it. There are cases in which children believed that their parents' reaction to the pet's death might be the same response if they might die. That, of course, is the very opposite of what we want them to feel. Trivializing death reinforces and encourages insecurity. There are better ways to simplify and adapt ideas.

At a very young age, children should not be troubled with complicated explanations or discussions about death. But they should not be excluded or made to feel left out of family conferences, even at their immature levels of comprehension. Let them sense how you respond to the death. They will rely on your example as a positive, safe role model—and love you better for this.

Somehow, children must learn that death is the normal ending to life, just as birth is the beginning. Every living thing experiences both. It should be made clear that death can be very upsetting, but it is not bad, and it is not to be feared. Too often, a parent's irrational dread of death is unintentionally revealed at this time, and that can disturb children for the rest of their lives. If you have strong religious views that help you ease your pain, then share these with the child. In issues dealing with death, children need and readily accept answers that are given with the security of your authority.

Usually, a child has a very personal relationship with a pet. This is very different from what parents usually experience. Be frank with children, and stay at their levels of comprehension. Ask questions to get feedback and an understanding of how your attempt at communication is succeeding, or not. Share everything, even the tears—and guide, but don't shield, children. If you make it easy for them to ask questions, they will be better able to grasp what they need to know. And as mentioned earlier, they also need to suffer some bereavement, to be able to reach their own sense of resolution. You should not try to shield them from that.

THE SPECIAL ROLE OF A PET

Pets can be silly, childlike, playful, and joyous. A pet makes a perfect companion for a child, who will learn about love, trust, and loyalty from the relationship. Pets also provide a sense of security and continuity when the parents are not present. The animal friend is there for the child, no matter what the trouble or how badly he or she may have behaved. And that bond seems even stronger after a punishment. Troubles are shared with these companion animals, who also serve as adoring siblings. In the long run, when a child cares for a pet, a healthy sense of responsibility and self-esteem develops. This becomes a basic component of the young person's developing self-image and attitude toward life. When that bond is finally broken by death, the child may grieve in very personal ways that even a parent does not expect. This relationship was often a profound one.

Children have great fun and escape, playing with their pets! There are countless pained adults undergoing psychotherapy who wish they could have had such a love and release. Children are not inhibited by the false sense of dignity that adults sometimes display. A pet supplies refuge and love, and it does not judge or criticize. It gives a sense of complete acceptance and security, obeying and loving the child as nothing or nobody else can. It is loyal and will stay close and supportive during hard times. In all, the pet becomes a powerful symbol of emotional security in an unsure world. Those are the wonder years for a child, before death must inevitably introduce a new awareness of life and reality.

WHAT CHILDREN MIGHT ASK

The kinds of questions most frequently asked by children include: "Where is my pet now?" "Why did she die?" "Is she happy now?" "Who takes care of her now?" "Will I ever see her again?" You must understand what the child is driving at and needs to know. Too often we answer in adult ways that do not satisfy the original question, as the child meant it.

Examples of bad and misleading answers to children include statements such as:

1. "Your pet was loved so much that God took it back to heaven." The child may wonder if God will take him or other dear members of the family back, as well.

2. "The animal doctor made a mistake and the pet died." A child may think that this may happen with people and their doctors, too.

3. "The pet ran away." This is tacitly understood by children to be untrue or improbable, at best. The child will sense being excluded from honest communication. Again, such an attempt at deception may easily lead to distortions, causing feelings that he or she is undeserving or guilty and cannot be trusted with the truth. It can also teach the child that you are not truthful.

4. "The pet got sick and died." The misperceived notion that dying is a result of getting sick may be very upsetting. Children and loved ones also get sick.

5. "The pet went to heaven" or "The pet went to sleep forever" can create frightening associations in a child's mind concerning heaven or even going to sleep.

These are only a few examples of common replies that can have dangerous implications. There are so many others like these that you need to become sensitized to before they are inadvertently used and create potential harm.

Euphemisms such as, "The pet was put to sleep," have created frightening associations with sleep or surgical procedures, during which a person has to be anesthetized. Attempts at sanitized verbal expressions can easily be misunderstood by a child, who understands words more at their face value. At a young age, minds do not work as well in verbal metaphors.

Some of the upsetting responses by children to the death of a pet have been, "I was bad, so my pet was taken," and, "If I am good, maybe he will come back to me." This is related to the bargaining phase that adults may experience during early bereavement. What happened to the pet may convince the child that the world is not a safe place. Any such fears of insecurity will surely be triggered by future stressful experiences. They need to be addressed now. Family discord at this time will certainly hinder any adjustment to bereavement.

As we all know a pet's disobedience sometimes causes its accidental death. There are countless examples of this. And it could be particularly stressful to the child. Obedience to authority is always part of any training, for a child or a pet. Certainly, no child is perfect in obeying rules. At some time or other all youngsters experience some feelings of shame or guilt at having been disobedient. Youngsters may secretly fear they could deservedly meet a similar fate—death—since they also disobey. Such a rationalized response instills an irrational fear, and it may remain with them for a very long time. There may even be times when that causes disruptive social behavior, since the child feels he or she is already guilty and going to die anyway. How sad that a child should be made to feel such things! Responsible parents should be sensitive to that and try to correct any misperceptions.

HELPING A CHILD ADJUST

One constantly hears of ideas and suggestions that have helped a child adjust to the death of a beloved pet. Some possible considerations include the following:

1. Hold a ceremony for the pet that includes the child. This also helps him or her bond more closely to the parents. That need not necessarily be at the gravesite. It serves to include the child in a positively structured bereavement activity. Shared rites and rituals on a very personal level help put the grief and death into some greater objectivity. Such an experience strengthens a child's sense of family unity as well as self-reliance during the mourning process.

It also can aid in immunizing him or her from some of the scary, unspoken, subjective confusions of death that he or she will eventually have to confront again.

2. Reminisce fondly with the child about the pet. Use pictures, if possible. Associate positive, happy events with the pet's memory. Emphasize that as long as we remember and love the pet, it will always be part of us. Associate happiness, not sadness, with this.

3. Ask the local librarian to suggest children's books that include the death of a pet in the story line. There are growing numbers of these in print. Any competent book dealer can help, as well. And read these with the child, sharing it all, together. A bibliography can be found on the website of the Association for Pet Loss and Bereavement (APLB) at www.aplb.org.

4. Discuss with the child the possibility of eventually getting another pet. Emphasize that this is not to try to replace the beloved pet or the memory, as that can never be done. This is to have another animal friend—but only when the child feels ready. Explain that it is like loving more than one person at a time. The new pet will be a different one, but the dead one is still loved and remembered. Suggest that the child could tell the pet loving stories about the deceased one—and that they could have been wonderful friends if they had lived at the same time. This is good advice for adults, as well.

    Ask how the child feels about the pet's death and why. With older children, never argue about views you don't like. If there is a conflict between your ideas, suggest that you both think it over and discuss it again at another time. And remind them that this should be about the pet, not them. Be supportive but not critical. Teenagers tend to perceive things very defensively. They crave feeling respected—as well as loved.

5. Visit an animal shelter with the child. Explain in advance that you will not adopt any animal during this visit. You are going for the special experience that only such a visit can

give. Encourage the child to ask questions and make comments on what you both see. Discuss this experience later. This will help put the child's grief and needs into a much more objective perspective. It will ease the bereavement.

6. Inform the child's teacher about the death of the pet and its effect on the child. Ask for advice. You may get some good suggestions, based on sound developmental, educational training. But even if nothing new is suggested, you can feel more secure that the teacher will probably be paying special attention to the child's behavior and needs during this critical period. Ask that the teacher schedule a class discussion about pets and petloss.

7. If the child is old enough, he/she should have an opportunity to ask your family's veterinarian questions about the pet's death. You should be present to add supportiveness and explanations, when needed.

8. In instances where euthanasia is necessary, include the child in a family discussion about this and the pet's quality of life. Share and explain your thoughts and feelings. Keep the understanding at the child's level. Explain that different people react in many different ways to this loss, and each of us needs space, love, and respect for our personal pain. But be sure to make the child feel he or she is part of the decision-making process, before euthanasia. If presented well, the child's opinions will reflect your own.

Of course, the death of a beloved pet presents problems even for a well-adjusted adult. But the child looks to us for guidance and security in our words and deeds. Too often we are at a loss ourselves, and may lose perspective on the effects of our behavior during this stressful time. Special care should be taken to be open, supportive, and especially sensitive to the different perceptions of children, during what is also their bereavement.

A comprehensive essay on children and the death of their pets would take an entire book to give the subject justice. This relatively short chapter is not an attempt to be all-inclusive. Considerations that may have been omitted are not necessarily of lesser importance.

As in all studies of a psychological nature, there are so many possible varieties of experiences and responses.

The ultimate consideration here is that you are always the authority in your child's life, as well as the role model. There is an important difference between the two. See to it that the child senses that he or she is included in your confidence. Treat the death of a pet with understanding, love, and care, allowing the child to benefit from your example and strength. The death of a beloved pet is a dramatic, instructive experience that will never be forgotten. Its effects will influence how your young person will respond to the death of a significant human, at some later date.

Children see tears and grief, and they also learn firsthand what bereavement means. This can teach them compassion for the needs of others, as well. Don't try to protect or shelter them from this reality. Let them share your feelings to a reasonable degree, according to their maturity and ability to understand. Share your experience and general responses with them, but always bear in mind that you are the example of how they are to behave. Avoid the mistakes that may have been made in your life concerning the understanding and fear of death. Children are the future. We love them dearly, and want only the best for them.

CHAPTER 13

Euthanasia

To every thing there is a season,
and a time to every purpose under the heaven:
a time to be born and a time to die.

—Eccles. 3:1

*E*uthanasia is a word derived from the Greek, literally meaning "good death." It is a matter of ethical and practical necessity, and one of the most difficult decisions anyone can ever make for a pet who is a beloved friend. Although the decision is demanded by humanitarian obligation, it is always traumatic for the person who must finally make it. It is perhaps the ultimate heartbreak we must be willing to endure for our dear companion animals.

Euthanasia should be used to put an end to terminal suffering and a negative quality of life. This choice is highly subjective and often difficult to make, but it is part of ultimate responsibility. We are morally obliged to protect and support the lives of our animal friends. A compassionate necessity to end a pet's life must not be avoided or procrastinated. Unfortunately, some people abuse this sacred trust by putting their own feelings above the needs of their pets—and they almost always sorely regret that later.

This is almost never a foreign concept to pet owners. From our earliest days as stewards, most of us have given it some fleeting thought, perhaps unconsciously preparing for this possible need. That, however, is always an abstraction before the grim reality forces itself on us. It is normal to want to turn one's back on this, when there is no compelling need for it. We are accomplished at not thinking about death until forced by circumstances to face it.

A COMPLEX DECISION

Although it is the right thing to do for the animal, euthanasia can be a psychological nightmare of confusion, guilt, and final responsibility for the owner. To opt for it, you must truly believe that it is the only recourse to ease a pet's pain and suffering. Once you accept that, be steadfast in your belief that it is appropriate. As part of the bereavement process, most people will invent some guilt and second thoughts about this later—although it is not merited.

The fear of death can be immobilizing to some. Anticipation of the death of the pet can be so overwhelming that one may be sorely tempted to delay making the necessary decision. But the pet suffers much more than the owner. Fatal accidents and death while undergoing surgery sometimes take the responsibility of the decision away from us. Otherwise, we are honor-bound to exercise this ultimate trust and duty in a timely way. That will be one of the most painful moments in your life. And it will always be one of the most loving.

To some people, the decision to employ euthanasia is a convenience and is as easy and simple as throwing away an unwanted toy. To others it is a desperate, necessary resolution they want but cannot easily confront. Fortunately, most of the rest of us fall somewhere between these two extremes. Choosing euthanasia is probably one of the most upsetting decisions one will ever have to make. But to own and care for a pet, we must accept the dreaded responsibility of possibly being forced to make this upsetting choice some day.

HAVING MERCY

Palliation is a term for positive medical intervention in terminal cases. It will usually prolong life, but always at additional financial and emotional expense to the owner. But the first considerations should be for the animal. Most of us certainly don't want our beloved pet to have to endure extended pain, dysfunction, and additional stresses—even for a little while—for our own sake. That's why we speak of giving our beloved animals the chance for death with dignity, before it is too late. Ultimately, the disease is killing your pet—not the mercy afforded by the euthanasia process.

ASPECTS OF EUTHANASIA

As difficult as it is, we must try to separate emotion from the decision-making process when contemplating this necessary alternative. It may help to keep in mind that there are three basic aspects of the distressing subject of euthanasia: *practical*, *ethical*, and *psychological*. In most cases they are all vitally interrelated, and each can be overwhelming. From the practical point of view, euthanasia may be the only answer to how one should humanely deal with the degenerating quality of the pet's life.

For example, it is practical to euthanize a dog who turns vicious. Here there is no margin for an alternative choice. Another practical consideration can be that an owner may not be able to bear the overwhelming emotional stress caused by a slowly dying pet. One of the most practical considerations is financial. The vet may offer the hope of temporary recovery if very expensive procedures are implemented. That can cost thousands of dollars—far beyond the ability of most pet owners. Under this circumstance it is understandable when they must opt to euthanize, although it is especially heartbreaking for them. Also extensive surgery and procedures such as chemotherapy can be very painful as well as upsetting for an animal. That must be taken into consideration, as well.

The ethical aspects are theoretical and more easily accepted. They make perfectly good sense, but the loving owner of a euthanized companion animal may suffer deep psychological distress from this. Tragically, the beloved pet must have its life terminated by the one person who loves it most. This is both an irony of fate and an extreme act of love, and this emotional strain is like nothing else.

JUST KEEPING A PET ALIVE IS NOT ENOUGH

The list of practical considerations can become a long one. There are many instances of pets suffering from extreme "separation anxiety"—to the point where they are destructive to themselves, the household, and the owner's nerves and lifestyle, as well. In cases when this behavioral problem cannot be successfully treated by an animal behaviorist or medication, euthanasia is a valid option for the heartbroken pet owner. When surrounded by their human family, these otherwise pathological pets can be very loving and dear. But when left alone they suffer enormous stress and can run amok—even to the point of

155

damaging themselves. It is very rare that the owner of such a disturbed pet can find another home that could provide constant attention and love. And even with that option, the sudden sense of abandonment by its loved family would surely cause new emotional trauma and behavioral problems. Just keeping it alive is not enough. Middle-aged pets who develop unusual or problem behavior should be examined by a vet for possible growths or lesions on the brain—or even a shift in neurochemical balance.

In older pets we sometimes see radical behavior changes that can be very upsetting—or even dangerous. This includes biting, aggression, and loud vocalizations. In almost all cases that is caused by the aging and deterioration of brain cells. Just as we see various forms of Alzheimer's disease affecting people in different ways, the effects in animals can be even more noticeable and troublesome. Medication usually is no help, as it dulls all the pet's senses, effectively turning it into a mere shadow of its former self. And in time the condition worsens. There is no cure.

In the long run, once it is decided that euthanasia is the only option, these considerations clearly demand that the owner should no longer be concerned with *if* it should be done, but *when*. The psychology involved in making such a life-death decision is always distressing. Sometimes that determination can be more easily made with the support of people who are close to you. It is wise to get professional guidance or counseling if this proves to be unduly disturbing. But the final decision always has to come from the owner—nobody else.

A CHILD'S PERSPECTIVE

As mentioned in the previous chapter, children should not be over-protected, they must not be made to feel left out of what may be very important to them. Their love of the pet should be fully respected by the parents. Depending on their age and ability to reason, they should be made part of what they feel is the decision-making process. Even if you have privately made up your own mind about what is to be done, make the children feel as though they have contributed good ideas to the discussion. Gentle persuasion is the rule here. Arguing with an older child about this always causes resistance, and sometimes creates emotional scars that last a lifetime.

MAKING THE DECISION

At what point has the quality of your pet's life degenerated to the critical point where you have the ethical responsibility and the obligation to end it? This is a terrible crisis for you, as well as your beloved animal friend.

Certainly, you should consult your veterinarian and others whom you trust to give objective, sound advice. One sometimes hears the suggestion to refer to an additional veterinarian for a second opinion. Although this has some merit, most practitioners will ask what the first one had said and will usually agree. Unless there is an emergency, most veterinarians will not suggest that you euthanize a pet. But under less dire conditions they may advise you to *consider* this. It may help you to ask what they would do if this were their pet. Once you make the decision, the veterinarian and staff merely do the physical job. Most can give you excellent support on this, but there are some who do not. For your own sake, ask around beforehand, if possible.

Some veterinarians will make an exception for their regular clients and come to your house for the procedure. Most will not do this, but may refer you to colleagues who make themselves available. It usually is more expensive, but the home environment can help this to be less traumatic for everyone concerned—especially the pet. Consider this, and make your tentative arrangements in advance, if possible.

As painful and difficult as it is, the final decision must be yours. The value of euthanasia is well accepted and appreciated, but this option must never be arrived at hastily. Once acted on, it cannot be reversed. This is a terrible, heart-wrenching conclusion that has to be fully confirmed in advance. Once chosen, it must be embraced as the appropriate and final decision. But don't delay unnecessarily. Dragging it out can cause preventable suffering for the pet.

What should be the considerations for euthanasia during a medical emergency? If the pet is in terminal pain or bodily dysfunction, we owe that pet the dignity of a painless and dignified death. Since its end is imminent anyway, we can be more philosophical about it and accept it a little earlier. Is there any realistic chance of a spontaneous recovery or cure? How much pain is the animal in now, and will its suffering increase? Are the medical expenses going to be hard on you? What about the prolonged emotional strain for you, as well? All of these considerations are highly subjective and wrought with emotion.

But using your best judgment, make a decision. It is a normal part of the grief to later question yourself about your decision to euthanize your pet; you should be ready for these doubts.

In considering euthanasia, we go through an intensely shocking decision-making period. During this time, the veterinarian may use some terms and even euphemisms that the pet owner may not fully understand at this highly confusing and unstable moment. There have been cases in which clients have been told that their pet should be "put to sleep" or "put out of its misery." The pet was euthanized without the client's full comprehension at the moment of what that meant. The intense guilt and anger that resulted from these instances could have been avoided. When we are very upset, we frequently do not make good sense of metaphors. We are more literal-minded and may entirely miss the point. This is another strong case against the use of euphemistic terminology and verbal manipulation.

Even when the word "euthanasia" is used, emotional blocks sometimes interfere with the full grasp of its meaning. If we go into denial concerning its necessity, we can set ourselves up for a terrible aftermath of guilt and soul-wrenching grief. We must be on top of the situation. As already mentioned, it may be advisable to have someone you trust with you when you are faced with the decision. Later it is too late to change your mind. The suffering, terminally ill pet may be ready for it, but too often the owner is not.

THE EUTHANASIA PROCESS

The expression "putting an animal to sleep" is quite literal, in addition to being the most frequently used euphemism. The euthanasia process itself is designed to be as quick and peaceful for you and your pet as possible. Ideally, euthanasia solution is injected intravenously, usually in the animal's front or back leg, and is a fast-acting sedative which stops the heart within a very short period of time. When the veterinarian is ready to begin the procedure, an assistant will usually be asked to help hold your pet. After shaving the area, the veterinarian inserts a needle or catheter into the vein. He or she will test it first, to make sure it is in the vein and that the solution is administered as desired.

Your veterinarian may choose to sedate your pet or place an intravenous catheter beforehand, to help ensure a smooth procedure. If sedation is used, it will be administered first, allowing the animal to relax and fall into a comfortable deep sleep. A veterinarian may also choose to administer the euthanasia solution into the vein, by itself. Discuss this in advance with him or her. Once the euthanasia solution is given, the animal's muscles will relax and the heart will stop beating.

Most owners are surprised at how quickly death comes—in seconds. In some instances, the muscles may contract or relax briefly, after the heart has stopped. At that time the pet may void urine and/or stool. Other involuntary contractions may occur, such as appearing to gasp, or moving the extremities. But it is important to realize that this is strictly a muscle reflex, and the life is already gone. Also, the eyes may not close. Try to remember that your pet is not aware of any of these things, as they happen after death has occurred. At this time most veterinarians will ask if you would like to spend a few moments alone with your pet.

Some pet owners initially think they will be more comfortable if they do not observe their pet's final moments, and would rather be in the waiting room (or elsewhere) during the procedure. But bear in mind that those who opt for not being present often later feel a terrible sense of guilt about this. If possible, discuss this with your veterinarian or the office staff before the appointment is made. Learn exactly how euthanasia is performed at that particular office. Your pet's health, temperament, and your preferences should all be considered. For very small, young, or exotic animals, there may be some exceptions to the procedure just described. Be sure that you are comfortable with the methodology that you and your veterinarian choose. You may need to find another veterinarian to do the procedure the way you prefer.

As terrible and difficult as it is for each pet owner, most will want to be present for this simple procedure. They prefer to hold the pet in their arms, calming the animal and expressing their own final loving farewells and tears. The moment is so intensely personal and emotional that it often becomes overwhelming. It is an experience that is never forgotten. Your veterinarian may prefer that you do not hold the pet at this time, as sometimes an overwrought owner will interfere with the procedure—and even possibly hurt the pet. Ask about this beforehand. If you are capable, and the vet still will not allow this, you still have the option to find another vet who will permit you to hold your dear pet in its final moments of life. Some shelters as a rule do not permit an owner to even be in the same room at the time of the procedure. Always check on this well in advance.

Veterinarians and their staffs find euthanasia very upsetting, despite their frequent need to perform it. A few, however, have developed an office rule that the pet owner may not even be present during the actual procedure. Experience has taught them that owners can suffer from a variety of unexpected, strong emotional responses. And that can make an already terrible but necessary procedure absolutely horrible for them. After a while, euthanizing so many dear pets can cause professional burnout. This is often professionally referred to as "compassion fatigue," and additional stress to the veterinary staff needs to be avoided at the time of the procedure.

Also, these veterinarians have a concern for financial liability. They may be sued. Some owners may faint, hurting themselves in the fall. Others might get hysterical, grow irrational or destructive, or even suffer a heart attack from the exceptional stress. It is best to discuss this first with your veterinarian and ask for advice. Again, if it is necessary, you may have to choose another veterinarian for the procedure. But only you should make the decision. You will have to live with yourself and the memory.

In dealing with the euthanasia of our beloved pets, our emotional composure is sacrificed. This is the last testimonial to our lives together. Intense personal grief is the price of that necessary, humane action. However, it is not uncommon to hear that this special moment together is sometimes experienced as a very spiritual, loving, transcendent episode. Many report that this unexpectedly gave them a profound and quieting sense of completion. So for some it may not be so dreadful after all.

If you opt for this act of mercy, it is good to close this chapter well. Say your personal, tearful good-byes. Understand that there is a unity in all things. When you die, your oneness with your beloved pet will be even more complete. But for now, it must be over—except in your heart.

Yet, there are people who cannot bear to experience this, and there should be no shame. Witnessing the moment of death is far too upsetting for them. This can make their bereavement worse because it adds to the confusion of guilt and irrational reasoning later. Opting to be present or not is a very painful and important decision. What is best for you should be taken into consideration, as well. But once done, honor the action. Then move on with your own life, and honor the beloved pet's memory, as part of your evolving self.

YOUR RESPONSIBILITY

In being the provider of all things to your pet, you have assumed a godlike role. From your pet's point of view, you are the source of everything and the cause of all that it understands. In addition to the love the pet knows, this includes everything from obedience, tricks, and toys to food, medical care, shelter, company, and every experience it has had.

But, as stated earlier, with this role you also took on the awesome responsibility of possibly having to make that final decision of life and death someday. As much as you don't want to have such an obligation, you do. There is no one else who has this moral and legal responsibility to decide or act accordingly. You must make that informed choice and be able to live with it. And you have to be absolutely right in your conclusions, out of love for your pet. Later on, this must not become distorted into some neurotic challenge to your own decision making. This is always painful and fraught with emotional pitfalls. When done for the pet's benefit, it is always the right decision.

It is regrettable, but most organized religions use generalities and euphemisms regarding this relatively new problem of the death of pets. They find many reasons for sidestepping the issue and avoiding real answers. We are too often forced to make religious interpretations that fit the times but have no biblical precedent. What can be wrong with "playing God" during an emergency if God doesn't act? Perhaps the deity sees it as *your* responsibility. There are many who now believe that the moral requirement demands humane action from the divinity within each of us. Chapter 16 of this book offers some innovative insights to this problem.

A PERSONAL DECISION

Before resorting to euthanasia, it is helpful, if time and circumstances allow, to consult as far in advance as possible with a few trusted friends or family, as well as at least one veterinarian. Ultimately, however, this decision must be made subjectively in the deepest, most private soul-searching you are capable of. The intimacy of your relationship with your pet may demand that no one else can be part of this intense personal morality. But what always should be foremost in your mind is the terrible negative change in the quality of life of your pet.

Perhaps the best source of information and support can be found on the website of the Association for Pet Loss and Bereavement (APLB): www.aplb.org. In addition to a special page on euthanasia, there are several three-hour supportive chat rooms each week. Everyone there has known petloss, from all perspectives. And now, they are all there for each other, as well.

Postponement may provide some more time for you, but is that the proper concern? This can be really just another way of trying to avoid and delay the inevitable. Such a stay is only temporary, at best, and may only be serving a self-defeating emotional denial of the grim reality. Thus, the practical approach usually helps make the decision for us. It then becomes a matter of getting it done and minimizing the shock to yourself. If this must be, then respect it. Honor your pet and yourself in this ultimate private salute to its life with you. And have it done right away.

When upset patients come to me after euthanizing their pets, they always fall into one of two categories: those who agonize over having possibly waited too long, or those who torture themselves for having possibly done it too soon. Many of these people had lifelong histories of indecision and self-doubt. As with other unresolved problems, euthanasia served as a psychological trigger mechanism to set them off.

Our feelings cannot be spared when making this ultimate consideration. It is one of the most distressing actions we will ever have to take. We should always bear in mind that no one else can legitimately pass judgment on us for deciding on euthanasia. People should respect our grief and painful decision with silence or supportiveness. If there are some in our lives who are critical, we must be able to ignore them, correct them, or discard them. This is essential for our own sake. However, beware of hasty emotional overreactions to these people. Quick anger at this time can destroy longstanding good relationships.

ETHICAL CONSIDERATIONS

From the ethical point of view, do we have the right to take away life? In the animal and pet world, this was settled long ago, in the name of humane action. But it is argued that life is life—and the life of a beloved pet is in many ways equated with our own. Because there are still many who feel that we do not have the right to euthanize ourselves, this argument can be weakly carried over to pets.

It is interesting to look at the history of American laws concerning cruelty to children. Essential new statutes were passed only on the strength of already existing laws protecting animals. These were the necessary legal precedents. We protected our animals better than we did our own young. Something is very wrong here.

In the last few years, euthanasia has started to become a high profile issue for ourselves, as well. Ironically, "humane" action was originally intended for animals, not us. With the proper ethical safeguards and conditions, human euthanasia is legal in only one state at this time. But there are some people who would not allow this if they had the power. Keep your mind open. It is the most compassionate and moral ultimate decision we can make for ourselves as well as our beloved pets—who in many ways are extensions of ourselves.

Related to this is the concept of the living will, which is only a modern social phenomenon. Sometimes this is referred to as an "advanced directive." The writer of such a document is, in effect, giving legal permission to be indirectly euthanized—under specific, dire medical circumstances. We have all read or heard of instances where people were kept on life-support machines for years, while actually being brain-dead or terminally comatose. This document gives the individual some measure of personal protection in being able to decide how to die with dignity. We are currently witnessing the curious social phenomenon of rapidly increasingly numbers of new cases of people who are now writing these living wills for themselves. But many do this only after first experiencing the soul-wrenching ordeal of having to euthanize a beloved pet. The analogy seems clear here. Our beloved companion animals teach us many things, and—perhaps not so surprising—this is one of them.

Whatever decision you make, if considering this necessary option for a pet, be sure it is your own decision, not someone else's. You will have to live with it after it is too late to change your mind. There always will be some who will criticize you, despite their lack of moral right to do so. Let reality and compassion guide you in evaluating the situation and need for euthanasia. What is right cannot be called wrong, unless you are looking for justification to be miserable.

In the final analysis, if the decision to euthanize a pet is made for the proper reasons, there can be no legitimate challenge to its morality and ultimate ethical nature—even from the narrowest of religious or even bigoted interpretations. Is it not vile and immoral to condone and perpetuate pain and suffering in animals—as well as people? And is the option to euthanize a pet less necessary or moral than that for a human? Can we ethically sidestep this responsibility? The time for moral cowardice is over. We must make the right decision now. Times are changing. But unfortunately, there will always be some highly prejudiced individuals who will say this is wrong, under any circumstances. Sadly, many of those same people are dangerous zealots who even deny their children and other family members critical medical attention—trying to substitute prayer, instead. The news media regularly feature horror stories of manslaughter cases against defendants who caused unbelievable terminal physical pain and suffering in others, claiming that was the way God wanted it. Extreme personal religious fervor has no place in determining medical care and attention. And of course, this applies to euthanization of our beloved pets, as well.

Sometimes after the euthanizing of a dear pet we experience a delayed emotional reaction. Perhaps the least considered and the most striking one is the sudden onset of unexpected depression and feelings of guilt. Being human, we suffer, and are normally bereft at the death of a loved one. But being actively involved in this we can also create unnecessary torment in our lives, and that is always a mistake.

There are cases of people who later regretted having agreed to euthanasia—rationalizing that they were under great stress at the time. If possible, this should always be an informed decision, made beforehand—or after a reasonable waiting period. But emergency decisions during exploratory surgery are another matter, as they must be made immediately. In some instances, however, the real issue for these pet owners is selfish preoccupation with their own feelings and personal problems. The pet comes only after themselves, in every circumstance. Other bereaved pet owners may be ambivalent and overly insecure, lacking emotional stability under the pressures of the moment. But regardless of the personal discomfort, we must be strong enough to put aside our own emotional baggage, for the sake of our beloved pets.

A HUMAN RESPONSE

We all respond individually, and sometimes irrationally. The death of a loved one will put us into a state of mourning. Whether the end was spontaneous or humanely produced, the human equation is not changed. Because of the intensity of our emotions, the clarity of our thinking is usually lost for a brief while. The confusions of guilt often distort our lives. In this instance, guilt is a response to handling responsibility and not being able to bear up under it.

The subject of death has always upset, intimidated, and confused us. Who is to say what it really is or what it means? In our frightened search for insight into the unknown, assurance and justification often elude us. Being forced by love and morality to become the angel of death for our pets is often overwhelming, or unsettling at best. But it serves two necessary and good purposes: We do what is right for the pet, and we ourselves are forced into an enormous existential growth step. We go on wiser and more mature than before.

Those who suffer most terribly in this role frequently created their own pitfalls by having allowed themselves to become too emotionally dependent on their pets. Sometimes our intense love for our companion animals eclipses much of the responsibility and love we should have for ourselves, as well. Intimate lifestyles and complex psychological interdependencies affect each of us in different ways and degrees.

The beloved pet frequently becomes a means of unconscious escape from a deep personal need or perceived inadequacy. We allow our animal friends to give us a sense of personal transcendence. This is not at all uncommon, but it is seldom recognized and rarely admitted. In many ways, the relationship may actually be more intimate than with other humans.

All humans experience some neurotic needs—each one very personal and unique. These responses can span the spectrum from harmless to pathological. The real measure of our "normalcy" is how we respond to stimuli, while maintaining our usual lifestyle. Since pets become extensions of ourselves, their innocence in such a world of complexities and troubles often represents the good part of ourselves, which we inwardly love and isolate. This constant supportiveness from a pet may offer a small escape from painful reality. The interrelationship between master and pet often becomes a living exercise in creative fantasy, as well as improved self-esteem. Thus, the decision to euthanize can be all the more agonizing.

There is another important consideration in the decision process that must be addressed here. There are some unique situations where the pet's degenerating quality of life may not yet be fatal. But the extreme heroic measures that might be required to maintain this

This memorial statue, by French sculptor Jules Moignez, entitled "Pointer Marking a Pheasant," was valued at $25 when purchased by Geraldine Rockefeller Dodge in 1921. Valued at over $4,000 in 1976, it now graces the entrance to St. Hubert's Giralda, an animal shelter, museum, and education center on the grounds of the former Dodge estate in New Jersey. *Photo by W. Sife. Courtesy of St. Hubert's Giralda, Inc.*

strained life could prove to be too harrowing to the pet owner—emotionally or financially. It also should be kept in mind that most often they are very painful and debilitating for the pet—making its last days terrible. As an example, chemotherapy might offer some hope, but it is too often a horrible experience for the pet. In addition, as much as we adore our companion animals, it may be unreasonable to sacrifice one's financial security to try to temporarily stave off the inevitable. It is not selfish or unloving to decide against these expensive palliative treatments. But again, only the individual may make a legitimate judgment on this. The decision to euthanize is heartbreaking, but necessary.

Also, by having to become the angel of death to that beloved pet and extension of ourselves, we are each tasting a bit of our own demise. And that is always very upsetting. We are forced back to the existential reality of being truly alone on our life journey, despite all the friends and family we may have. Death is so upsetting and confusing. All life is a kind of metaphor. How can we look for answers when we can't even comprehend the basic questions? But there is so much potential learning and growth to be gleaned from it. Each of us plays a role in this, with our beloved pets—getting occasional hints, but not ever really understanding the larger picture.

In having to euthanize, we must come to an existential turning point in our lives—ever seeking self-understanding and justification. In meeting ourselves in this darkness, we learn that we can go on. We are strengthened by that particular living, loving enrichment that we shared for a few wonderful years with our beloved pet. It lives on in us. And now we have to be better people because of it.

WHAT DO ANIMALS EXPERIENCE?

Some people fear that their pets know what is going to happen when they take them out on that final trip. The companion animals may sense that their time has come and that their human companion is helping them. There have been reported cases in which a pet who was about to be euthanized showed signs of being greatly upset because the owner was in another room. In all those instances, when that person joined the pet and veterinarian, the animal grew calm, and waited to be helped out of all its pain and misery. It seems that they need us for this parting.

The pet may seem anxious, but that is almost always because it recognizes the veterinarian's office and smells the fear of other animals. It will also be reactive to the owner's intense tension, and it can respond strongly to that. At such times—through our tears—we have to give it loving permission to let go. Animals are not frightened by the prospect of their own death—unless they are being attacked by a predator. When their time comes, they sense it and often go off by themselves, accepting death as normal. Our pets do not get upset or sentimental at the prospect of their own death. That is a projection of our own fear. We have so much to learn from them, even after they leave us.

When we project our dread of death to our pets, we are incorrectly attributing human qualities to them. In reality, at this time there is no regret or sadness in their minds. Unless they have been made to feel they still need to protect our feelings, the pet and owner need to say goodbye and give each other permission to let go. We should not torture ourselves during our grief by agonizing about this and distorting the final memories of our beloved companion animals.

ADDITIONAL THOUGHTS

With all of our humanitarian considerations, there are still some who claim that euthanasia is always wrong. These people are usually the "holier than thou" type and feel that they are superior to others in their moral, religious, and ethical values. That is nonsense. But it still can be very upsetting.

All life is precious and should be respected. While considering euthanasia and its critics, we also have to be concerned with the killing of other animals. What about proposed slaughterhouse reform, and *canned hunts* among other things? Don't we have a moral obligation to act to remedy these daily horrors? Or is it easier to turn our backs on this? As stewards of all other life on this planet, don't we have a responsibility to prevent the cruel conditions and very inhumane ways of "dispatching" these other animals? Think about that.

Have you become aware of the rapidly increasing trend toward vegetarianism? Why are so many people turning away from eating animals and wearing furs?

Did you ever think that even the bait worm is screaming on the hook, but you can't hear it—and you won't allow yourself to observe or even acknowledge its agony?

If an individual is not concerned with these and similar considerations, then the argument can be made that this person has no moral right to criticize or oppose euthanasia.

Much of the world remained passive to the Nazi holocaust while it was rampant. And many of the same horrors are being committed today in several parts of the world. If any individual can turn away from these with "studied ignorance" and denial—preferring to remain noncommittal—then what happens to that person's claim to be able to ethically judge or condemn euthanasia?

Humane care and consideration for our pets is our direct responsibility. The life and death of all creatures is our moral concern and responsibility. Even the Bible says that man is the steward of all the animals.

In this grievous forced encounter with death, we can learn new things. But there are some questions and personal problems about pet death, bereavement and euthanasia that cannot be satisfied by this or any other book. We must reach down deep into our innermost selves for those answers. They are there, if we really look for them.

OUR LOVED ONE

GRUMPY

AUG. 4, 1913
SEPT. 20, 1926

HIS SYMPATHETIC LOVE
AND UNDERSTANDING
ENRICHED OUR LIVES

HE WAITS FOR US

EMMA AND HENRY BIGALLION

"Enriching Our Lives."

Photo by W. Sife. Courtesy of
Hartsdale Canine Cemetery, Inc.

CHAPTER 14

Final

Arrangements

(Aftercare)

Break, break, break,
At the foot of thy crags, O Sea!
But the tender grace of a day that is dead
Will never come back to me.

—Alfred, Lord Tennyson

W e love our pets dearly, and go well out of our way to see that they get everything they could possibly need or want. It can be said that America is a nation of pets, and we treasure them above even jewels. Astonishing published figures show that in 2003 people all over the world spent about $11.4 billion on the purchases of gem diamonds. Yet Americans spent over $24 billion on food and veterinary care just for cats and dogs. And that number is constantly growing with the increasing numbers and varieties of animals in our pet population. Today, these expenditures are nearly double what they were only eight years ago.

A devoted pet ever mourned.   *Photo by W. Sife. Courtesy of*
                                               Hartsdale Canine Cemetery, Inc.

Ossuary for beloved cremains.   *Photo by W. Sife. Courtesy of*
                                               Abbey Glen Pet Memorial Park

Final Arrangements (Aftercare)

The annual dollar amount spent in the United States on mortuary care for all pets has been roughly estimated at between $9 million to $11 million, but pet cemeteries have existed here for over a century. In the last twenty years or so, their numbers have rapidly increased. There is now one major organization, the International Association of Pet Cemeteries (IAOPC), that is an umbrella association for most aftercare services. Judging by the careful maintenance and respect for the innumerable gravesites in these pet cemetaries, it is obvious that the loving care we give our companion animals does not end when their lives do. Their cherished memory lives on in us, and it seems fitting that we memorialize their remains the same as we do our dearly departed fellow humans.

We learn from our mistakes, though, and have come to realize that looking for a cemetery or crematorium just after the pet's death can be the hardest and most inefficient way to go about this task. And it also usually proves to be the most expensive. Generally, it makes more sense to get an overview of the establishments that are available in your immediate area and the services they provide. Long before your pet's death is the best time to obtain option and price brochures. Charges will vary from place to place. After going over the listings in the appendix of this book, check out the Yellow Pages in your local telephone directory; look under "Pet Cemeteries and Crematories." Or visit the Association for Pet Loss and Bereavement's website: www.aplb.org. They maintain the most updated list of all aftercare services. Information is also available free, on request, by contacting the IAOPC.

Your veterinarian should also be able to give you some suggestions, without having to make a profit on this. Keep in mind, though, that most vets receive a referral fee from the cemetery or crematory they send the bodies to. Some even sell urns, caskets, and other mortuary paraphernalia. So your best financial interest may not be served in this manner. Also check out your local SPCA or Bide-A-Wee Foundation, if there is one in your vicinity. Fellow pet owners are another good source of information regarding pet cemeteries and crematories, and their expenses.

All of this advanced preparation may seem a bit unsettling to the pet owner, who probably hates giving even a brief thought to the pet's eventual death. This makes perfectly good sense, however. Checking these things out beforehand can sometimes be an unexpected stimulus to loving one's pet even better than before, and cherishing every last day with it. Whatever your action or inaction on this early preparation, it is important to know in advance not to be caught totally unprepared and ignorant when that time actually comes—and it will. This chapter will also help you with your decision, if it isn't already too late.

AFTERCARE OPTIONS

Several options are available in the handling of the deceased pet. As with humans, burial and cremation are two choices. Now, with pets there are new choices—freeze-drying and taxidermy. These may seem repulsive to many, but there is always going to be someone who will opt for them.

There have been recent developments in the freeze-drying of animal corpses, which seems to preserve them perfectly. Sometimes this is combined with taxidermy for added durability and realism. The rationale behind this is that some people would love to have their pet still with them, in body if not in spirit. This can seem a bit ghoulish to many, but who is to criticize anything benign if it makes people feel better? However, having a dust-catching, fading image made of your pet's body may be seen as disrespectful of the pet and its death. It can also negatively affect the owner's full bereavement process. These services are advertised in pet mortuary publications and can be located through most of them. Some may even be listed online and in your local Yellow Pages.

INTERMENT

Burial is the most common preference, but it can get complicated. Most people like to bury their pets in very private sites on their own property. That makes excellent sense, but unfortunately it is illegal in most of the country. But this is "more honored in the breech than in the observance." Laws are supposed to be made to serve us, not the reverse. Nevertheless, check out your local statutes on this. It is remotely possible that variations exist in your favor.

Today there are many pet cemeteries throughout the world. Most of them seem to be in the United States, however. As a rule, these places are spacious, beautifully landscaped, and legitimate. Almost all of them also take pains to make legal provisions against the land ever being reused in the future for any other purpose. Whenever visiting or inquiring, ask what guarantees they provide, if any. Regard this as a very important consideration in choosing. Occasionally we read in the papers about a pet cemetery that is being dug up to make way for "development." We don't want that for our pets! If the owner or representative cannot provide written documentation of legal protection from this, walk away; there are others. But destruction of these properties is becoming more of a rarity today, among the more truly professional ones. Be wary, though. Every few years we see in the news that another one is being destroyed—along with all the graves in it.

If a burial is chosen over the other options, then you will have additional considerations and expenses to deal with. Prices range widely, for coffins and gravestones—according to size, materials, and workmanship. Just as with human burials, you must make personal decisions depending on what you want and can afford. But if you had time to comparison shop earlier, a substantial amount of money can be saved. Some places are just more expensive than others. Check out the Internet. You can find a wealth of choices and excellent prices there. But as mentioned earlier, immediately after the pet's death is not the right time to have to make these kinds of difficult decisions—just as with human burials. Fortunately, the legitimate pet cemetery will not pressure you to make an immediate choice. But the urgency is there, nevertheless.

You will probably want to hold some sort of private service at the gravesite. Sometimes it is good to have this led by a professional, especially when the mourner is so distraught as to be a bit dysfunctional for that moment. But the most touching memorial services I ever attended were conducted privately, with plenty of tears and hesitations. There are a few good books in print, with fine suggestions for this. Consult the bibliography list on the Association for Pet Loss and Bereavement's website (www.aplb.org).

If you can organize a funeral in advance, invite a very limited group to attend. Make sure that this includes only people who hold the same views as you do regarding the death of your beloved pet. It can be very upsetting to have someone present who may feel you are being overindulgent with this kind of ceremony. Such people stand out badly, and the ceremony may be diminished or even blemished because of them. Definitely bring the children who loved the pet. If you can, say some prepared thoughts about the pet and your special love for it. Tell everyone why you loved this dear one so very much. It might make you cry and lose control for the moment, but it is good. If you need to, read your thoughts from a paper that you prepared in advance. Nobody will mind. Sometimes religious considerations will be brought into the service. That is a personal decision. Regardless of its design or handling, you will feel much better for having such a service.

CREMATION

More and more people today are opting for cremation of their own bodies after death. And this is becoming increasingly popular for pets, as well. At the present time, about 45 percent of pet deaths are treated in this manner. It has some advantages that you may wish to consider. Starting at the very beginning, cremation is another service your veterinarian can help provide. Of course, there will be a kickback fee. Pet funeral parlors, cemeteries, and crematoriums will also offer these services at varying prices. They will most often be lower than if you had signed a contract with the veterinarian, who is only an intermediary. Ask for this.

Many humane societies, as well as pet cemeteries and some veterinary clinics, operate their own crematoriums. They usually provide informative brochures that you should obtain well in advance of any need for their use. The choice of individual or communal cremation should be explained to your satisfaction.

The ashes may also be buried in the same way that a body is interred. Some cemeteries reserve special columbarium sections just for this. Others will allow either type of burial anywhere on the premises. It was interesting to learn that in many states, people may not have the ashes of their pets buried along with theirs. The interment of bodies is even more restrictive. There is no logic to these arbitrary laws, and they need to be changed.

There are two basic types of cremation services available. Mass cremation is the less expensive, of course. This is when your pet's body is incinerated with many others and the ashes are usually returned to you. Check on that, first. But, even if the cremains are returned, there is no guarantee that they are your pet's. The other option is the more costly private procedure. Many people prefer this for a few reasons. The cremation is not shared with others, and you are less prone to worry that the ashes are not wrongly identified or mixed up with another pet's.

Final Arrangements (Aftercare)

You will also need to choose the kind of container to keep the ashes in. Keep in mind that this is also a business, so the styles, sizes, and prices will vary—competitively. There is nothing wrong with keeping the cremains in a cardboard box for burial or scattering. It certainly is not disrespectful to your pet. This is purely a personal decision, and nobody can judge you for your choices.

Most pet cemeteries have columbariums (ossuaries) where the cremains are stored permanently in prominent vaults. Of course, that is a different expense, but it might be just the thing you feel comfortable with. Some of these are quite beautiful and worthy of their precious contents. However, many people prefer to keep the cremains in some lovely urn or box, to be later buried with them. This is often set aside in some prominent place in the home, and it becomes the pet's permanent place there. Some people make a provision in their wills to have the pet's cremains mixed with their own. Others will scatter the pet's ashes in some special place that they both loved. There is no "proper" way to handle this. Whatever feels right *for you* is good.

Depending on the size of the pet, private cemetery costs vary from a few hundred dollars and up. Options of community or individual burial are offered by many pet cemeteries and humane societies (such as the Bide-A-Wee Foundation). These nonprofit organizations provide similar memorial facilities that are considerably less expensive, while preserving the dignity of your pet's memory. Your veterinarian should be able to advise you about this, if asked. But always keep in mind that this is a business, and there is a profit incentive here. It is always wise to do some comparison shopping, and contact other pet owners for advice.

If you should have a reasonably strong feeling about what action or selection to take, don't hesitate. Put it into effect right away. You may get well-intended conflicting and disturbing opinions later. What other people may think should be of lesser value than your own feelings and well-considered decision.

At present, there are only about half a dozen pet cemeteries in the United States that have adjacent plots for their owners as well. Most states and communities absurdly outlaw this practice. Indeed, as stated earlier, in nearly all areas of the country, people may not even legally bury a beloved pet on their own private property.

INVESTIGATE WITH CARE

Caveat emptor! "Let the buyer beware." You should know that some pet cemeteries and mortuary facilities have been run by unscrupulous, unfeeling people. This is increasingly rare today, but all it takes is one! These few scoundrels deliberately mislead and cheat the credulous pet owner, who unfortunately is not in any position to objectively evaluate things at the time of bereavement. These corruptors of an otherwise honorable profession have been prosecuted in court and found guilty of violating many laws. They are con artists—deliberate criminals who prey on very susceptible people at their most vulnerable time. But they get rich quickly as a result of their vile scams.

In 1991, there was a scandal involving a pet cemetery in Long Island, New York. Heartbroken mourners who believed their pets had been buried or cremated according to contract were shocked to discover that there were mass burial pits. These contained the unprotected decomposing bodies of beloved pets who were supposed to have been treated in completely different ways. These cemetery profiteers were tried and found guilty on several counts of criminal behavior. They were also sued in civil courts by hundreds of bereft pet owners. Although these criminals served jail terms, the irreversible damage had been done. Admittedly, this is a rare example, but it may not be the last one. To their credit, most pet cemeterians now try to police their own industry in order to prevent this sort of thing from ever happening again. Unfortunately, a similar incident took place in Florida a few years later.

It would be completely wrong to brand the entire pet mortuary profession with the same stamp. Most of these businesses are very ethical, with fine reputations. A few of the more outstanding ones have been in continuous existence for nearly a century. They are eager to prove their value. Most families have human burial plots already assigned to their still living members. This also makes sense for pets, and when visiting most pet cemeteries today you will see many reserved empty plots.

VISITS

It is good to visit any pet cemeteries that are in your vicinity. Walk around. Look and feel how other loving pet owners have felt. Read the inscriptions. You will be moved and strengthened by them. If there is one near you, it can be a very poignant occasion to visit an older one. The aging and varied grave markers, stones, and monuments, along with their heartfelt inscriptions, are a powerful testament to our lasting love of all types of pets. Many burial plots have impressive markers and inscriptions memorializing different pets who belonged to the same owner or family. Each of these was buried years apart, and the stone had those later names inscribed, accordingly. In these serene places there is a strange sense of spiritual community and intense love. This will be a visit of great positive value to you, regardless of how you decide to care for the body of your beloved pet. There are no other places like these.

In 1986, a team of archaeologists unearthed a pet cemetery in Ashkelon, a port city of the Persian Empire that had been inhabited by people in what is now southern Israel. The skeletal remains of about one thousand dogs, from puppies to old ones, were found. They had been individually buried over a long span of time. The cemetery dated back to what is called the Persian Period, which lasted from about 500 to 332 B.C. All indications suggest that each dog freely roamed a sacred precinct and died of natural causes. The plots had been cared for and protected from scavengers and human interference. This unexpected find is the oldest surviving record of a pet cemetery ever discovered. But these memorialized free-ranging dogs were not actually pets, as we have them today. They probably were revered as religious icons. From ancient Egypt there are even older remains of individually mummified dogs and cats, along with their carved and inscribed sarcophagi and wooden coffins. But these were not in cemeteries.

MAKING A FINAL DECISION

If you have just experienced the death of a beloved pet, you are probably faced with the need to make an immediate decision. Delay it at least for a few hours. Talk with trusted, concerned people. Ask them about their feelings and opinions. In addition to these people whom you know, there are professionals at the pet cemeteries and pet funeral parlors who are usually well-prepared to give you sound advice and counseling. Although they also want to sell you a product, for the most part they are very good at what they do. If you have certain financial or other limitations, explain this to them. These people are also pet lovers and humanitarians. They really want to help. Don't hesitate to say when you are not comfortable with anything they suggest. A good pet cemetery or funeral parlor has a reputation to make and keep, which can be to your advantage at this time. But to feel safe, be sure your final decision is your own, regardless of who does or doesn't seem to agree with it.

In the long run, all of this is only a temporary turbulence in your life. Whatever final arrangements you decide on, will be made with your undying love. And that is the greatest memorial anyone can ever give to a beloved pet. Whether cremation or burial, it is all only symbolic. Your pet has passed on to a higher plane, and the grave sites or cremains can be only a poor reminder. Now that sweet soul is memorialized in your heart, forever. You bless each other that way.

Here is text taken from a memorial:

" . . . *For if the dog be well remembered, if sometimes she leaps through your dreams actual as in life, eyes kindling, laughing, begging, it matters not where that dog sleeps. On a hill where the wind is unrebuked and the trees are roaring, or beside a stream she knew in puppyhood, or somewhere in the flatness of a pastureland where most exhilarating cattle graze. It is one to a dog, and all one to you, and nothing is gained and nothing lost—if memory lives. But there is one best place to bury a dog.*

"*If you bury her in this spot, she will come to you when you call—come to you over the grim, dim frontiers of death, and down the well-remembered path and to your side again. And though you may call a dozen living dogs to heel, they shall not growl at her nor resent her coming, for she belongs there.*

"*People may scoff at you, who see no lightest blade of grass bent by her footfall, who hear no whimper, people who have never really had a dog. Smile at them, for you shall know something that is hidden from them.*

"*The one best place to bury a good dog is in the heart of her master.*"

—Anonymous

Kitten mummy: Egyptian, Ptolemaic-Roman;
Linen; Height: 20.5 cm., Width: 4.5 cm.,
Max. depth: 6 cm.

Photo by W. Sife. Hay Collection,
gift of Granville Way, courtesy of
Museum of Fine Arts, Boston

CHAPTER 15

Supportive Counseling

Sweet are the uses of adversity.

—William Shakespeare

The loss of a pet is an extremely difficult subject that traditionally has been glossed over for many reasons. Aside from the intolerant criticisms of the arrogant few who claim that this kind of loss means nothing, we live in a society that passionately avoids thinking or speaking about any death. Even the word and concept have been avoided and replaced with polite, more socially acceptable expressions. In many circles we must not even use the words "die" or "death," and we are required to avoid many other direct terms, as well. It becomes necessary to say something such as "pass away" or "gone on to his/her maker." As mentioned in previous chapters, we still tend to hide behind euphemisms and avoidance. Despite our feelings of condolence when someone else grieves over any death, we tend to remain cautiously apart. Death scares most of us, and we don't know how to handle it.

Psychologically, we feel threatened and unable to cope with this subject that nobody wants to talk about. It is a topic that most of us are terribly uncomfortable with. People don't know how to examine their feelings about death without confusion, embarrassment, and even fear. Our culture has evolved many taboos concerning our

Bless these pets, O Lord.

*Photo by W. Sife. Courtesy of
Abbey Glen Pet Memorial Park*

responses. Euphemisms ease our somewhat Victorian reluctance to deal with these upsetting and unacceptable words or ideas. This foolish consistency is a self-made hobgoblin still mocking us, even now at the start of the twenty-first century.

TRADITIONAL RESPONSES

Death is too upsetting a subject, and Western society has traditionally avoided it as much as possible. We leave its handling to the professionals—the clergy and mortuary specialists. Since nobody knows the answers or even the right questions, we tend to evade its consideration or discussion, keeping our private passions, hopes, and heartbreaks to ourselves. When it comes to the death of a beloved pet, however, there is the additional problem of being intimidated by those who tend to belittle this. Up until recently, it was tacitly accepted by nearly everyone, including the bereaved, that there must be something wrong with us if we grieved so deeply for a mere animal. But the reality is that the death of any loved companion—pet or person—will cause bereavement and heartbreak. People with little or no compassion take a perverse pleasure in criticizing bereaving pet owners for their feelings. Almost invariably, these self-styled critics lack sensitivity or do not understand this experience, and they are too quick to condemn others. Yet, in our grief, we still have to hide our feelings from people who have prejudices. We owe these critics nothing, but of course we are vulnerable—especially during this period of intense heartache. Yet it is natural to want to hide this insecurity.

It had been generally presumed that the death of *only a pet* should be less meaningful than that of a human. This kind of grief was an easy target to criticize. Bereaving pet owners in the midst of their overwhelming sorrow had to become defensive and apologetic, for fear of being ridiculed and ostracized. But now, at last, because of broadened exposure to these experiences, the mass media are starting to cover the subject of pet death with an increasing sense of humanism and awareness. The Internet really gave this a great boost. There, bereaving pet owners were able to express their feelings and post very personal and loving memorials. And a few special chat rooms were formed to serve this need. When so many people openly experience this kind of grief, it becomes a major social phenomenon that gradually must make itself better understood, despite all the older traditional pitfalls.

You are not alone in your grief. The time has finally come to realize and be comforted by this. There are millions of us, and our numbers are ever increasing. Because of the escalating visibility of such experiences, the problem is becoming much more accepted as a normal living experience. Bereavement for a beloved pet is no longer ridiculed and ignored, as it had been. Indeed, in some circles it is even becoming an honored and respected experience. Unfortunately, this is a special rite of passage for pet lovers everywhere.

THE FIRST BEREAVEMENT CLINICS

The first four pet bereavement clinics were established in the 1980s, and, of course, they were an immediate success. Only ten years later, about twenty-five major pet bereavement clinics, with specially chosen counselors had been established around the United States. Now nearly every large city in the country has some social worker or trained therapist offering help in this newly recognized category. But most prominent and effective is the recent strong presence of petloss-related websites on the Internet. Good old pragmatic Yankee ingenuity is one of our national hallmarks. Necessity has always been the mother of invention, here.

CHOOSE WITH CARE

Now there are hundreds of other people suddenly appearing on the pet bereavement scene. Although most of them are very well-intentioned, they have little or no appropriate training or experience, and are calling themselves pet bereavement counselors. They love animals, have good hearts, and are driven by personal motivations and needs to help other people control their lives.

Unfortunately, among these many there are some who have extremely unusual views and feelings about life. Their varied passions for such esoteric interests as crystals, aromas, pyramids, aliens, numerology, astrology, séances, and so on have convinced them that they can help soothe the aching heart of the person bereaving for a pet. There is an amazing spectrum of arcane approaches, some of which may be effective, while others may well cross the border into some form of self-delusion or even harmless psychosis. Although these counselors themselves are probably in no apparent danger from this, the people they counsel may be placed in jeopardy.

It must be admitted that an approach to counseling in pet bereavement based on radical religious or "spiritual" views may well work wonders for a small population of mourners. But some extreme approaches that rely, for example, on crystals or chants under a pyramidal structure raise many doubts. Of course, a *placebo effect* can have its effect under the right conditions. If a client truly believes a treatment will work, the healing may actually occur—regardless of the methodology or anything else involved.

There is an astonishing variety of approaches being offered by this recent influx of well-intentioned people. It is also unfortunate that they use no discretion when dealing with their clients. Too many of these consultants will try to prescribe their way of life to anyone who is grieving for a beloved pet, regardless of that person's beliefs or attitudes. Under conditions of such stress and grief, these self-styled "counselors" take unfair advantage of their clients' extreme vulnerability, and impose their strong personal views on them. This can be seen as an ego trip and expression of power in an extremely sensitive, emotional environment. It also violates basic counseling standards and ethics, and in some cases, it can even do harm. On a few occasions, I have been called in on emergency sessions to perform damage control. As indicated in previous chapters, people under severe stress usually have repressed acute psychological problems that are triggered by just this kind of emotional intensity. Clients who are prone to hysterics, suicide, or aggravated depression are especially endangered by these advisors who do not know the danger signs. Some of these consultants are in actual denial about the limits of their ability to help or damage. A well-intentioned self-image as a healer is not enough—despite their passionate surety. Watch out!

In most states no regulations exist to prevent anyone from hanging up a shingle as a "psychotherapist." That is bad enough, but now along comes this horde of individuals who are starting to call themselves pet bereavement counselors. Unfortunately, there are no formal standards or requirements of any kind, and anybody can do this! One need not even have a grammar school education for this. The final choice in counselors should always be up to the enlightened prospective client, though.

It is heartening to note that since its inception in 1997, the Association for Pet Loss and Bereavement (APLB) has been training counselors and developing a set of high standards for this new profession. They also conduct several three-hour specialized chat rooms each week on the Internet, helping thousands of bereaving pet owners who have no other place to turn for help. Visit their website: www.aplb.org.

Even licensed psychiatrists with M.D. degrees may not be good counselors for this still new and very specialized field. There have been cases when patients of very reputable psychiatrists have found it necessary to find experienced pet bereavement counselors who *really* knew how to help them. Book training and degrees do not create a compatible or sensitive personality. Other personal characteristics based on loving animals and people are absolutely essential, as well. Some important human qualities cannot be created by university diplomas. We have a very strange mixture of advisors out there.

A good petloss counselor must be an animal lover, just for starters. He or she must also have reasonable training and experience in the loss of a pet. And then there are other less definable personal characteristics that create a warm, positive, interpersonal relationship. There has to be a good level of respect and responsiveness between counselor and client. Some people are natural helpers, and others will never be, despite degrees, education, or even experience.

The honor of being called a healer is a great one, indeed. It is one of the finest compliments anyone can be given. This is an achievement that takes a long time to accomplish. In addition to loving what one does, the practitioner must be successful at this. There is no room for self-deception or ego here. Dedication to the cure, not the method, is what sets the most accomplished counselors aside from the others. Unfortunately, too many who advise in pet bereavement do not measure up to this requirement—regardless of their credentials, or lack of them.

Perhaps, not so surprising, there are many good, concerned "naturals" who successfully advise others. It is heartening to realize that their ranks are increasing. With the proper training and experience, they often make the best petloss and bereavement counselors.

Supportive Counseling

A GROWING SUPPORT

Starting in the 1980s, we have seen a growing and open support for pet bereavement. This all too human expression used to be socially frowned upon. What we really have here is the beginning of a revolution in thinking and public attitude. Others are beginning to realize that mourning is not a privileged commemoration to be reserved only for the loss of human loved ones.

History, art, and literature provide us with many glimpses into personal memorials to beloved dogs. These emotional expressions have been successful because of their great human-interest and artistic value. The concept of a hero weeping for a faithful dog is dramatic and even poetic. It has a classic and universal appeal to our basic love of all animals.

As household pets became more common, the problem of bereavement for them increased greatly. This once occasional, secret tragedy has changed. Now we are faced with the misfortunes of millions who are dealing with this shock. Despite our advances, many individuals still tend to hide their distress from those who have no understanding or sensitivity to their problem. That can make good sense, in certain social situations. But as with some other important contemporary social issues, pet bereavement is finally "coming out of the closet." The stigma is finally losing its effectiveness.

SEEKING HELP

Most often our grief responses need sharing and good counsel. That certainly does not mean that one is in need of psychotherapy. However, if we do opt for trained help, it also does not imply that we are weak or emotionally defective. On the contrary, when we seek answers and objectivity it is usually a sign of good mental health. Professional petloss guidance could offer just the boost we need in helping ourselves attain some positive direction during this particular time of trial and suffering.

We need good people around us during this personal crisis. Anyone who is truly sympathetic can be a good listener and helper. But the death of a beloved pet is so deeply personal that we also need some very private time away from others. It becomes a time for an existential search alone—deep within ourselves and our pain.

189

Don't feed your depression. Sidestep it or even try to avoid it. Here are some helpful practices the person in mourning should consider:

1. If you live alone, try to change your daily patterns slightly. Make an effort to be with others more often, and stay away from sad and stressful people.

2. Watch different television programs, and listen to other radio stations. Vary your selections.

3. Avoid certain types of movies that may be upsetting, and actively seek out other ones that are entertaining. Try to enjoy them with someone who is sensitive to what you are going through.

4. Although you may feel some initial resistance, arrange to visit others. Get out of the house more frequently. You can still take memories with you and share them, if you choose.

5. At this time, avoid social situations that may prove upsetting—for any reason.

6. Meet with other pet owners and talk about your beloved pet, and what you are going through.

7. Attend pet bereavement support group sessions or online petloss chat rooms. They are a wonderful sharing and healing experience.

COUNSELING

Until recently, professionals with psychological and psychiatric training had not been forced to consider the unique complexities of pet bereavement. The truly understanding counselor can be a rare, personal treasure. Unfortunately, many of these professionals with no personal experience or understanding of pet bereavement offer their general, well-intended guidance that is often too shallow and inadequate. Those who are not pet people themselves lack a basic understanding of the depth of the love that others have for their pets. Now this is starting to change for the better. The Association for Pet Loss and Bereavement (APLB) was recently formed in order to train professional counselors in pet bereavement. You can read more about the APLB at the end of this chapter.

Today, the specialty of health and death care for pets has become a multi-billion-dollar business. With such increased visibility and growing socio-economic pressure, it is natural that there should be a much greater positive response to the needs of so many. Unfortunately, in the past, this had always been rare. Even veterinary colleges used to give little or no instruction on pet death counseling and sensitivity. Now that is all changing. Within the past decade or so, there has been a growing movement to correct this condition to better provide for the bereaving pet owner. Most veterinary colleges and pet hospitals have recognized this and the need to train themselves, as well as the general public.

It used to be that the only source of advice was pet cemetery personnel, whose sheer volume of varied experiences with bereaved pet owners had created an accumulated base of wisdom and philosophy. These people and their establishments may help with good, practical advice and support, but their business is primarily the mechanics of burial or cremation. Indeed, some clients still hesitate to ask for help there because they feel that the interest of these places is strictly that of a financially motivated business. In some instances this is true, but there are many wonderful exceptions. Aside from all the other counselors, professional pet cemeterians have a great deal of experience and compassion, and they can be very supportive and helpful. Some of them have even received training in counseling. This is something you can ask about when you visit or call.

THE HUMANISTIC VIEW

The growing humanistic view of bereavement places the pain and grief of mourners as the prime focus, with all other considerations secondary. There is absolutely no tolerance for those who are judgmental here. This approach to understanding bereavement is helping us to overcome the enormous historic inertia and stagnation that was imprinted on our collective social awareness. Times are changing and our values with them—to our credit as a civilization. But this is happening slowly and not without great labor and pain.

Today, the deeply bereaved mourner for a beloved pet has some organized help available. At this writing, there are at least twenty-five centers across the United States where one may speak with counselors who are experienced and trained for this specific problem. Most of them also offer wonderful group support sessions that are unmatched in the good they do for pet bereavement. Also, such help is usually free. These centers are listed at the end of this chapter. Some are telephone "hotlines" with specially selected and trained personnel.

As stated earlier, there is a wide spectrum of counselors in this field, and their numbers are rapidly increasing. It is important to take warning, though. The newly bereaved are especially vulnerable and easily duped. There is an ever-present danger of the few unscrupulous people who enter this field only for personal reward, without appropriate qualifications or experience. Too many of these enjoy the sense of power, control, and ego involvement that counseling offers them. Others love the thought that they are helping people. As mentioned earlier, in the past few years we have seen a rash of new kinds of "therapies" being foisted on unsuspecting and very susceptible pet owners. These include "aroma therapy", numerology, spiritualism, and perhaps most deceiving of all, "animal communication." But we all will believe what we want to believe, and in some instances hard contrary facts and evidence will not dissuade. Most of these self-appointed "counselors" are good people, and caring pet lovers, as well. They are convinced of the truth that they want and need to see. *Caveat emptor*—"Let the buyer beware." Much emotional damage has been done by many of these "counselors". They were not trained to identify and deal with certain powerful emotional needs and failings in those who are in deep bereavement for a beloved pet.

RELIGION AS A MEANS FOR SUPPORTIVE COUNSELING

We reach out for any help and guidance available. Unfortunately, until very recently there had been precious few helpful responses from the established Judeo-Christian theologies. Fundamental faiths are not concerned with the death of companion animals. They are too rooted in tradition and the past. Their view is understandable since civilization in biblical times had no pets, and there was no need for such considerations.

Fortunately, many modern members of the clergy are taking brave new stands and interpretations on the death of our companion animals. The next chapter will expand on this with some specific examples.

Certain Eastern philosophies and religions hold that all life is precious and intrinsically one and the same. It is part of the great unity of being. Thus, the passing of a pet is also respected as important. Here we can find a new perspective and solace in our bereavement. There is much to be considered and learned.

Islam, to its credit, respects the souls of all living things. But you will never see a pet in the home of a fundamentalist. The Koran, like the Old Testament, makes no reference at all to pets. A strong general concern for the humane treatment of all animals is emphasized instead.

For thousands of years, Native Americans have revered life and spirit in all animals, especially in those that they had to hunt. Although dogs roamed freely through the camps and belonged to no one, they were respected and treated almost like members of the tribe. It was generally believed that death took the dogs to the same "happy hunting grounds" that they went to.

Unfortunately, most organized religions may not be able to help, since they are not philosophically or historically oriented in this specific direction. The rare exceptions lie with a few variant attitudes. In Christianity, St. Francis is the patron saint of animals and pets. Here, the individual priest has extreme latitude. But no guidelines exist that define a clear position about whether pets have souls, go to heaven, and so on. When offering solace to the person mourning for a pet, each cleric may deal with this as he/she sees fit, in accordance with personal preference and practicality. The compassionate priest who is a real pet lover may be a fine counselor in pet bereavement. But that is only because of one's unique personality and approach. Unfortunately, this too often an exception.

Take heart, however. Some major denominations are just beginning to follow the fine example of the Episcopal Cathedral Church of St. John the Divine, in New York City. They have set the modern standard for loving respect and consideration of pets and the effects their deaths have on us. Their very impressive annual St. Francis Day celebration is begun with a blessing of an amazing host of animals, and it is always a major feature on the local television news of the day. In the last decade we have seen many different denominations starting to make a big festival with a blessing of the animals on St. Francis Day. There was a great popular need for this. Many are starting to respond and deal with it in appropriate modern ways that were never dreamed of by their more traditional clergy.

Dealing with death is a profoundly spiritual experience, and most people in pet bereavement feel a great need to turn to their spiritual leaders. But too often the help needed for these mourners is not sanctioned. Rather than appearing pessimistic when viewing the historical record of religion, a comprehensive study has been made for your consideration. The next chapter is designed to give a more in-depth perspective of the positive role that religion may still play for the grieving pet owner. Pastoral counseling, if available during the mourning period, can offer unique and very effective help and hope. But too often, it is difficult or impossible to find. A sense of spiritual uplift is particularly beneficial and often desired at this tragic time. Perhaps by surveying some of the best contemporary religious thinking concerning the death of pets, one may find some important insights and self-counsel, as well.

COMFORT IN PHILOSOPHY

There is also consolation to be found in philosophy. Metaphysical philosophers and transcendental poets offer beautiful hope in this area. In addition to their other merits, they are well worth reading for this inspiration and incidental support. This is especially important to those of us who do not believe in any kind of afterlife—for ourselves and our pets, as well. These good people do not have the sense of security that others find in formal religion. So they must rely on their own solitary convictions and philosophies to help them put an appropriate perspective on the meaning of their lives—and their beloved pets. In some ways their mourning can be even more grievous.

COUNSELING CENTERS AND HOTLINES

IN THE UNITED STATES

Arizona

Companion Animal Association of Arizona
Scottsdale
(602) 995-5885

California

The Grief Recovery Institute
Beverly Hills
(888) 773-2683

University of California School of Veterinary Medicine
Davis
(530) 752-4200

Colorado

Colorado State University School of Veterinary Medicine
Fort Collins
(970) 491-1242

Florida

University of Florida School of Veterinary Medicine
Gainsville
(352) 392-4700, extension 4080

Illinois

C.A.R.E. Pet Loss Helpline, University of Illinois
Urbana
(217) 244-2273 or (877) 394-2273 (toll-free)
www.cvm.uiuc.edu/CARE/

Chicago Veterinary Medical Association
Chicago
(630) 325-1600

Iowa

Iowa State University School of Veterinary Medicine
Ames
(888) 478-7574

Massachusetts

Tufts University School of Veterinary Medicine
Grafton
(508) 839-7966

Michigan

Michigan State University School of Veterinary Medicine
Lansing
(517) 432-2696

Minnesota

The Broken Bond Pet Loss Hotline/Support Group
Rochester
(507) 289-8169

University of Minnesota School of Veterinary Medicine
Minneapolis
(612) 625-1919

New Jersey

Pet Friends, Inc.
Moorestown
(800) 404-7387

St. Hubert's Giralda
Madison
(973) 377-7094

New York

Animal Medical Center
New York
(212) 838-8100

ASPCA
New York
(212) 876-7700

Bide-A-Wee Foundation
New York
(212) 532-6395

Capitol Region Pet Loss Network
Albany
(518) 448-5677

Cornell University
Ithaca
(607) 253-3932

Ohio

Ohio State University
Columbus
(614) 292-1823

Pennsylvania

University of Pennsylvania School of Veterinary Medicine
Philadelphia
(215) 898-4525

Virginia

Virginia-Maryland College of Veterinary Medicine
Blacksburgh
(540) 231-8038

Washington

Washington State University, College of Veterinary Medicine,
Pet Loss Hotline
Pullman
(509) 335-5704
E-mail: plhl@vetmed.wsu.edu
www.vetmed.wsu.edu/plhl

Wisconsin

The Rainbow Passage, Pet Loss Support and Bereavement Center
Grafton
(414) 376-0340
E-mail: douglasc@execpc.com

INTERNATIONAL

Australia

The Australian Centre for Companion Animals in Society (ACCAS) operates a national petloss grief hotline in Australia between 7 p.m. and 9 p.m. every evening (local time). (02) 9746 1911; 1800 704 291 (toll-free)

England

The Pet Bereavement Support Service
0800 096 6606 (toll-free)

Note: There are several other listings for individuals or groups that are not associated with established institutions or organizations, and they are not posted here. Some of these have been found to represent only the personal, untrained approaches of the individuals in charge of them. Although others may be very helpful, the above listing is only of authenticated institutions known at the time of this writing.

Other organizations such as the Delta Society compose paid listings of pet bereavement counselors, but there is no authentication of their verifiability as bona fide practitioners in this field.

Also, you can check the various online listings by searching for "Pet Bereavement." There are many interesting services and chat rooms, as well as offerings for counseling and products. But it is always advisable to verify the personal credentials of anyone claiming to be an authority or counselor in pet bereavement.

THE ASSOCIATION FOR PET LOSS AND BEREAVEMENT (APLB)

The Association for Pet Loss and Bereavement is a confederation of diverse and concerned members who are experienced and knowledge-able in the area of pet death and its varying effects on those who acutely mourn this loss.

The purpose of this nonprofit organization is to coordinate people who are suffering from pet bereavement with appropriate counseling and other services, according to their individual needs. In serving as a clear-inghouse for all pertinent information, the APLB prepares and publishes continually updated bibliographies and reports assessing all therapies currently in use in this field. Their highly acclaimed newsletter is the only one of its kind.

The APLB recognizes that there are several controversial or even questionable approaches to this specialized counseling, and that there are always going to be some adherents who feel assured that their methods work for them. This association favors therapies based on more conventional counseling techniques for pet bereavement analysis and treatment, but it registers online anyone who conforms to reasonable standards of preparation and experience, regardless of methodology. It regularly upgrades that registry of practitioners with information on each counselor's background, training, experience, and method of therapy.

The APLB is continually open to suggestions, recommendations, and petitions from additional individuals desiring to be listed as counselors. It also offers special services such as several three-hour online chat rooms, publications, and internship training, as well as conferences open to the general public. At the time of this writing, the APLB is the only approved organization to help teach and advise pet bereavement counselors. Special training seminars are made available to a variety of learners.

For more information about this outstanding Internet organization and its activities, contact:

The Association for Pet Loss and Bereavement
P.O. Box 106
Brooklyn, NY 11230
(718) 382-0690
E-mail: aplb@aplb.org
www.aplb.org

CHAPTER 16

Religion
and the
Death
of Pets

A righteous man regardeth the life of his beasts.

—Prov. 7:10

*T*raditionally, our understanding of death had been a subject that fell solely within the province of religion. With the exception of a few metaphysical philosophers, our religious leaders were the only acknowledged authorities on the subject. Historically, however, since the Industrial Revolution our lifestyles have been changing, dramatically affecting this situation.

SOCIAL CHANGES AND EFFECTS

With the onset of the growth in the size and population of cities, there came a corresponding decline in rural population. As a result, there was the rapid disappearance of the extended family, and a diminishment of the traditionally powerful influence of organized religion on

201

its members. The previously unchallenged regulation of the church over everyday matters is also strongly affected by dramatically changing socioeconomic conditions. A more modern example of this is that in the last decade, we have witnessed an unprecedented explosion in the means and ease of communications between people—as well as entertainment and distraction. This has an indirect effect of diverting and diminishing reliance on religion. It also has the capacity to drown out personal introspection and spirituality. We are vulnerable to becoming dependent on sound-bites, superficialities, and instant gratification. Society is in danger of becoming alarmingly short-sighted. Now, in this increasingly distracted and hectic world, Western religion is losing even more of its needed influence.

Historically, the keeping of pets for pleasure and companionship had originally been the practice of rich and powerful men. As populations started to shift to the cities, basic lifestyles changed, and more people began to discover the gratifications of having a companion animal. With the advent of increased personal wealth and leisure, this natural source of human pleasure began to gain even more popularity. Within the span of just a few hundred years, pet dogs and cats were beginning to be seen everywhere. A graphic illustration of this is New York City. At the turn of the twentieth century there were only a few thousand pet dogs there. Today there are well over one million, with even more cats. And who can begin to guess at the great numbers of other living animals who are also being kept as pets? Of course, the human population has exploded, as well. With all these pets dying, it is not so surprising that there is an even greater need for spiritual guidance and counseling today.

Modern times have also seen a great increase in zoos of all kinds and wildlife refuges. Pet owners are not the only people to mourn the loss of an animal. The people who dedicate themselves to stewarding these institutions and their wards also form powerful emotional and spiritual bonds with their wards. And they grieve their losses, too. Unfortunately, organized religion has generally shown no regard for this modern social phenomenon. These special people are considered merely shepherds who lose a favored one of their flock. Here is another modern phenomenon of good people in bereavement for animals of all kinds, feeling abandoned by their religion when they need it most.

DO ANIMALS HAVE SOULS?

The eventual death of a beloved animal raises profound personal questions about whether such a sentient, loving animal also has a soul that would find its reward in heaven. This presents a theological problem that had been ignored or scoffed at, at best, until very recently. Organized Western religion had no doctrinal authority or precedent. As a result, it was unable to offer solace to people mourning the death of even their companion animals. Emphasis needs to be placed again that the concept or word *pet* is not mentioned in the Bible or New Testament. Reference is made only to animals in general, with instruction that they should be treated with humane care. In effect, religion turned its back on this evolving theological problem and human need.

WHAT DOES THE BIBLE SAY?

In biblical times farm animals often shared the same shelter as their masters. But the harsh demands of survival required that even the most lovable of these animals first serve their utilitarian functions. Many were raised for slaughter, others for milking. Certain animals, especially their adorable young, must have elicited affection and some special regard from their masters and their families. We find constant instruction in the Old Testament for the humane treatment of animals. But the concept of companion animals that we have was still in the future, and the word "pet" did not yet exist. The first documented use of that term was made much later, about A.D. 1000.

All religions with a basis in fundamental interpretation of the Bible have no literal criteria to deal with anything concerning the subject of pets. Despite biblical interest in humane treatment of animals, until only very recently a pet's death seemed unworthy of religious consideration. Disappointingly, even at this time there are too many clergy who believe that only the life and death of humans should merit their involvement and concern. So where can the pet owner turn for spiritual help when a beloved animal dies?

With the recent increased awareness of this problem, concern is growing among a few modern spiritual leaders. Their responsibility includes caring for people when they are in deep distress. That now is logically extending to the legitimate, passionate question about the meaning of death for our pets, as well. Humans have a natural craving for some spiritual guidance and uplift, and this is a problem that demands attention. Fortunately, some of our more modern religious leaders are taking notice and are starting to do something positive.

WHAT RELIGION CAN OFFER US

What can organized religion now do to help deeply bereaving pet owners? Unfortunately, many people have felt abandoned by their faiths at this very critical time of their lives. They sought wisdom, solace, and counsel from their traditional source of spiritual support but they were turned away without any prospect of hope or help. Religious leaders could not offer anything better than generalizations. Some even dismissed the bereaver with a chastisement that they were thinking blasphemous things. But, where was their love and responsibility? As a result, many of these bereaving individuals turned away from religion to some degree because they felt bitter and painful resentment at being abandoned. A spiritual perspective is especially needed at this time.

When preparing this chapter, many telephone calls and visits were made, and letters were sent to leaders of the major religions of the world: Catholicism, Protestantism, Judaism, Buddhism, and Islam. After a while it became evident that those faiths based upon a fundamentalist point of view felt that they had nothing to say about the problem and refused to participate in this endeavor. It was also disappointing that the Catholic Archdiocese of New York suggested that this chapter be printed without their point of view because of their "time constraints." It seemed as if they didn't want to touch the issue at the time.

The following is presented with hope that these considerations offer you some spiritual guidance and uplift. Each gives its unique direction and perspective, proffering you with potential new ways for seeing and dealing with your bereavement.

THE JUDEO-CHRISTIAN PHILOSOPHY AND THE BUDDHIST VIEW

Judeo-Christian theology is based upon a God of love, who created all things lovingly. In Genesis, it is established that we are to care for the rest of God's creations, as stewards of the earth. He made a covenant with us to that effect. We are to have a loving relationship with all of His creations. We are obligated to treat them as lovingly as we can, as we know He does. That is part of our responsibility and what it means to be alive, here, created in God's image.

In the Old Testament, after the flood, God further revealed His intention concerning the Covenant, in Genesis 9:8-17: "And God spake unto Noah, and to his sons with him, saying, And I, behold, I establish my covenant with you, and with your seed after you; And with every living creature that is with you, of the fowl, of the cattle, and of every beast of the earth."

Later, in the New Testament, in Matthew: Verse 29, Jesus says "Are not two sparrows sold for a cent? And yet not one of them will fall to the ground apart from your Father." In this quotation, Jesus is saying that not even a sparrow can die apart from the notice and will of God. Unfortunately, the Covenant that God made with all living animals is something that seems to have been overlooked by us, only up until recently. Yet even today too many claim that only humans have souls, and can go to heaven. Why is this? There is no biblical support for such an attitude. If a sparrow dies and that is heeded by God, then certainly all other creatures—including our beloved pets—are blessed by this, as well.

In another translation of the story of Noah, we are told, "Behold, I establish my covenant with you, and your descendants after you, and with every living creature that is with you; the birds, the cattle and every beast of the earth with you. This is the sign of the covenant, which I make between Me and you and every living creature that is with you. For all future generations I set my rainbow in the cloud, and it shall be a sign of the covenant between me and the earth."

God's loving contract is not made exclusively with just humans, but with all living creatures. There is a kind of equality established that we must take into account. He has made us his stewards, and after centuries of disregard, religion is slowly taking up the contemporary issue of man's struggle to better understand his bereavement for a beloved pet. Some modern spiritual leaders have offered us their thoughts on this, for your consideration here.

THE JEWISH PERSPECTIVE

"While Judaism does not address itself specifically to the subject of the concern for or care of pets, it is deeply concerned about the humane treatment of all living things. In English, the principle would be called 'pain to living things.' Animals are a part of

God's creation. Humanity has a responsibility to protect them, to avoid bringing unnecessary pain to them, and to treat them without cruelty. Thus, we find a biblical prohibition against plowing with an ox and an ass together (Deut. xxii, 10), on the assumption that the ox, being stronger, would bring pain to the ass. Sabbath laws of rest also apply to the animal kingdom (Exod. xx, 10; Deut. v, 14). From an application of humane consideration it is even forbidden to slaughter an animal and its young on the same day (Lev. xxii, 28). This same concern is exhibited in such biblical laws as the ones demanding that an animal struggling under too heavy a load have the burden removed (Exod. xxiii, 5), and releasing the parent bird from the nest before taking the young (Deut. xxii, 67). Indications of this same consideration for the welfare of animals can be seen in such narrative tales as when the angel rebuked Balaam for beating his beast, an ass (Num. xxii, 23), and when God chastised Jonah for not having compassion for the residents of Ninevah, 'that great city, wherein are more than six score thousand persons . . . and also much cattle' (Jonah iv, 11).

"The rabbinic tradition expanded on the biblical compassion for all living things. One of the seven Noachian Laws (laws that were to be observed universally, not just by Jews) prohibits the eating of the flesh of a living animal. While the rabbis were not opposed to the killing of animals for food, that act had to be performed with the greatest of compassion and speed. It was regulated with strict detail. It was forbidden for a man to eat before he had fed and tended to his animals, and it was out of this same consideration for their welfare that 'a man is not permitted to buy animals unless he can properly provide for them.' The compassionate consideration for the welfare of animals, codified in Jewish law, also finds its expression in legendary material of the Jewish tradition. For example, it is said that Moses and David were considered fit to be leaders of Israel only after they had been shepherds.

"Out of this tradition, it is legitimate to extract an attitude of sympathetic response to the loss of a pet and to the tender

administration of a pet's remains. A pet, having brought joy to the life of its owner, is as deserving of loving care in death as it was in its lifetime. However, after its death and disposal, one is not expected to mourn excessively or become involved in bizarre or unnecessarily expensive practices, any more than such expressions would be tolerated after the death of a person.

"Death is a part of life, and after death and reasonable mourning, life is to continue normally as quickly as possible."

Rabbi Balfour Brickner
Senior Rabbi Emeritus
The Stephen Wise Free Synagogue
New York City

HONORING A LOVING RELATIONSHIP

Believers should consider their personal reaffirmation of the relationship between God and all of creation. If we, alone, are given the particular gift to understand this, then we have the responsibility to help bring it about. We must care for all other living things, as well. When any part of creation dies, we must treat it as lovingly as the Creator would. Whenever there is a death in any loving relationship, it must be dealt with in a respectful manner. That is in honor of the loving relationship, which is also God's.

We know how it feels to grieve over the loss of something we love. God's love is demonstrated through us. It is godly to grieve over the loss of a pet because He grieves over the loss of any life.

Our grief is terrible enough without self-imposed guilt. The necessary taking of a pet's life, by euthanasia, can upset the religious harmony within some people. Despite the dire and demanding circumstances, it could be felt that God's commandment, "Thou shalt not kill," may have been taken in vain. But if the act is truly one of mercy and compassion, then God's love is expressed in this performance of duty, and there should be no thought of sin and guilt. Clergy are fond of saying that they are doing God's work. And history is filled with fine examples of good people being called to do this, also.

This "mercy killing" falls into a special category, far from the otherwise sinful act of indifferent killing. We express God's love in preventing any further unavoidable pain and suffering, and actually bestow a personal blessing on the pet. This is, in effect, an intense act of love. Indeed, it is God's love expressed through us in a very disturbing and extreme private sacrifice. We must wrap ourselves in the beauty and love of that life, keep it with us and go on as better humans because of it. It does, however, still cause us untold grief.

The Christian point of view emphasizes resurrection and the life that comes out of death. It is taught that the God of creation is always making new life and new relationships. But it is important not to get mired in our grief. We must allow the remembrance and understanding of that love to give birth to new opportunities for us to grow and love. We can do this only when we travel through the painful valley of the shadow of death. We must come out of it. The grieving process must be lived through, from beginning to end. If not, we create trouble for our inner selves.

There is nothing in the scriptures that suggests that any living thing other than man has a soul. To wonder about this is a projection of our anthropomorphic fantasy, but we are confined to our limited human perspectives. It must also be said that there is nothing in the *scriptures that denies* the existence of a soul for any other creature of creation. We are just not privy to God's larger view of truth. Things are not as obvious as they seem, and many important meanings are hidden from us.

Much of the Bible's wisdom is expressed in parables and metaphors. Wisdom is derived from a diligent search for their interpretations. Talmudic scholars spend their lifetimes in this pursuit. The Creator made a covenant with the whole of the animal kingdom, including man as steward. There has always been a strong bond between many of us and our charges. We have come to know that there is a capacity for animals to love, and it is natural for us to wonder if they could possibly possess some spirituality unknown to us. One may easily conclude that there is some spiritual dimension to the life and death of other life forms in God's creation. But that would be a personal assumption.

THE HEREAFTER

We get solace from thinking about meeting again in some afterlife. Our earthly image of heaven is really a wonderful conceit—based on our very limited perceptions. We conceive of paradise in earthly forms, but that next level of existence is probably on such a greater dimension that it is nothing at all like what we know. What actual "appearance" that may have is probably well beyond our imagination and perception. But each of us gets pleasure and reassurance from imagining what it must look like. And that is good. The concept of a heaven is a metaphor of Oneness, a loving unity of all things with God. So whatever forms we envision can't really be wrong.

All earthly sentience transcends this life and becomes part of a great love and Oneness that is called God by many names. So if we hope to meet with our beloved deceased pet again, that can make a lot of sense. They are pure love, and that is what heaven is all about.

The human condition is one of passion, and this insatiable desire to know is very important, as an afterthought of our love for our pets. We pose the question as a reflection of the grief and urgency of today. We must live through the period of grief and mourning, affirming its value for now. But each of us must also be concerned with what is now done with the love for and from that pet—and how that love has improved his/her life. But in our minds, we tend to create hellish, as well as heavenly, conditions.

Most religions would affirm that the real question is how to accept and deal with the pain that comes from such a profound loss, resulting from the love of a pet. A funeral is all about putting away the body, saying goodbye to the physical form, and giving thanks for the spiritual. But since nothing is known about the spiritual dimensions of the animal kingdom as well, many religions still do not officially sanction such considerations or services for them. There are many possible liturgies that can be used in the death of a pet, without getting involved with official religious approval. We can write them ourselves, or even find some fine examples in many books starting to come out on this subject.

St. Francis of Assisi (1182–1226) was a lover of creation. He felt that we are all part of nature and are interrelated. We are one with all of creation. He understood the Creator's love to encompass all living things, including man. He believed that God, man, and nature were all part of the same truth. And a growing number of modern clerics are now beginning to incorporate these considerations into their regular services. Perhaps it was not such a coincidence that Christ was born in a manger, surrounded by animals. Nobody has ever given that much serious consideration. Possibly there is a profound metaphor and lesson in this, as well.

SOME EPISCOPAL REFLECTIONS

"For people of faith, especially of the Judeo-Christian traditions, creation is the living act of a loving God. And for those persons who have special relationships with various members of the animal kingdom, it is important to understand the creatures of this world, big and small, as wonderful manifestations of that creative act. That which is before us, after us, above us, below us, beyond us, within us; that Mother/Father of all life is called by many different names, yet experienced by a majority of the human beings of this earth as that one true origin of all life. Plant, animal, or human, no matter what the name of the child, one must wonder if it is truly possible for the Mother/Father to care more for one than another. Can the love of the Creator for that which is created be unequally given? I think not, if I am to trust my own feelings as a parent, and am a product of the Creator's will. ('Let us make man in Our image.' Gen. i, 26.)

"The Judeo-Christian tradition leads me and many others to believe in God's love for all living things. It also reminds people of our role as stewards of that creation, of all living things. Therefore, we are to act lovingly to all life, as would God.

"It is natural to grieve; it is the loss of that which is love. Again and again, scripture reminds us that God grieved and still grieves for that which is created, when it is no longer truly alive. So it is not only natural but right that, created in God's image, we too grieve when life is lost, any life—all life. It is natural and right to grieve over the loss of a pet that we loved, as God loves. Would the God of love expect anything less of us? I think not.

"There are those who ask the question, 'Do animals have souls like ours, and will they be with us in an afterlife?' In a loss situation this question is best heard as an expression of the deep love for that which is lost in death. It is not so important to search for the answer to that which only God knows, as to trust

*that which God loved is always under God's care. We, as a peo-
ple of faith, are our own proof of this comforting truth."*

*Reverend Canon Joel A. Gibson
Subdean, The Cathedral Church of
St. John the Divine
New York City*

A UNITARIAN-UNIVERSALIST PERSPECTIVE

*"In the statement of Principles and Purposes of the Unitarian
Universalist Association we affirm the inherent worth and dignity of every person, and the interdependent web of existence,
of which we are a part.*

*"In the first of these two affirmations, Unitarian
Universalism tells us that each one of us has the freedom to
decide what is true and right for herself or himself, and the
responsibility to act according to these beliefs. In the second we
are reminded that what is true and right for each of us must take
into account our place in the interdependent web. Both principles can guide us when we are with one who is grieving over the
loss of a beloved pet.*

*"Humans and animals are part of this web—and it is a spe-
cial strand of love and companionship that links pet and pet
owner. Pets are important life companions. They take us out of
ourselves by calling us to respond to them, watch them, engage
with them. They demand of us responsibility, that we attend to
their needs with care. They give to us joy in life, a different perspective, a relief from loneliness, along with their love.*

*"When that connecting strand is broken—when a pet dies—
the resulting feelings of loss are real and significant. And, in that
moment, we must attend to the brokenness, guided by the principle of inherent worth and dignity. The person who is grieving
knows what the loss means for him or her. And this is the starting point. In our respect for them we can participate in acknowl-
edging the reality of the loss, affirming the feelings of bereavement, of emptiness, in remembering the happy moments, and in
learning to say goodbye.*

"In the spirit of earth-centered religious traditions, we take time to honor and acknowledge our animal brothers and sisters with whom we share this planet. In the tradition of St. Francis we set aside a time to bless the animals who are part of our lives. We find ways to celebrate the intertwining of these strands of life. And so it is fitting that we also take time and find ways to mourn the loss and share the grief that the death of a pet brings."

—Reverend Dr. Tracy Robinson-Harris
Unitarian Universalist
Community Church of New York

Eastern philosophy and religious practice has always offered enriched perspectives to the traditional Western ways of looking at things. Although there are many differing sects in Buddhism—Zen being the best known—they all follow the basic teachings of Buddha, each with some variation. In its fascinating wisdom, the viewpoint offered here can offer hope to the bereaving pet owner.

A ZEN BUDDHIST PERSPECTIVE

"Being human, we love. Healthy love—caring deeply for another—is good. It brings richness and fulfillment to our lives. Yet the object of our love must eventually die, for all things are transitory. Impermanence is a natural law or truth of the universe. All things are in a constant state of change—of becoming.

"The Buddha taught that all things that are born are subject to the laws of causation and impermanence. All living beings must grow older, experience sickness and infirmities, and ultimately must die. This is true not only of living beings but of the many other 'beings', as well. Mountains, rivers, stars, and even the universe, are all in the process of growing old. All will eventually cease to exist.

"A monk once asked a Zen Master, 'What is the fundamental constant principle?' The Master said, 'Moving.'

"If all things are subject to this natural law, why do we, as humans, struggle so in the face of our own death, and those we love? The other living creatures of the world seem able to live, experience the challenges of life, and die with equanimity. We

see this most clearly perhaps with our beloved pets. As they age and grow infirm, or suffer from illness or accident, they seem to accept these changes with ease. The cat continues to purr when her ears are stroked; the dog still wags his tail when his back is scratched. Why is it so difficult for us to accept the constant flux within life and death as a natural aspect of our humanity?

"In the Buddha's enlightenment, he realized that the cause of our suffering is based in our attachments and grasping at things. In trying to hold on to something good we want to fix it in time and space. We would like to preserve this feeling of love, or this creature, or our relationship with it, forever—or at least for as long as possible. Yet everything is in flux, and nothing remains the same, even from one moment to the next. So as things change according to the nature of causation, we tend to struggle against that change. This can reach a peak with the ultimate change that comes with the death of an animal that we have known, loved and lived with for many years. In death, we cannot turn away from the loss of what we have been trying to preserve. In death, the fragile, precious and transient nature of life—including our own—comes starkly into the front of our consciousness.

"It is natural to have feelings of sadness and grief when we lose a loved one. Let's investigate how our naturally arising feelings of sadness transform into a more debilitating experience of suffering through our attachments. When grief arises, if we can recognize it, in our mind then when the crushing wave of feeling has eased we can let it go and return to the present moment— the place where our own life is taking place. If the feelings of grief are too strong to let go of, then we can still allow them to be present, and bear witness to them without being overwhelmed by them. With time they will soften and fade, allowing us to let them go more easily. If we are in a highly emotional state we may have difficulty observing our thoughts and feelings in this way. Instead, we may find ourselves being drawn into these emotions and losing all awareness of what is happening. When this happens, we can try to notice what we are feeling and open our awareness so we can maintain this awareness.

"Why is this important? When we become attached to or mired in those feelings, then that simple memory or feeling becomes imprisoned within us and begins to tear at us and create unnecessary misery. It's also important to observe how we personally respond to our loss, either by actively holding on to those feelings, or by pushing them away, denying or trying to ignore them. In either case, we are fighting against our grief and ourselves, and are essentially refusing to accept the reality of this present moment. The result is what follows any conflict—more grief. Learning to be at peace with loss, as with any moment, begins with understanding that equanimity comes not from satisfying our desires, but from being intimate with our life—and death—moment after moment. This intimacy arises from being fully present and aware to our world both internally and externally.

"Many may feel that if they let go of the feelings of sadness rather than cling to them, they will in some way be dishonoring the memory of their loved one. On the contrary, it is in holding on that we trap both them and ourselves. Death is a time for letting go. We must let go of the deceased so they can be free in death. We must let go of our feelings of loss, so we can be free in life. What better way to honor the life and memory of someone we love."

Geoffrey Shugen Arnold
Zen Mountain Monastery
Mount Tremper, New York

As the reader already well knows, there is no simple or single answer to our questions. But the collected wisdom of the ages should be of assistance in our search. This chapter is designed to lend some spiritual perspective to the bereaved person, regardless of what religion he or she elects to observe—or not observe. One may well be an agnostic, yet believe that there is some sort of all-pervading and unifying force within the cosmos. However this may be perceived, it offers reassurance, which is the balm and nourishment we need at this critical time. That is a great gift to us, and it should be used to improve our ongoing lives.

Whether we call it religion or any other word, our search for spiritual values and help is a prime factor in our existence on this plane. Especially during bereavement each person's personal odyssey is integral to his or her deeply personal sense of self and continued growth.

It is hoped that the viewpoints presented in this chapter offer some help in this search. The continuity of life is all around us. As a part of that, in time each of us can help ourselves grow better in our own renewing lives.

◈

ALL PETS GO TO HEAVEN

Can you imagine a heaven without pets?

There is a very special place where beloved pets go after they die. This is only a temporary location. But there are trees and grass and lakes and everything they love. Here they can play and eat and sleep, even better than they did before they died. Now there are no aches or worries or dangers of any kind to trouble or threaten them. The only joy missing is their beloved human companion, you.

All health is restored completely, and all injuries are healed. Dogs and cats play and are at peace with each other, and they do not feel lonely for you. They miss you, but with the special wisdom that animals have, they trust that this condition will get better. And they confidently wait as they frolic.

A wonderful day will come for each of them, when in the middle of their peace, they will suddenly feel something is different. And all their senses will peak at the height of excitement and exuberance. They will sniff the air and look off in the distance where they recognize that dearly loved, very special presence. Then they will call out in elation and, with eyes shining and tail going wild, tear off at a full gallop, almost flying over the green grass.

Your expected eventual arrival has been sensed, and now there is nothing that can keep the two of you apart ever again. As you run toward each other, the tears jump from your eyes. Your pet leaps into your arms, and you cling together in jubilant reunion. The joyous kisses rain on your face, and you kiss back just as ecstatically. Your hands so lovingly caress once more the beloved fur, the head and neck and body you knew so well. And you look into each other's loving eyes and know that now everything is put aright.

And then something will call the both of you on to a different field of warmth and nurture, where all the love you knew now comes to fruition. With your pet, you leave that special waiting area, pass into the main part of heaven, and begin a new existence there, together.

If you accept that pets can love us as much as we love them, then the logic is clear and cannot be denied. If you believe that there is a heaven for people, then they must also be there, waiting for us, when we cross over. Heaven is love, and pets will always share that with us.

This was written by Wallace Sife in the early 1970s for the California Dog's Club newsletter. It has since appeared as many forms, ascribed to an anonymous author.

"Our soldier's friend."   *Photo by W. Sife. Courtesy of Hamilton Pet Meadow, Memorial Park and Crematory*

CHAPTER 17

Some

Practical

Suggestions

Build thee more stately mansions, O my soul!

—Oliver Wendell Holmes

*I*n concluding this book, it is fitting to list some practical suggestions that have been gleaned over years of experience. Not all of them may seem right or timely for you, but most will. Whatever you choose to do at this time of extreme heartache is very private and not to be judged by anyone else. The only thing that should be criticized is inaction to help yourself. Your pet would have wanted you to heal yourself as quickly and well as you could. These suggestions will help you do that:

1. Find sympathetic and supportive people, and let your feelings out. Cry. Don't hold back. Your emotions have to come out. After that, the pain and confusion will start to get sorted out. If you suppress your feelings, that will only delay the healing and mourning processes. Sometimes it is advisable to allow yourself some sort of personal indulgence to loosen up. If you

In memory of all those who have gone before us and remain in our hearts and minds.

Photo by W. Sife. Courtesy of Hartsdale Canine Cemetery, Inc.

drink liquor, take a little wine or other spirit. Drink a toast to your beloved pet and its memory. Share this with others, but don't overindulge.

2. Write a letter or will from your pet to yourself. Do this over several sittings, and constantly update it. Keep this as a permanent memory. You may be amazed at how much this reveals to you about yourself. Years later this will become a very valuable personal reminder.

3. Dedicate something in your pet's name and memory. Donations to worthy causes are very appropriate. Usually gifts that require a plaque or permanent label give great satisfaction. If your pet was a show animal, then donating a memorial trophy to a pet club is very gratifying. Humane organizations will appreciate a donation in your pet's name and memory.

4. It is never too late to say something to your deceased pet. Over a period of time, compose a log of all the loving memories you have of your pet. Constantly amend this list. Then write a letter to your pet, remembering all these intimate smiles and tears. Keep this as part of your loving goodbye in this life. But remember, these memories live on forever with you, so something of your beloved pet will never die and leave you. Letting go of the pain does not mean that you are letting go of the cherished memories. This list and log will take on added value with time.

5. Make an audio recording of yourself, reading these memories and saying whatever emotional, private things you feel. Listen to it a few times during your mourning, and add to it whenever it feels right. Keep this as a permanent part of your personal memorial to your beloved pet. You may be surprised at how effective this is when you play it back.

6. At home, establish new routines. Change or vary the old ones. (We fall into the usual emotional responses when we follow old patterns.) Deliberately do things in a changed order as soon as you get up in the morning. At home, try sitting in a different chair or place on the couch. Try new things, such as rearranging your furniture. Work, shop, meditate, attend social functions, walk, jog, run, bike, and partake in special events, sports, or concerts with other people. Exercise and physical activity help reduce depression and help promote emotional healing. Most importantly, start meeting with people again. Avoid being alone too often.

7. Invite friends, relatives or good neighbors to visit you in your home. Visit other pet owners and their pets. Return (with company?) to some of the sites you shared with your

pet. This will help you accept how separate the past is from
the present. Embrace resolution and "closure" with your
loving memories, knowing that you can keep your remembrances without their fading in the future. As time goes on,
they become even more enriched.

8. Treat yourself to things you would have liked, but couldn't
    or wouldn't do before your pet's death. Imagine his/her
    spirit advising you how to ease your pain. Do some enjoy-
    able things—with your pet's blessings. Certainly you
    deserve them. As soon as you can, go on a trip or vacation.
    If it appealed to you before, now is the right time to seri-
    ously consider relocating or changing your job.

9. Avoid keeping *many* conspicuous reminders of your grief.
    One by one, get rid of your pet's toys and other things that
    you may have wanted to keep as mementos. They are
    mostly painful and not good for you at this time. If you
    can't throw them out yet, then store them out of sight in a
    drawer or a box in a closet or basement. When you are
    ready, they could make a fine gift an animal shelter. The
    real memory is in your heart. You don't need to rely on
    items to remind you of your love and years together.

    Don't make it hard to recover. Give yourself permission
    to heal. Embrace your memories and strong feelings. Share
    them with people who understand, but don't get morbid.

10. Go to pet bereavement group support sessions and tell your
    feelings to others who are undergoing the same misery.
    When you feel their tears, you will realize you are not alone.

11. As soon as you can, talk to your veterinarian. Make a list,
    in advance, of any questions or doubts you may have about
    your pet's death. This will prevent you from forgetting
    items while you are still experiencing strong emotions.
    This planned conversation should clear up any possible
    doubts about everything.

    Such a meeting should be warm and informational. Do
    not abuse it as a means to vent anger at your pet's doctor or
    staff. Ask his or her advice about any special problems or
    questions that have been bothering you. Veterinarians have

had considerable experience with other clients who have been through this. They may be able to offer you some practical information. Usually, most veterinarians try to stay clear of individual bereavements unless they are asked for advice. Keep in mind, however, that a vet is a medical authority, but not a trained counselor.

12.   In advance, unless there is an emergency, avoid the administration of euthanasia on special calendar dates such as birthdays or anniversaries. This could be upsetting in the future. Prevent yourself from linking unhappy associations with happy ones.

13.   Learn to understand and respect your own mourning. If your grief is intense, take some time off from work. Tell your employer that there has been a death in your immediate family. This certainly is true. Most employers provide a specific brief leave for this. Don't try to explain or give excuses. Even if you are prodded to say who died, you don't have to tell. Just say it is very personal, and walk away. Be firm and insistent, but not confrontational. Assert yourself at this time. You deserve it. If you cannot get any time off, at least you tried. If you still really feel you need it, take the time off without pay. Most likely, you will be respected for this, not criticized. But, be prepared; that may not always be the case at your place of employment.

14.   When you are ready, visit an animal shelter to look around—not to adopt. You have to be firm with yourself about this. It will help you in many ways if you write down your feelings after this visit and read them again later. What new thoughts or feelings are stimulated by this visit? Don't give in to any sudden impulses to adopt any of the animals you see there. If such a response remains with you, go back a second time and see if you still feel that way.

15.   Hold some sort of private service for your beloved pet. You will have wonderful, permanent memories of this. Only friends and family who would appreciate such a ceremony should be invited. Children definitely should be helped to feel they are a basic part of the family in planning and

carrying out such a ceremony. This is a very positive activity that could to be one of the healthiest parts of your mourning process. A private service will help you better understand your underlying feelings. It need not be of any traditional religious nature. Its purpose is to express your own personal spiritual values in a loving retrospective. Be careful not to invite anyone who is not sympathetic to your mourning. If you like, a few words from some of those people present, followed by your eulogy, should be sufficient—that is up to you. This will almost assuredly help you through the worst parts of your grief and healing process. Such a ceremony will enrich you and become an important part of your loving memories.

16. List your major thoughts and feelings, but keep it brief. If you feel that you want to write at length on the subject, do that separately. Perhaps that could be the basis for an interesting magazine article, essay or short story. Such a journal will become a treasured part of your memorial to your pet. It will also be of great personal value to you in gaining insight and objectivity into your own thoughts and feelings. (Later, reading parts of it to others in bereavement for a beloved pet might offer hope and comfort to them, as well.)

17. Make a list of the smart and funny things your pet did that used to make you laugh or smile. Add to it as often as you can, even if it takes weeks. Review the items. When you can share these good memories, laughs, and tears, read them to someone who has been supportive during your mourning.

   This is part of your healing. It is good medicine. With many healing tears, you will be happier and stronger after each reading of the list. Put it away and keep it forever, along with photographs and other memorabilia. You will treasure reading these precious memories in the future. This is an excellent and very loving memorial, as well.

18. Don't live the life of a hermit or of one who is atoning. Mourning pain is normal and inevitable, but extended misery is optional. We can help ourselves with that. Give yourself permission to heal. Feeling better is not disrespectful to the memory of your beloved pet. Get out of the house. Go to a movie or museum. Fight the depression, and don't allow yourself to feel you are a victim of circumstances. Turn on the television, instead of sitting in a silent room. Expose yourself to distractions and possible pleasure again. This is life. You deserve it.

19. If you get a new pet, tell it bedtime stories about your beloved one who died. This will bring tears, but they will also be healing tears. This storytelling will be a living memorial. And it also will help the bonding for the both of you. This can also be done with pets in the household who were already there.

20. If possible, make a memorial garden spot. There are good books that can help you better plan this. Planting a tree or other beautiful symbolic plant life can be a wonderful living memorial.

21. Visit the website of the Association for Pet Loss and Bereavement (APLB) at www.aplb.org.

These suggestions can be of great assistance for helping yourself. Be assured that from the very start of your bereavement your love and tender memories will live on with you. The pain will diminish as a sense of resolution or closure starts to transform it into cherished memories. In letting go of one thing, you are reaching out and grasping something else that is very precious. And that will never leave you. It will enrich and bless you, as you go on in your life and personal evolution.

"Gift of Love Memorial"—testimony to many pets that enriched their owners' lives.

Photo by W. Sife. Courtesy of Abbey Glen Pet Memorial Park

Memorial to fire dogs. *Photo by George Wirt. Courtesy of Bide-A-Wee*

Resources

> But if the while I think on thee, dear friend,
> All losses are restored and sorrows end.

> —"Sonnet number 30," William Shakespeare

S everal different kinds of resources are available to the bereaving pet owner. There are support groups, emergency telephone hotlines, pet bereavement counselors, legal counselors, pet cemeteries, crematories, funeral parlors, and online websites and chat rooms. Since the availability of all of these keeps changing, we list only aftercare services for pets here. Counseling centers and emergency hotlines are listed in chapter 15, "Supportive Counseling." To view a full, updated listing of all the different resources, go the website of the Association for Pet Loss and Bereavement (APLB) www.aplb.org.

AFTERCARE SERVICES

Pet Cemeteries, Crematories, and Funeral Parlors

There are many pet cemeteries, crematories, and funeral parlors, and it is logical that they have formed a specialized professional association to represent themselves. The International Association of Pet Cemeteries (IAOPC) will be glad to assist you in answering questions and choosing one of their members. They can be reached at (800) 952-5541.

Some of the aftercare facilities listed below are not IAOPC members, but they are all listed here for your convenience. For possible additional facilities, it is advisable to look in your local Yellow Pages under "Pet Cemeteries," or other similar listings. All the Internet search engines such as Google and Yahoo also have many listings under this category. In addition, you can find a constantly updated list on the website of the Association for Pet Loss and Bereavement: www.aplb.org. Click on their Aftercare Page link.

When choosing a cemetery or crematory, the following list is only offered as a general guide. Keep in mind that it will become outdated as soon as this book is printed. After finally finding one it is essential for the prospective client to make a reasonable analysis and inspection of the property, operation, and legal protections that should be available. It is strongly advised to do this first to avoid any possible disappointments later. This is the last thing we do for a beloved pet, and it must be done right.

UNITED STATES

Location	Name	Phone Number
ALABAMA		
BIRMINGHAM	Alabama Pet Cemetery	(205) 870-5010
COTTONDALE	Loving Companion Pet Cemetery and Monument Co.	(205) 554-0670
FAIRHOPE	Fairhope Pet Cemetery	(251) 928-2603
SPRINGVILLE	Pets At Peace	(205) 467-7695
ALASKA		
ANCHORAGE	Harthaven Pet Crematory	(907) 563-1801
ANCHORAGE	Pet Cremations	(907) 274-5637
SOLDOTNA	Twin Cities Pet Cremation Service	(907) 562-2999

LOCATION	NAME	PHONE NUMBER
ARIZONA		
KINGMAN	Griffith Pet Cremation Services	(928) 757-7869
PAYSON	Lynn Andrew	(520) 472-8063
PHOENIX	Pals, Inc.	(602) 455-6677
SUN CITY	Sunland Pet Rest	(602) 933-0161
TUCSON	The Pet Cemetery of Tucson	(520) 566-4242
ARKANSAS		
HEBER SPRINGS	Pet Cremation Services	(501) 831-4562 (Little Rock number)
HOT SPRINGS	Pet Lawn	(501) 623-7078
LITTLE ROCK	Pet Land Memorial Park	(501) 565-1619
MAYFLOWER	4R Pets - Pet Cremation Services	(501) 470-0403 or (501) 733-3351
ROGERS	Rest Haven Pet Cemetery	(479) 636-3738
CALIFORNIA		
ALTADENA	Faithful Friends Pet Cemetery at Mountain View	(626) 794-7133
CALABASAS	Los Angeles Pet Memorial Park	(818) 591-7037
COLMA	Pet Rest Cemetery	(650) 755-2201
HEMET	Circle of Life Crematorium	(800) 791-0906
MERCED	Franklyn Pet Cemetery	(209) 383-4582
NAPA	Bubbling Well Pet Memorial Park	(707) 255-3456

UNITED STATES *(continued)*

LOCATION	NAME	PHONE NUMBER
CALIFORNIA		
PETUMA	My Pet's Cemetery	(707) 762-6743
ROYAL OAKS	Monterey Bay Memorial Park	(831) 722-8722
SACRAMENTO	Sierra Hills Pet Cemetery	(916) 732-2037
SAN DIEGO	AA Sorrento Valley Pet Cemetery	(619) 276-3361
SAN DIEGO	San Diego Pet Memorial Park	(858) 909-0009
WHITTIER	Sycamore Canyon Pet Memorial	(562) 692-1212
COLORADO		
COMMERCE CITY	Denver Pet Cemetery	(303) 288-0177
EVERGREEN	Evergreen Memorial Park, Inc.	(303) 674-7750
GRAND JUNCTION	Final Paws	(970) 242-7417
PUEBLO	Roselawn Cemetery Association	(719) 542-2934
CONNECTICUT		
BETHANY	Keystone Memorial Park	(203) 393-3126
GAYLORDSVILLE	Balmoral Pet Cemetery	(860) 354-3433
GLASTONBURY	Forest Rest Memorial Park	(203) 659-0784
NORWALK	Harperlawn Pet Memorial Gardens	(203) 846-3360
WESTBROOK	Trail's End Pet Crematory	(203) 399-5420

LOCATION	NAME	PHONE NUMBER
DELAWARE		
MIDDLETOWN	Abendblum Crematory	(302) 378-8400
WILMINGTON	Delaware Pet Cremations	(302) 322-9749
FLORIDA		
APOPKA	Greenbriar Memory Gardens for Pets	(407) 886-2620
BELLEVIEW	Central Florida Pet Cemetery and Crematory	(352) 307-2256
GAINSVILLE	Garden of Love Memorial Park	(352) 373-4252
GREEN COVE SPRINGS	Plumtree Pet Services	(904) 284-5700
INDIANTOWN	Twin Oaks Pet Cemetery	(651) 597-5270
KISSIMMEE	Trail's End Pet Crematory	(407) 396-6385
LAUREL	Driftwood Pet Memorial Gardens	(813) 485-6672
MIAMI	Oaklawn Pet Cemetery	(305) 696-0800
MIAMI	Pet Heaven Memorial Park, Inc.	(305) 223-6515
OKEECHOBEE	Twin Oaks Pet Cemetery and Crematoriums	(941) 467-6377 or (877) 332-3738
ORLANDO	ALL Crematory	(407) 886-0777
PENSACOLA	Gulf Coast Pet Crematory	(850) 437-9639
PENSACOLA	Pet Cremation Network	(850) 477-2563
PINELLAS PARK	Pinellas Memorial Pet Cemetery	(813) 544-1051
PLANTATION	Broward Pet Cemetery	(305) 476-0743
TALLAHASSEE	Laurie Daynon Affiliates	(904) 877-6053

UNITED STATES *(continued)*

LOCATION	NAME	PHONE NUMBER
GEORGIA		
ATLANTA	Atlanta Pet Cemetery & Crematory	(770) 333-3332
CHAMBLEE	Deceased Pet Care / Oakrest Pet Gardens	(770) 457-7659
SAVANNAH	Savannah Pet Cemetery	(912) 233-3767
SNELLVILLE	Pet Cremations of Georgia	(770) 985-9898
WATKINSVILLE	Memory Gardens for Pets	(706) 769-7386
HAWAII		
KAILUA	Oahu Pet Crematory	(808) 371-7531
KANEOHE	Valley of the Temples Pet Memorial	(808) 239-8811
IDAHO		
BOISE	Pet Haven Memorial Gardens	(208) 342-3938
MERIDIAN	Memorial Pet Care	(208) 887-7669
SANDPOINT	Celebration Forest	(877) 245-7378
ILLINOIS		
BLOOMINGTON	Faithful Friends Memory Gardens	(309) 828-8424
CARY	Fawnwoods of Windridge Memorial Park	(847) 639-3883
CHICAGO	Illinois Pet Cemetery	(773) 549-1154
COLLINSVILLE	Herr Funeral Homes	(618) 344-0187
JOLIET	Kozy Acres Pet Cemetery	(815) 723-9588
LEXINGTON	Bluegrass Pet Crematorium	(847) 639-3883

Location	Name	Phone Number
ILLINOIS		
MELROSE PARK	Chez Paw Gardens	(708) 343-7896
MONEE	Evergreen Pet Cemetery	(708) 534-5700
MURPHYSBORO	Pleasant Grove Memorial Park	(618) 687-2500
ROCKFORD	Arlington Pet Cemetery	(815) 399-5011
ROMEOVILLE	Forest Crematory	(800) 452-1957
SPRINGFIELD	Kirlin-Egan and Butler Funeral	(217) 544-4646 or (877) 724-6381
VERNON HILLS	Aarowood Pet Cemetery	(847) 634-3787
WEST CHICAGO	Paw Print Gardens	(630) 231-1117
WILLOWBROOK	Hinsdale Animal Cemetery	(630) 323-5120
WOOD DALE	St. Francis Pet Crematory	(630) 766-3646
INDIANA		
BLOOMINGTON	Precious Memories Pet Gardens	(812) 824-3950
EATON	Union Cemetery Association	(317) 396-3177
INDIANAPOLIS	Memory Gardens Cemetery for Pets	(317) 895-0955
MOUNT VERNON	Peaceful Pets Cemetery	(812) 838-0811
SALEM	The Farm Pet Cemetery	(812) 967-2119
IOWA		
BOONE	Boone County Humane Society Affiliates	(515) 432-8985
TIPTON	Pet Memories	(319) 886-3128
URBANDALE	Loving Rest Pet Cemetery	(515) 278-4230

UNITED STATES *(continued)*

Location	Name	Phone Number
KANSAS		
TOPEKA	Hope Mount Cemetery	(913) 272-1122
TOPEKA	Pet Lawn Memorial Gardens	(913) 478-4925
WHITING	Meadowlark Pet Cemetery	(913) 873-3568
WICHITA	All Pets Crematory	(316) 832-1500
WICHITA	Dog-Voted Pet Cemetery	(316) 733-1631
KENTUCKY		
LEXINGTON	Bluegrass Pet Crematorium	(859) 258-2052
LOUISIANA		
BREAUX BRIDGE	Mickey Bassford Affiliates	(202) 544-3960
HARVEY	Agee's Pet Crematorium	(504) 362-3311
METAIRIE	Heaven's Pets	(504) 835-9188
PRAIRIEVILLE	Pet Memorial Gardens	(225) 673-8991
SLIDELL	Unforgettable Pets Crematory	(985) 639-3393
MAINE		
EAST EDDINGTON	Blueberry Ridge	(207) 843-5331
ENFIELD	Wildwood Pet Cremations	(207) 732-5483
LITCHFIELD	Fluke's Aftercare Pet Cremation Services	(207) 268-2912
MARYLAND		
BARNESVILLE	Sugarloaf Pet Gardens	(301) 972-8555
ELKTON	Family Pet Cremations	(410) 996-8883
FREDERICK	Resthaven Memorial Gardens	(301) 848-7177

Location	Name	Phone Number
MARYLAND		
SILVER SPRING	Aspin Hill Memorial Park & Pet Cemetery	(301) 871-6700
TIMONIUM	Dulaney Pet Haven	(301) 666-0495
WALDORF	Friendship Pet Memorial Park	(301) 843-2651
WILLIAMSPORT	Valley Pet Cemetery	(301) 582-3320
MASSACHUSETTS		
DEDHAM	Pine Ridge Pet Cemetery	(781) 326-0729
METHUEN	Hillside Acre Pet Cemetery	(978) 687-1140
MIDDLEBORO	Angel View Pet Cemetery	(508) 947-4103
NEW BEDFORD	Donna M. Marks Affiliates	(508) 985-9607
PLYMOUTH	Pleasant Mountain Pet Rest & Crematory	(508) 746-5550
MICHIGAN		
BYRON CENTER	Sleepy Hollow Pet Cemetery	(616) 538-6050
DIMONDALE	Country Meadows Pet Cemetery	(517) 646-8043
GRAND RAPIDS	Noah's Gardens Pet Cemetery / Mortuary	(616) 949-1390
KALAMAZOO	Precious Pets	(616) 399-7387
TAYLOR	AAA Dog & Cat Cemetery	(743) 946-5555
YPSILANTI	Whispering Pines Pet Cemetery	(734) 547-0083
MISSISSIPPI		
COLUMBUS	Countryside Pet Cemetery	(601) 328-4384
JACKSON	Pet Paradise	(601) 366-2000

UNITED STATES *(continued)*

LOCATION	NAME	PHONE NUMBER
MISSOURI		
BRIDGETON	Order of the Golden Rule	(314) 209-7142
JOPLIN	Agape Pet Cremations	(417) 782-8498
KANSAS CITY	Rolling Acres Memorial Gardens for Pets	(816) 891-8888
KANSAS CITY	Peaceful Meadow	(816) 761-8151
MONTANA		
BILLINGS	Yellowstone Valley Memorial Park	(406) 252-3024
BOZEMAN	All Paws Great & Small Pet Crematory, Inc.	(406) 582-0705
BUTTE	Bill & Micki Best Affiliate	(406) 494-7942
NEBRASKA		
LINCOLN	Rolling Acres Complex	(402) 483-7001
OMAHA	Tully's Pet Cemetery	(402) 397-3077
NEVADA		
CARSON CITY	Carson City Pet Cemetery	(702) 887-2171
LAS VEGAS	Craig Road Pet Cemetery	(702) 645-1112
LAS VEGAS	Pet Cremation Services	(702) 683-9941
PAHRUMP	Pet Cremation Services	(775) 727-0920
NEW HAMPSHIRE		
HOLLIS	Animal Heaven	(603) 465-2577
KEENE	Final Journey Animal Aftercare	(603) 357-2020
NASHUA	Proctor Animal Cemetery	(603) 889-2275
NORTHFIELD	Birch Hill Kennels Crematorium	(603) 286-3901

Location	Name	Phone Number
NEW JERSEY		
BERLIN	Pet Lawn Memorial Park	(856) 767-1564
HAMILTON	Hamilton Pet Meadow	(609) 586-9660
LAFAYETTE	Abbey Glen Pet Memorial Park	(800) 972-3118 or (973) 579-2171
TRENTON	Precious Funerals For Pets	(609) 989-7494
NEW MEXICO		
ALBUQUERQUE	Best Friends Pet Cremation Service	(505) 345-5615
ALBUQUERQUE	Albuquerque Pet Memorial Services	(505) 550-4793
NEW YORK		
ALBANY	Memory's Garden	(518) 355-4030
BERLIN	Pet Lawn Memorial Park	(609) 767-1564
BROOKLYN	All Pets Go To Heaven Funeral Home	(718) 875-7877
ELLENBURG DEPOT	Drownwood Forest Pet Cemetery	(518) 594-7500
ELMIRA	Best Friends Pet Cemetery, Inc.	(607) 734-8754
HARTSDALE	Hartsdale Pet Cemetery	(914) 949-2583
HUNTINGTON	Sheltervale Pet Cemetery	(631) 368-8770
HYDE PARK	Faithful Companion Pet Memorial Park	(914) 452-1654
LATHAM	Rolling Acres Pet Cemetery	(518) 785-8305
MIDDLE ISLAND	Regency Forest Pet Memorial Park	(516) 345-0600

UNITED STATES *(continued)*

LOCATION	NAME	PHONE NUMBER
NEW YORK		
MONTGOMERY	Abbingdon Hill Pet Cemetery	(845) 361-2200
SOMERS	Garden of St. Francis Pet Columbarium	(914) 277-3122
STEPHENTOWN	Breezy Nook Pet Crematory	(518) 733-5488
SYRACUSE	Pet Haven Cemetery	(315) 469-1212
UTICA	My Pet Memorial Park	(315) 732-8440
WEST BABYLON	Pet Crematory Agency, Inc.	(631) 293-2929 or (718) 234-3653
WEST RUSH	Rush Inter Pet Cemetery & Crematory	(585) 533-1685
WEST SENECA	Pine Rest Pet Cemetery	(716) 674-9470
NORTH CAROLINA		
ASHEVILLE	Forever Friends Pet Memorial Gardens & Cremation Center	(828) 281-0005
JAMESTOWN	St. Francis Pet Cemetery	(336) 887-1442
NEW BERN	Lynaire Crematory	(252) 633-6225
RALEIGH	Pet Rest Cemetery	(919) 596-3895
WEST END	Good Shepard	(910) 673-2200
NORTH DAKOTA		
MINOT	Country Meadows Pet Cemetery	(701) 852-6379
WILLISTON	Eagle View Pet Cemetery	(701) 875-4278

Location	Name	Phone Number
OHIO		
COLUMBUS	Pet Cremation Services	(614) 272-6550
COLUMBUS	Schoedinger Pet Crematory	(614) 224-6105
CRIDERSVILLE	Bayliff & Son Pet Crematory	(419) 645-6700
FINDLAY	Coldren Crates Funeral Home	(419) 422-2323
GRAFTON	Western Farm Pet Crematory & Cemetery	(440) 748-1716
GROVE CITY	Pet Cremation Services	(614) 272-6550
LEBANON	Pines Pet Cemetery	(513) 932-2270
MIAMISBURG	Robert T. Bell Affiliates	(937) 866-2444
NAVARRE	Woodside Pet Cemetery	(216) 484-3378
ONTARIO	Angel Refuge Pet Cemetery	(419) 529-2229
PICKERINGTON	Veterinary Cremation Services	(614) 837-0947
PROCTORVILLE	Rome Pet Cemetery	(740) 886-9888
RICHFIELD	Paws Awhile Pet Memorial Park	(216) 659-4270
WHITEHOUSE	Karnik Memorial Gardens	(419) 878-9796
OKLAHOMA		
LAWTON	Pet Memorial Cemetery	(405) 536-1221
SPENCER	Precious Pets Cemetery	(405) 771-5510
OREGON		
CENTRAL POINT	Green Acres Pet Cemetery	(541) 772-5947
TUALATIN	Dignified Pet Services	(503) 885-2211

UNITED STATES *(continued)*

Location	Name	Phone Number
PENNSYLVANIA		
BLAIRSVILLE	Chestnut Ridge Pet Cemetery	(412) 459-7750
BREINIGSVILLE	Cloud Nine Pet Services at Kimberly Memorial Park	(610) 285-2720
CONESTOGA	Green Hill Pet Cemetery	(717) 871-3254
CONNEAUT LAKE	Forever Friends Pet Memorial Park	(412) 931-2909
FOGELSVILLE	Kimberly Memorial Park	(610) 285-2720
FRAZER	Great Valley Pet Cemetery	(610) 647-3330
HAZLETON	Lacey Memorial Pet Cemetery	(717) 454-6655
HALLIDAYSBURG	Chimney Rocks Animal Rest, Inc.	(814) 695-2591
LANCASTER	Greenwood Cemetery	(215) 826-2803
PITTSBURGH	Pet Memorial, Inc.	(412) 421-6910
QUAKERTOWN	Abbey Glen Pet Memorial Services	(888) 651-7555
QUAKERTOWN	Bucks County Pet Cemetery, Inc.	(215) 257-9584
ULSTER	Faithful Companions Pet Cemetery, Inc.	(570) 596-3192
UNIONTOWN	Faithful Pets Memorial Gardens	(412) 245-8524
WATSONVILLE	Pet Rest Memorial Park	(717) 538-2008
WELLSBORO	Pennsylvania SPCA	(717) 724-3687
YORK	Brookside Pet Cemetery	(717) 845-6618

238

Location	Name	Phone Number
RHODE ISLAND		
CRANSTON	Dignity Pet Cremation Service	(401) 641-3966
PEACEDALE	Rose Hill Pet Cemetery	(401) 789-1345
SOUTH CAROLINA		
BEAUFORT	Rainbow Bridge Pet Aftercare	(803) 521-9494
GOOSE CREEK	Pet Rest Cemetery & Cremation Service	(803) 797-5735
GREENVILLE	Saint Francis Columbarium Guild, Inc.	(864) 244-0709
GREENVILLE	Saint Francis Pet Services	(864) 232-0311
GREENVILLE	Top Dog, Ltd.	(864) 288-7282
LEXINGTON	Midlands Pet Care, Inc.	(803) 356-1610
WILLISTON	Plumtree Pet Services	(803) 266-4293
SOUTH DAKOTA		
HERMOSA	Memory Hills Pet Cemetery	(605) 484-2413
TEA	Forever Friends Pet Cemetery	(605) 368-2090
TENNESSEE		
HERMITAGE	Faithful Companions Pet Crematory	(615) 872-9221
MILLINGTON	Dixie Memorial Pet Cemetery	(901) 873-4127
NASHVILLE	Faithful Friends Pet Memorial	(615) 403-8020
NORMANDY	Pets Forever Crematory	(931) 581-3733
OOLTEWAH	Pet Haven Cemetery & Crematory	(423) 396-9877

UNITED STATES *(continued)*

Location	Name	Phone Number
TENNESSEE		
PREMIUM SPRINGS	Little Angels Pet Crematory	(615) 794-4370
SEYMOUR	Resthaven Pet Cemetery & Crematory	(865) 577-2900
TEXAS		
AZLE	Smoke Rise Farm	(817) 270-0491
CANYON LAKE	Paws in Heaven	(830) 964-2210
CARROLTON	Toothacres Pet Care Center	(214) 492-3711
FORT WORTH	Faithful Friends Pet Cemetery & Crematory	(817) 478-6696
GRAPEVINE	All Paws Go To Heaven	(817) 690-1560
HARKERS HEIGHTS	Rolling Hills Pet Cemetery	(817) 699-6365
HOUSTON	Bit of Heaven Pet Cemetery	(281) 999-2002
HOUSTON	Chester Cloudt Affiliates	(281) 861-0913
MCKINNEY	Green Oaks Pet Memorial Park	(972) 548-7757
MIDLAND	Pets At Peace	(432) 685-3306
WACO	God's Creatures Pet Cemetery	(254) 836-4484
UTAH		
KANAB	Angels Rest Memorial Park	(801) 644-2001
KANAB	Best Friends Animal Sanctuary	(801) 644-2001
OGDEN	Ogden City Cemetery	(801) 629-8231
VERMONT		
BRATTLEBORO	White Rose Pet Memorial Services	(802) 254-4749

Resources

Location	Name	Phone Number
VIRGINIA		
ALEXANDRIA	Pet Remains by Beverly	(318) 449-4780
AMELIA	Sweet Dreams Pet Cemetery & Crematory	(804) 561-6096
GLEN ALLEN	Bean and Company	(804) 553-0669
LEESBURG	The National Humane Ed. Society	(703) 777-8319
NEWPORT NEWS	Peninsula Pet Rest	(757) 599-0661
SANSTON	Faithful Friends Pet Cemetery	(804) 737-6046
WASHINGTON		
ABERDEEN	Petland Cemetery, Inc.	(800) 738-5119
KENT	Pet Haven Cemetery, Inc.	(812) 838-0811
TACOMA	A.R.C. Northwest	(253) 536-8775
WEST VIRGINIA		
ALBANS	J.L. Bowling Pet Cemetery	(304) 727-1362
ELKINS	Willowood Pet Cemetery	(304) 636-4449
SCOTT DEPOT	J.L. Bowling Pet Cemetery	(304) 757-7044
SHADY SPRING	Rainbow Retreat Pet Cemetery	(304) 763-2757
WHEELING	Ohio Valley Pet Crematory and Cemetery	(304) 232-7210 or (888) 816-9323
WISCONSIN		
DENMARK	Pets at Rest	(920) 863-3584
GREEN BAY	Forever Friends Pet Cremation Services	(920) 884-6060
MADISON	Westport Pet Memorial	(608) 249-3278
MILWAUKEE	Pet Lawn	(414) 353-9387

UNITED STATES *(continued)*

LOCATION	NAME	PHONE NUMBER
WISCONSIN		
MOSINEE	Peaceful Pines Pet Memorial Park	(715) 693-4693
OSHKOSH	Petland Memorial Garden	(414) 236-2828
PICKETT	John A. Dudzinski Affiliates	(414) 922-5110
POYNETTE	Midwest Cremation Services of Wisconsin	(608) 635-7270
SHERWOOD	Forrest Run Pet Cemetery	(414) 989-2600
UNION GROVE	Paris Pet Crematory	(262) 878-9194
WYOMING		
CASPER	Angel Companions Pet Cemetery	(307) 237-5744
GLASGOW	Kanawha Valley Memorial Gardens	(304) 595-6753

CANADA

LOCATION	NAME	PHONE NUMBER
ALBERTA		
CALGARY	Country Club Pet Memorial Park	(403) 256-4433
BRITISH COLUMBIA		
ABBOTSFORD	Allcare Pet Services	(888) 743-9988
COURTENAY	Pet Crematoria Services	(250) 334-7111
MANITOBA		
HEADINGLY	Domestic Animal Cremation	(204) 864-2815

LOCATION	NAME	PHONE NUMBER
NEW BRUNSWICK		
SUMMERVILLE	Cherished Pets Memorial Services	(506) 763-2252
NEWFOUNDLAND		
ST. JOHNS	Devonshire Pet Memorial Services	(709) 754-2384
NOVA SCOTIA		
ONSLOW	Donall Memorial Pet Cemetery	(902) 897-0534 or (902) 897-9442
SYDNEY	Faithful Friends Pet Memorial Service	(902) 567-2900
ONTARIO		
BROCKVILLE	Lakeview Haven Pet Cemetery	(613) 342-6806
BURLINGTON	Bill Halfpenny Affiliates	(905) 634-8339
EDEN	Sandy Ridge Pet Cemetery	(519) 866-3243
ELGIN	Little California Pet Cemetery	(613) 539-2264
GUELPH	Gateway Pet Memorial Services	(519) 822-8858
MORRISBURG	Helene Aub Affiliates	(613) 543-3010
PEMBROKE	Veterinary Referral Cremation Service	(613) 732-3614
TORONTO	Pet Loss Services	(416) 250-7388
QUEBEC		
VERDUN	Montreal Pet Cremation and Cemetery	(514) 766-2400
VIMONT	Toujours Present Crematoire d'Animaux de Compagnie	(450) 975-7738

OTHER INTERNATIONAL

Location	Name	Phone Number
AUSTRALIA		
BOOVAL, QUEENSLAND	Brisbane Pet Crematorium	61 7 3222 4322
NEW SOUTH WALES	The Animal Memorial Cemetery	45 72 5333
WALKERVILLE, SOUTH AUSTRALIA	Atkinson's Pet Crematorium & Cemetery	61 8 8342 9477
ENGLAND		
IPSWICH, SUFFOLK	Ipswich Pet Cemetery	+44(0)1394 213079
ROSSENDALE, LANCASHIRE	Rossendale Pet Crematorium and Memorial Gardens	07106 213810
SURREY	The Surrey Pet Cemetery & Crematory	01342-893069
NEW ZEALAND		
ALBANY, AUCKLAND	Auckland Pet Funerals	0 9 415 9949
RONGOTAI, WELLINGTON	Animal Cremation Services	0 4 387 9009
S.A.M.C., AUCKLAND	Pet Cremations, Ltd.	0 9 263 8782
WHANGAREI	Stardust Cremation Services, Ltd.	0 9 436 1333
U.S. VIRGIN ISLANDS		
ST. THOMAS	Philip E. Davis Affiliate	(284) 494-2120

Glossary
of
Terms

ABERRATION—Deviation from normal mental activity or from some standard of what is right or correct.

ALIENATION—Withdrawal or detachment of affection or feelings.

ANTHROPOMORPHIZE—To assign human characteristics to non-human things.

APATHY—The absence or lack of feeling, emotion, or caring.

ARRESTED—Stopped, halted progress of normal functioning.

BATTERED—Subjected to strong or overwhelming attack, not necessarily physical.

BEREAVEMENT—The emotional state resulting from being deprived of a loved one because of death.

BLOCK OUT—To be unable to recall something because of related emotional stress.

BONDING—Emotional attachment.

CLOSURE (RESOLUTION)—This term refers to the final stage of a predicament, where one can finally feel comfortable with it. It was formerly used to signify the final stage of pet bereavement, but has been replaced by *resolution*.

COLUMBARIUM—A vault or special repository for storing the ashes of cremated bodies. (also referred to as *ossuary*)

COMPENSATE—To make amends, an adjustment, or supply an equivalent need.

CONDITIONED—Developed or modified by frequent usage or practice.

CREMAINS—The ashes of a body after cremation.

DEFENSE MECHANISM—A psychological reaction in which one defends oneself emotionally.

DEPRESSION—A mental state characterized by very low spirits, sadness, and feelings of inadequacy.

DYSFUNCTION—Impaired or abnormal functioning.

ETHOLOGIST—A person who studies the behavior of animals.

EUPHEMISM—The substitution of an agreeable word or phrase for one that feels uncomfortable.

EVOLVED—Gradually changed or transformed. Adapted over a period of time to progressive development or evolution.

EXISTENTIAL—Dealing with personal existence and being.

FALLIBLE—Capable of error or misperception.

FANTASY—A pleasant mental image created by the imagination to satisfy some need.

Glossary of Terms

GUT FEELING—An extremely subjective, intuitive, personal response or appraisal—lacking suitable explanation, yet profound in its effect on an individual.

HUMANE—An attitude marked by compassion, sympathy, and consideration for other beings.

HUMANIST—A person characterized by compassion, respect, and strong interest in others.

INHERENT—Belonging by nature or settled habit.

JUDGMENTAL—Of or relating to judgment or criticism arising from a strong personal point of view.

JUSTIFICATION—Vindication or proof of usefulness; explanation or grounds for defending an action or behavior.

MAUDLIN—Gloomily tearful; miserable or excessively sentimental.

METAMORPHOSIS—A stage of growth in transition to higher development.

METAPHOR—A word or phrase used to imply a comparison or special concept.

MIND SET—An attitude of being close-minded, opinionated, or having a preconceived set of ideas or views on a subject.

MISPERCEPTION—The incorrect understanding or discernment of an idea.

MORBIDITY—A state of intense misery, discomfort, and pain, resulting from disease or upset.

MORES—The binding customs or traditions of an established society.

MORTALITY—Fatality caused by a disease, drug, or action.

MORTUARY—A business dealing with death and burial or cremation.

NEUROTIC—Describing a personal pattern of behavior caused by conflict and insecurity, and marked by tension.

OBJECTIVE (adj)—Clear; able to make an independent appraisal of an idea or situation without being affected by personal feelings or prejudices.

OBSESSIVE—Excessive in some interest or repeated action, sometimes to the point of abnormality.

OSSUARY—A vault or receptacle for the cremated body. (also known as *columbarium*)

PARADOXICAL—At first, seemingly contradictory or opposed to logic, yet valid.

PATHOLOGICAL—Unhealthy; damaging to physical or mental well-being.

PERCEPTION—Individual awareness or intuitive recognition; insight or intellectual grasp.

PERSPECTIVE—A view of a whole entity in relation and proportion to all its parts.

PLACEBO EFFECT—Physical or psychological reaction caused by presumption that a specific medicine or treatment will have its effect, regardless of its actual capability. (This demonstrates unconscious mind over body control, allowing counterfeit remedies to sometimes be effective if they are believed to be real.)

POST-TRAUMATIC STRESS—Exceptional stress that was caused by a severe emotional shock.

PROGNOSIS—The foretelling of how a condition or disease will change over time.

REPRESS—To exclude from conscious awareness.

RESOLUTION—The final stage in bereavement, previously referred to as *closure*.

Glossary of Terms

ROLE MODEL—A person one looks up to and imitates.

SECONDARY ANGER—The release of pent-up anger, which is triggered by a completely different stimulus not meriting this response.

SELF-DEFEATISM—The act of defeating one's own purposes by unconsciously sabotaging what is thought or done.

SELF-RECRIMINATION—The act of accusing or blaming one's self.

SENTIENT—Aware; consciously perceiving, thinking, feeling.

SEPARATION ANXIETY—Anxiety or distress caused by death or separation.

SLAUGHTERHOUSE REFORM—Social reform to pass laws to remedy the horrible and inhumane conditions in slaughterhouses.

STIMULI—Things that rouse the body, mind, or feelings.

SUBCONSCIOUS (n)—The function of the brain in which mental processes take place just below the level of conscious awareness.

SUBJECTIVE—Describing a particular individual's perception, which is modified and defined by personal bias and limitations.

SUPPRESS—To unconsciously or subconsciously impede or inhibit from conscious thought or feeling.

SURROGATE—A substitute, or one appointed to act for another.

SYMBIOTIC—The positive mutual relationship of two dissimilar organisms, in which each helps the other in some way.

SYMBOL—Anything that suggests or associates other things or ideas.

SYNDROME—A group of related symptoms, collectively typical of a particular problem.

TACTILE CONTACT—Physical contact by touching and feeling.

THERAPEUTIC—Having to do with remedial treatment of a disease.

TRANSCENDENCE—The going beyond usual spiritual limits; excelling, surpassing.

TRAUMA—A state or condition of physical, mental, or emotional shock, produced by extreme stress or injury. Emotional stress or blow that may produce disordered feelings or behavior.

TRIGGER MECHANISM—A stimulus that acts as a psychological trigger, suddenly releasing other unrelated pent-up responses.

UNCONSCIOUS (n)—That function of the mind that operates completely beyond the levels of awareness.

VENTING—Providing an escape for the release of pressure or suppressed feelings.

VULNERABLE—Open to attack or possible damage; not defensive.

EPITAPH

These precious words can only say

You loved me well and are ever loved by me.

I know we will join again.

About the Author

*W*allace Sife, Ph.D., has long been in the private practice of psychotherapy, specializing in educational psychology, biofeedback, and behavior modification. He has also trained and counseled in human bereavement. The untimely death of his beloved miniature Dachshund, Edel Meister, motivated him to make a major change in the direction of his life, as well as his career. That resulted in his writing of this book, in 1993. He is now acclaimed as the leading authority on petloss and bereavement.

In 1998, at a book signing for the second edition, Dr. Sife was asked by several of those present if he would form a local petloss group. As a result he founded and is currently the president of the Association for Pet Loss and Bereavement (APLB). Now semi-retired, he is volunteering about thirty hours every week, managing this unique nonprofit organization. On their extensive website, www.aplb.org, he hosts the popular Friday night chat rooms, while supervising several other chat rooms. Each week he personally counsels about 25 bereaving pet owners, and oversees the guidance of over 115 visitors in all the APLB chat rooms. Dr. Sife has also developed a special APLB program for anyone wanting to start and manage a petloss support group. He has helped inaugurate many of these in the United States and Canada, with a few in other countries.

In addition, he designed and has personally taught his outstanding training workshop for pet bereavement counselors—which has received considerable praise for its success. He succeeded in personally establishing basic standards and codification in what had been a new, unregulated profession. This program is being offered as a ten-hour workshop at all APLB conferences. It is also being prepared in a special online curriculum for presentation on the APLB website. Dr. Sife is the mentor to several of today's most successful pet bereavement counselors—including the many interns he trains in his chat rooms.

Over the years he has also written columns for various pet clubs, and is now completing a lengthy article on pet death for a national magazine. He was active for twenty-two years in the Dachshund Association of Long Island (DALI) and is still involved in animal rights work. He writes and communicates extensively in all media on man's loving bond and stewardship of pets.

In the first edition of this book, Dr. Sife published and established a working modification for the stages of bereavement for a pet— derived from the stages created by Dr. Elizabeth Kubler-Ross for human loss. This is now considered to be the standard for all pet bereavement counseling. Dr. Sife is frequently interviewed in all the mass media, and has lectured extensively on pet bereavement and euthanasia. Before founding the APLB, he also helped plan annual Pets and People Conferences for a major northeastern university.

In addition to several other professional and personal affiliations, Dr. Sife has been a member of Delta Society, American Psychological Association, Biofeedback Society of America, and the Association for Thanatology. He was a successful breeder-owner-handler of miniature Dachshunds and an active member of the Dachshund Association of Long Island. Dr. Sife also counseled on problem behavior in dogs. His section on comments, advice, and responses to letters from members appeared as a regular feature in the bimonthly publication of the original Owner Handlers Association.

Dr. Sife has written several other books on different subjects. He is also an acclaimed poet, and his *Modern Rubaiyat* contains several quatrains on the death of beloved animals.

This book was originally dedicated to the memory of his dog, Edel Meister, CD, and to all other similarly loved pets throughout history. He now lives with his two adored miniature Dachshunds, Sheeba, 18, and her son, Pip, 13. Because of Sheeba's advanced age, Dr. Sife recently obtained a miniature Dachshund puppy, Phoebe, who will help ease and buffer the pain for him and Pip when their beloved Sheeba leaves them.

Index

Index

Index

resources
    aftercare services, 225–244
    supportive counseling, 194–199
responsibility
    care provision commitments, 27–29
    euthanasia, 153, 154, 159–161
    palliation, 154
    self-awareness, 29–34
    senior citizen exceptions, 33–34
    unhealthy relationships, 34–36

selective memory, denial/disbelief, 82
self-destruction, depression, 100–101
self-punishment, anger response, 63
separation anxiety, euthanasia,
  155–156
service animals, theft, 121
service dogs, 24–25
shelters
    animal lab providers, 121–122
    bereavement relief, 221
    children's loss adjustment, 150–151
    euthanasia observation, 159
    replacement pet, 129–130
shock/disbelief, 53, 55–56
snakes, lost/missing pets, 122
social support, 46, 47
SPCA, cemetery/crematoriums, 173
spiritual background, grief response, 46
spiritualism, denial/disbelief, 80–81
strays, lost/missing pet reason, 116
subconscious, bereavement, 18
suicidal feelings, depression danger, 100
supportive counseling
    benefits of, 217–218, 220
    bereavement clinics, 186–191
    cultural issues, 183, 185
    depression, 190
    humanistic view of bereavement,
      191–192
    Internet chat rooms, 185
    metaphysical philosophers, 194
    positive response to, 190–191
    psychotherapist qualifications,
      186–188
    public awareness, 189, 190–191
    resources, 194–199
    role of religion, 192–194
    transcendental poets, 194
supportive people, overcoming grief,
  41–42

tears (crying), healing process, 41
teenagers, death of pet, 141–142
terms, 245–250
theft
    lost/missing pet reason, 116
    preventable loss situations, 118
toddlers, death of pet, 140
touching (petting), fundamental human
  need, 16–17
training, as guilt justification, 95
transcendental poets, supportive counseling, 94
travel, lost/missing pets, 119

unworthy me syndrome, self-destructive
  attitude, 47, 78

vacations, bereavement relief, 220
veterinarians
    anger scapegoat, 62
    cemetery/crematorium, 173
    children's loss of pet assistance, 151
    compassion fatigue, 160
    euthanasia, 157–160
    malpractice actions, 70–71
    support counseling, 220–221
violation, disbelief/shock reaction, 55
visitations, bereavement relief,
  219–220, 223
vocalizations (loud), 156

weakly bonded, human-pet relationship,
  21
website, APLB (Association for Pet Loss
  and Bereavement), 4
Western cultures
    death acceptance attitudes,
      109–110
    death/dying perceptions, 39
    death preparation, 18–19
    euphemistic society, 77
    extended household disappearance,
      5
    pet death, 4
    undeserved guilt cause, 92–93
withdrawal, depression, 101–102
written memorials, bereavement, 219

young adults, death of pet, 142

Zen Buddhism philosophy, 212–214